THE UNIVERSITY OF MICHIGAN
CENTER FOR SOUTH AND SOUTHEAST ASIAN STUDIES

MICHIGAN PAPERS ON SOUTH AND SOUTHEAST ASIA

Editorial Board

Alton L. Becker
John K. Musgrave
George B. Simmons
Thomas R. Trautmann, chm.

Ann Arbor, Michigan

ECONOMIC EXCHANGE AND
SOCIAL INTERACTION IN SOUTHEAST ASIA:
PERSPECTIVES FROM
PREHISTORY, HISTORY, AND ETHNOGRAPHY

Edited by:

Karl L. Hutterer

Ann Arbor

Center for South and Southeast Asian Studies

The University of Michigan

1977

Michigan Papers on South and Southeast Asia, 13

Library of Congress Catalog Card Number: 77-95147

International Standard Book Number: 0-89148-013-7

Copyright
1978
by
Center for South and Southeast Asian Studies
The University of Michigan

Printed in the United States of America

Table of Contents

Plates	vii
Tables	vii
Figures	viii
Maps	viii
The Contributors	ix
Preface	xiii

I. Theory of Exchange, Models, General Problems

Trade, Social Conflict, and Social Integration: Rethinking Some Old Ideas on Exchange	B. L. Foster	3
From Stage to Development in Prehistoric Thailand: An Exploration of the Origins of Growth, Exchange, and Variability in Southeast Asia	J. Kennedy	23
Exchange at the Upstream and Downstream Ends: Notes Toward a Functional Model of the Coastal State in Southeast Asia	B. Bronson	39

II. Contributions to the Ethnography of Exchange in Southeast Asia

Ecotones and Exchange in Northern Luzon	J. T. Peterson	55
Contemporary Malay Traders in the Gulf of Siam	L. A. P. Gosling	73
East Timor: Exchange and Political Hierarchy at the Time of the European Discoveries	S. Forman	97
Trading Patterns of Philippine Chinese: Strategies of Sojourning Middlemen	J. T. Omohundro	113

III. Exchange and the Prehistoric and Historic Development of Southeast Asia

The Opening of Southeast Asia, Trading Patterns through the Centuries	J. K. Whitmore	139

Archaeology and Palaeogeography in the Straits
of Malacca   J. N. Miksic   155

Prehistoric Trade and the Evolution of Philippine
Societies: A Reconsideration   K. L. Hutterer 177

Markets and Trade in Pre-Madjapahit
Java   J. Wisseman   197

The Coming of Islam to the Archipelago:
A Reassessment   K. R. Hall   213

A Chinese Silk Depicted at Caṇḍi
Sèwu   H. W. Woodward 233

Ethnic Participation in the Export of Thai
Rice, 1885 -1890   C. M. Wilson   245

Bibliography   275

Plates

1. Salt Manufacture near Bara Laem 80
2. Loading Sand Ballast in Kuala Trengganu 80
3. Ship Owner Haji Awang 82
4. Malay Crew 82
5. The Perahu Pinas Gobel 86
6. The Perahu Pinas Dogor 86
7. The Harbor at Kuala Trengganu 93
8. Abandoned Hulls at Kuala Trengganu 93
9. Temple at Chaṇḍi Sèwu 234
10. Portion of Temple's Exterior Wall 235
11. Rosette and Animal Roundels 236
12. Rosettes at Prambanan 238
13. Circles and Medallions at Prambanan 239

Tables

1. Mechanisms for Controlling Exchange Conflict 20
2. Agta Food Production 60
3. Regional Origin of Fukienese Immigrants in Iloilo City, Dumaguete, Dagupan, and Davao 118
4. Regional Origin of Cantonese Immigrants in Iloilo City and Davao 118
5. Surnames of Fukienese Immigrants to Iloilo and Degree of Concentration by Home Township within Home <u>Hsien</u> 120
6. Distribution of Chinese Businesses in Iloilo City and Province, 1972 126
7. Degree of Interrelatedness of Iloilo Chinese Merchant Families, 1972 128

Tables, continued

8. Ethnic Participation in the Thai Rice Trade, 1885 through 1890 — 257
9. Ethnic Participation in the Thai Rice Trade by Individuals and Business Firms, 1885 through 1890 — 259-259
10. Rice Exports of Individuals and Firms, 1885 through 1890 — 260-267
11. Cooperative Relationships: Thai Rice Trade, 1885 through 1890 — 268-271

Figures

1. Abstract Model for Exchange between a Drainage Basin Center and an Overseas Power — 42
2. Agta-Palanan Food Production Interdependence — 61
3. A Model of Exchange and Ecotone Expansion — 68
4. A Cabacillo-Agent Network: The History of Mr. Lo — 122-123

Maps

1. Palanan Bay — 56
2. Ports and Sailing Routes Used by Trengganu Traders — 78
3. The Lesser Sunda Islands — 98
4. Southeast Asia — at back

The Contributors

BENNET BRONSON is Associate Curator of Asian Archaeology at the Field Museum, Chicago. He received his Ph.D. in Anthropology at the University of Pennsylvania with a dissertation on excavations at Chansen, a protohistoric site in central Thailand. He has also directed excavations in Sri Lanka, Sumatra, and Java and has published a number of reports on these, as well as several papers on early agriculture and demography. He is currently engaged in a long-term archaeological project in Java, in close cooperation with the University of Indonesia and the National Center for Archaeological Research.

SHEPARD FORMAN is Associate Professor of Anthropology at the University of Michigan. He received his Ph.D. from Columbia University and has done field research in Brazil and on the island of Timor. He has published a number of papers and two monographs on Brazilian peasants. At present he is heading the social science section of the Ford Foundation.

BRIAN FOSTER is Assistant Professor of Anthropology at the State University of New York, Binghamton. He conducted ethnographic research among the Mon people of Thailand and received his Ph.D. at the University of Michigan. His research interests include ethnic relations, family studies, population and social organization and social organization of commerce. He has published a number of papers based on his ethnographic work in Thailand. At present, he is engaged in research involving a mathematical social network study.

L. A. PETER GOSLING has conducted extensive field work in Malaya and Thailand, dealing with peasant economies and transportation systems. He has taught at the University of Malaya, and is currently Professor of Geography and Director of the Center for South and Southeast Asian Studies at the University of Michigan.

KENNETH R. HALL is Assistant Professor of Asian History at Elmira College, Elmira, New York. With a Ph.D. in pre-modern South and Southeast Asian History from the University of Michigan, he specializes in the epigraphic sources for the study of trade in India and Southeast Asia. He has published several papers and edited with John K. Whitmore a volume of essays concerning the origins of Southeast Asian statecraft.

KARL L. HUTTERER is Assistant Curator, Division of the Orient, Museum of Anthropology, the University of Michigan. He received his Ph.D. in Anthropology at the University of Hawaii. He has been involved in archaeological fieldwork in the Philippines, Hawaii, and Australia. He has written a number of papers on the ethnography and archaeology of the Philippines and Southeast Asia. His major interests include technology, trade, and human ecology in tropical regions.

JEAN KENNEDY is a Research Scholar at the Australian National University, Canberra. She received her Ph.D. in Anthropology at the University of Hawaii with a dissertation on Southeast Asian prehistory. She has done archaeological research in several areas of Polynesia and in Thailand and is now working in Melanesia. Her interests are primarily in the development of subsistence systems, in problems of variability and change, and the various theoretical problems posed in making sense of the prehistoric and protohistoric periods of Southeast Asia.

JOHN N. MIKSIC is a Ph.D. Candidate in Anthropology at Cornell University. He has participated in archaeological excavations in Canada and Honduras, and is presently pursuing an archaeological research project in Sumatra.

JOHN T. OMOHUNDRO is Assistant Professor of Anthropology at the State University College at Potsdam. He conducted ehtnographic fieldwork in the Philippines and received his Ph.D. in Anthropology at the University of Michigan. His monograph on The Chinese Merchant Community of Iloilo City is forthcoming. His research interests include intermarriage and cultural change among ethnic groups specializing in commerce.

JEAN TRELOGGEN PETERSON received a Ph.D. in Anthropology at the University of Hawaii and is an Assistant Professor at the University of Illinois at Urbana-Champaign. She has conducted ethnographic research with negritos in the Philippines and is currently back in the Philippines for continuing research work. She has a book on The Ecology of Social Boundaries forthcoming.

JOHN K. WHITMORE received a Ph.D. in Southeast Asian History from Cornell University. He is a specialist in the history of Vietnam and is also interested in geography, a field in which he is presently pursuing studies. His book on *The Transformation of Vietnam: Politics and Confucianism in the 15th Century* is forthcoming. He is an Associate of the Center for South and Southeast Asian Studies at the University of Michigan.

CONSTANCE M. WILSON received her Ph.D. in History from Cornell University. She is currently an Assistant Professor in the Department of History at Northern Illinois University. Her major interests are the social and political history of Thailand in the nineteenth century. She has made several trips to Bangkok to work in the National Library and the National Archives.

JAN WISSEMAN is a Ph.D. Candidate in Art and Archaeology of Southeast Asia at the School of Oriental and African Studies, University of London. She has done archaeological work in England, Java, and Sumatra. Her dissertation combines archaeological, historical, and epigraphic data on commerce in western Indonesia during the ninth through the twelfth centuries. She has published several articles on Indonesian archaeology.

HIRAM W. WOODWARD served in the Peace Corps in Thailand and has an M.A. in Southeast Asian Studies and a Ph.D. in Art History from Yale University. He has been teaching Art History at the University of Michigan since 1972. He is co-editor of a forthcoming volume of *Essays on Barabuḍur*.

Preface

This volume of essays on economic interactions in Southeast Asia is the result of a three day seminar, sponsored by the Center for South and Southeast Asian Studies at the University of Michigan and held in Ann Arbor from March 22 to 24, 1976. The topic of the seminar was chosen on the assumption that the investigation of economic interaction was of interest to a large range of social scientists, and that the archaeology, history, and ethnography of Southeast Asia offer an unusual variety of relevant data.

Economic behavior is governed by two major sets of boundary conditions: environmental and technological factors on the one hand, and conditions of social organization and social relations on the other hand. Indeed, the interrelationship between economic and social conditions appears so strong and obvious that some social scientists have advocated analyzing all social interactions within the framework of exchange relationships: exchange of goods, services, personnel, and information. But even if one does not want to impose an economic model on the totality of social organization and social relations, it is still true that the investigation of social interactions is of particular interest to social scientists: economic exchanges lend concrete manifestations to social relations which themselves may transcend the economic realm and which otherwise are often difficult to trace.

As for Southeast Asia, one of the most visible characteristics of the region is the tremendous diversity of its physical as well as human environment. The great potential of this diversity for social science research with regard to general problems of human organization and social evolution should be obvious, but it is fair to say that surprisingly little advantage has been taken of this opportunity. Particularly the area of economic studies has lagged behind in Southeast Asia; the majority of investigations have focused on the production process of agrarian subsistence and peasant economies, although some seminal market studies have been carried out (e.g., Dewey

1962), and certain aspects of ancient trade have received some more attention.

The present collection of essays was designed primarily to give some idea of the incredible diversity of economic and social systems that can be investigated in Southeast Asia. This diversity is all the more fascinating because, as a number of the papers show, many if not most of the systems organized on very different levels of integration interact with each other. A perusal of the titles of the essays will show that little effort was made to promote a theme more narrowly unifying than that expressed in the title of the volume. Still, the careful reader will find that a number of common concerns are articulated throughout the collection.

As already mentioned, the seminar as well as the publication of the papers has been made possible through the Center for South and Southeast Asian Studies at the University of Michigan. Professor Thomas Trautmann, formerly Director of the Center, must be thanked for his warm interest in, and support of, the conference and the resulting volume of papers. Professor Kenneth Hall, now at Elmira College, helped organize the conference from the beginning, and William Macdonald and Vincas Steponaitis provided very important assistance during the seminar itself. I thank all of them.

                                                           Karl L. Hutterer
                                                           Ann Arbor
                                                           December 1977

I.

THEORY OF EXCHANGE,

MODELS, GENERAL PROBLEMS

Trade, Social Conflict and Social Integration:
Rethinking Some Old Ideas on Exchange

by

Brian L. Foster

Systems of economic exchange have long occupied a central place in social theory, providing for many theorists the glue which holds societies together. Many anthropologists in their studies of primitive societies have taken this idea much further by generalizing the theories of economic exchange to include exchange of women and other material and non-material goods. This paper re-examines one such school of thought and proposes some very different perspectives on the topic.

My argument is two-fold. First, it is concerned with the mechanisms which produce social cohesion and stability (or dissolution and instability), and second with the relationship of economic exchange to these mechanisms. I begin with a brief discussion of the problem as it was posed by Durkheim and extended by Mauss and Levi-Strauss; the major elements of my own proposals emerge from the critique of their formulations. I argue that economic exchange does not in itself promote social solidarity or stability, but rather is fundamentally a dissociative, conflict relation which must be carefully regulated. The mechanisms by which it is regulated are the subject of my own proposals.

Exchange in the Theories of Durkheim and Mauss

The dominant problem in western sociology and social anthropology is the problem of order. The problem has been studied and formulated in many different ways, some scholars emphasizing stability and others change, some focusing on consensus and others on conflict, some on interaction and others on structural and/or functional considerations.

The problem is probably most usefully formulated, however, in its most general terms. We know empirically that some social relationships (and some complex systems of relationships) are stable in different ways and in varying degrees, and also that they change in different ways, in varying degrees, and at varying rates. The primary subject matter of sociology and social anthropology is this variability in the patterns, the persistence, and the change of social relationships; our goal is to understand that variability—to investigate the conditions of stability and change and the processes by which stability is maintained and by which change occurs.

The question has seldom been asked in this form. Most frequently the problem of order has been approached by addressing the question, "What holds society together?" Probably the most influential scholar who has dealt with this question was Emile Durkheim (1964) who, in The Division of Labor in Society, did so with particular reference to modern, highly differentiated (or, as he called them, the 'higher') societies. The main argument of Durkheim's book revolves around his discussion of two kinds of solidarity: mechanical solidarity, which stems from similarity and is characteristic of simple societies, and organic solidarity, which is somehow produced by the division of labor and is associated with more complex, differentiated societies.

Although this aspect of the book is widely known, Durkheim's argument explaining the association of the different kinds of solidarity with different types of society is frequently misunderstood. The substantive hypothesis most frequently attributed to Division of Labor is that the division of labor brings about solidarity through functional interdependence of the differentiated parts of a society—a proposition about which Durkheim is at best ambiguous. In some passages he seems to support this view (though not unequivocally), but in others he seems to rule it out quite explicitly. In his critique of Spencer's notion of contract, for instance, he says:

> If interest relates men, it is never for more than a few moments.... Consciences are only superficially in contact; they neither penetrate each other, nor do they adhere,... total harmony of interests conceals a latent or deferred conflict. For where

> interest is the only ruling force, each individual finds himself in a state of war with every other since nothing comes to mollify the egos, and any truce in this eternal antagonism would not be of long duration (Durkheim 1964:203-204).

And a few pages later:

> To be sure, when men unite in a contract, it is because, through division of labor, either simple or complex, they need each other. But in order for them to cooperate harmoniously, it is not enough that they enter into a relationship, nor even that they feel the state of mutual dependence in which they find themselves.... We must not forget that, if the division of labor makes interests solidary, it does not confound them; it keeps them distinct and opposite.... Each of the contractants, while needing the other, seeks to obtain what he needs at the least expense; that is to say, to acquire as many rights as possible in exchange for the smallest possible obligations (Durkheim 1964:212-213).

Moreover, Durkheim tells us that we can have a kind of false division of labor which does not produce organic solidarity at all, but which exists on the structural foundations of a segmental society. The division of labor, he says, is a "derived and secondary phenomenon"; it "passes on the surfaces of social life, and this is especially true of the economic division of labor" (Durkheim 1964:282). We can, therefore, have societies with a strong division of labor (at least in the economic sense) but with mechanical solidarity. His example is startling: England (Durkheim 1964:282).

The mechanism which seems to produce the division of labor and organic solidarity in Durkheim's sense is the struggle for existence. As societies increase in material density (by which he means primarily population density), the struggle for existence is intensified. But by division of labor, the parts of society are put in a relation less of direct conflict and more of cooperation.

> The division of labor is, then, a result of the struggle for existence, but it is a mellowed dénouement. Thanks to it, opponents are not obliged to fight to a finish, but can exist one beside the other (Durkheim 1964:270).

The argument, however, seems to rest primarily on establishing what Durkheim (1964:115) earlier called 'negative solidarity', which is abstention from interfering with others. Negative solidarity, he says, is a necessary condition for all other types of solidarity, but not sufficient—in fact, not really solidarity at all, strictly speaking. Nevertheless, "The first condition of total coherence is that the parties who compose it should not interfere with one another through discordant movements" (Durkheim 1964:119). In the end, it seems that one must agree with LaCapra (1972:127) that Durkheim remains unclear on how or whether the division of labor produces social solidarity.

Durkheim's own argument aside, the necessity for solidarity and cohesion by no means provides a satisfactory demonstration or explanation of their causal connection. Clearly the possibility exists for some societies which need solidarity to fail for lack of it. It might be argued that since those which lack it fail, its presence in the ones remaining is explained. The tautology in this argument is too obvious for it to be satisfying, and in any case it would be desirable to be able to determine the mechanisms by which the solidarity comes about.

An important extension of Durkheim's ideas was developed by Marcel Mauss who, in The Gift (1967), argued that certain kinds of exchange provide the mechanism for producing solidarity in certain kinds of differentiated societies. Mauss' attention focused on gift exchange in primitive and archaic societies—particularly on determining what force in a gift compelled a return gift. Such exchange is, he says, self-interested economic exchange, but unlike exchange in modern societies takes the form of the gift and is made to appear selfless and disinterested. Gifts are "total social phenomena," containing within them "all threads of which the social fabric is composed...religious, legal, moral, economic" (Mauss 1967: 1967:1). The gift economy, Mauss concluded, was the means of "setting up the will for peace against follies...," of "substituting alliance, gift and commerce for war, isolation and stagnation"—in short, it is "one of the secrets of their [the primatives] wisdom and solidarity" (Mauss 1967:80). Thus, for Mauss it was the gift which provided—at least for primitive peoples—the mechanism of solidarity which eluded Durkheim.

Mauss' argument has been taken up by many social theorists and for some has become almost an item of faith. Moreover, it has been generalized, primarily through the influence of Levi-Strauss, to include other kinds of exchange— especially of women. But although Mauss does provide the mechanism which was lacking in Durkheim, and although the analysis has stimulated a great deal of productive research, there seem to be a number of reasons for re-examining his basic proposition. The central question is whether exchange in itself is the glue which holds society together; I argue that it is not. Quite the contrary, exchange—at least of utilitarian goods—produces conflict which is destructive of social unity and stability. Mauss' argument can be approached from several different directions.

First, it is important to notice that in most of Mauss' major examples—the Kula being the most important—he focuses primarily on exchange of non-utilitarian goods, although, it is true, exchange of utilitarian goods often occurs, as with the Kula, in the shadow of the other. Although the utilitarian exchange is temporally and spatially associated with the ritual exchange or gift giving, the acts of exchange themselves, which provide Masss' mechanism for solidarity, are very different in character. While the one is pervaded by elaborate ritual etiquette and generosity, the other is characterized by fierce bargaining. This prominence of non-utilitarian exchange is surprising in view of Mauss' unwillingness to distinguish between exchange of different kinds of items—e.g., necessities and non-necessities. For example, he comments that the Trobrianders and other groups have a variety of terms for 'exchange' (1967:28-29) and exhibit a "strange incapacity for abstraction" (1967:30-31). In the light of these facts, the entire argument is called into question by Mauss' (and Durkheim's) recognition that economic exchange is a conflict relationship.

Where the Mauss (and Levi-Strauss) analysis goes wrong, I think, is in confounding exchange as an incidental part of ritual with exchange in itself. In a sense, Mauss was correct in focusing on the gift, but he focused on the wrong aspect of it in focusing on the exchange rather than the ritual aspect. An object which is exchanged and ritual acts of exchange themselves, just as other phenomena, can partake of the sacred and, in so doing, become a vehicle for both negative and positive solidarity. When this happens, though, the exchange act is only a by-product of the ritual activity in which it is embedded.

This characteristic of ritual exchange becomes clear when it is recognized that ritual is behavior, and that such behavior almost of necessity involves some kind of manipulation of material objects (dancing or other personal acts might not entail manipulation, but even these Mauss wishes to call gifts to gods). Anyway, there are strict limits to what one can do with physical objects; one can transform them (e.g., reshape, destroy, create), or one can give them to someone or something, or one can eat them, or one can look at them or fondle them; but beyond that, the options are few. No matter how one views the situation, exchanging the objects has an important place in the repertoir of possibilities. In any case, ritual objects must be disposed of somehow after the ritual is finished, and one way to dispose of them is to give them to someone. It seems, then, that in at least some cases, exchange can be separated from economics as well as from ritual, and the distinction may be an important one.

It is also important to distinguish between the notion that the act of exchange itself underlies solidarity and the notion that the results of the exchange underlie it. It is interesting to compare exchange of women and exchange of goods in the light of this distinction. Exchange of women (e.g., to cement a treaty, or in cross-cousin marriage) may well produce a set of circumstances which promotes cohesion and solidarity, but which in this respect is clearly distinct from the exchange act itself—e.g., by a process of crosscutting ties such as those described by Gluckman (1956). In such a case, the solidarity is produced by certain features of the social networks generated by the exchange acts rather than by the exchange acts themselves. But convincing mechanisms do not seem to exist which would

allow a similar interpretation of exchange of goods unless one
resorts to some kind of nearly mystical power in the object
exchanged, as does Mauss in some passages concerning the <u>hau</u>.

It seems, then, that although Mauss provided a mechanism
for organic solidarity, there are a number of serious problems
in his analysis. Moverover, these difficulties are futher
compounded by Mauss' and Durkheim's assertion that exchange
of utilitarian goods is basically a conflict relation. It is
necessary at this point to consider more closely the nature of
exchange-generated conflict and its consequences.

Exchange and Social Conflict

I use the term 'conflict' as does Dahrendorf (1959:135) "for
contests, competitions, disputes, and tensions as well as for
manifest clashes between social forces," although it will
sometimes be necessary to distinguish between different kinds of
conflict. Very generally, two parties are in a conflict
relationship when the action or predisposition to action of one
either potentially or actually injures or makes less effective the
ability of the other party to achieve its goals. Exchange which is
necessitated by the division of labor is clearly a conflict relation,
since one party to the exchange has control over something
needed and/or desired by the other—which is to say that one
party is dependent on the other. In a condition of perceived
scarcity, whether real or not, interests are still more unalter-
ably opposed, since either one or both parties must remain
dissatisfied with the exchange. These conditions are further
exacerbated by the fact that "violent coercion is always a
potential resource, and it is a zero-sum sort" (Collins 1975:59).

It is clear, however, that the intensity and consequences of
exchange-generated conflict vary greatly. Two considerations
seem to be expecially important for my arguments: the
destructiveness and the intensity of the conflict. It has often been
been argued that not all conflict is destructive of social
stability or unity (e.g., Coser 1956; Gluckmann 1956). Conflict
which is generated by exchange of utilitarian goods, however,
does seem to be of the divisive, dissociative kind for two closely
related reasons. On the one hand, the relationship between
parties to trade characteristically rests heavily—or primarily—

on the trade (see Coser 1956:73-75). This is particularly true in primitive societies, where little trade occurs within groups, and trade constitutes one of the most important inter-group relations. On the other hand, in more complex societies, trading specialists emerge who, along with political authorities and property owners, become major foci of conflict relations. By focusing conflict on themselves, the compensating effects of other, crosscutting conflicts, are diffused and their relative force diminished (see Coser 1956; Gluckmann 1956).

Although exchange-generated conflict tends to be destructive of social stability and unity, its consequences vary greatly with its intensity. The intensity depends largely on the degree to which the item being exchanged is a necessity, on its scarcity, on the proportion of the recipient's total resources devoted to acquiring it, and on the degree to which the quantity and quality of the goods are manipulable—all of which conditions can be directly derived from the definition of conflict. The relationship of these factors to intensity of conflict seems too obvious to elaborate here. Clearly, trade for an expensive, scarce necessity which is inherently manipulable in quality constitutes a highly explosive relationship; trade for an inexpensive object which is convenient but not necessary, and for which many suitable substitutes are readily available, is, however, likely to have minimal consequences, although the consequences may be dissociative.

These considerations bring us directly back to Mauss and Durkheim, for if this argument is correct, the classic sociological question, "What holds society together?" is only compounded by the existence of exchange and by the division of labor which necessitates exchange. We must, therefore, at the minimum ask what mechanisms alleviate the conflict produced by the necessary exchange in highly differentiated societies. What, in Durkheim's terms, are the mechanisms which produce negative solidarity, which is a prerequisite for positive solidarity? To answer this question, we must examine three different aspects of conflict regulation. It should be noted that I am speaking of conflict regulation, not resolution, since the conflict is inherent in the trading relation, which, in turn, is necessitated by the division of labor.

First, we must consider social mechanisms for regulating

the content of behavior associated with exchange relationships.
At the most general level, there seem to be two kinds of
mechanisms: prescription of content of interaction, and
proscription of certain acts. Prescription of trading behavior
occurs when it is standardized or stereotyped according to a
detailed set of rules. Trade carried out in this way can, in the
broadest sense, be said to be ritualized—a ritual being "any
practice... regularly repeated in a set or precise manner so as
to satisfy one's sense of fitness" (Webster's International
Dictionary, quoted in Rappaport 1971:62). Ritualization gives
trading behavior an affective dimension and in many cases
provides supernatural sanctions. The complexity of prescription
of an elaborate kind of interaction makes supernatural sanctions
of affective 'sense of fitness' an ideal means of enforcement,
since deviation can take an indefinite number of forms. A more
modest way of regulating the content of interaction—at least in
scope—is to proscribe certain very specific acts. This kind of
regulation is more amenable to enforcement by coercive
sanctions.

A second aspect of conflict regulation concerns amount and
kinds of interaction which are possible. Conflict can be
regulated by putting distance between the parties, on the
assumption that manifest conflict behavior cannot occur if the
parties do not interact. This can be accomplished to a limited
degree by social distance, which restricts certain kinds of
interaction; but, it can be accomplished more effectively by
putting spatial distance between the parties.

The third aspect of conflict regulation concerns the target
of conflict behavior. It is well known that conflict (especially in
the sense of hostile sentiments or tensions) can be displaced to
targets other than those which form the basis for realistic
conflict (Coser 1956:39-48). Displacement can have several
very different outcomes. On the one hand, conflict can be
displaced in such a way that it can be more easily controlled by
other mechanisms or, perhaps, can be resolved. On the other
hand, displacement can result in highly explosive situations
(Coser 1956:39-48).

These three types of mechanisms combine in different
ways under varying socio-economic conditions to regulate trade-
generated conflicts. Although different manifestations of the

three can be combined in many different ways, three combinations stand out as especially common, and they represent a three-stage evolutionary sequence of exchange systems; to put it another way, the three respective combinations are characteristically associated with societies at different levels of complexity.

Mechanisms for Alleviating
Exchange-Induced Conflict

<u>a</u>. <u>Tribal Societies</u>

In tribal societies, trade is characteristically ritualized; that is, the trade is embedded in a larger ritual context. Real trade, moreover, is usually not carried out within primitive groups, since there is little or no division of labor; it generally occurs between groups, and some measure of spatial distance is often also present. The classic description of such a system remains Malinowski's (1961) account of the Trobriand <u>Kula</u>, in which exchange of utilitarian goods (<u>gimwali</u>) took place in the shadow of an elaborate, simultaneous ritual exchange of ceremonial objects. Trade between African pygmies and Bantu often carry the spatial separation to a bizarre extreme in the well-known practice of 'blind trade', in which the partners never meet.

Although trade occasioned by the division of labor usually occurs between local groups in primitive societies there are some occasions in which extensive exchange of food and other necessities occurs within groups. This is often the case, for example, among very primitive groups who live in environments where distribution and exploitation of resources is uneven, or for whom hunting larger animals—for which kills are sporadic— is a major source of food (Lombardi 1975). Such exchange is very similar to that which is brought about by the division of labor insofar as one party is dependent on others at various times for desirable or even necessary goods; such exchange generates precisely the same kinds of conflict as does trade, and it must be carefully regulated in similar ways.

As would be expected from the previous discussion, within-group exchange for necessities is usually heavily ritualized.

In addition, direct, two-way exchange (balanced reciprocity) generally does not occur for scarce necessities because, I would argue, of its potential to develop into overt conflict (negative reciprocity, in Sahlins' [1965] terms). Rather, generalized reciprocity, which is usually the rule, separates the parties to the exchange in the critical matter of reckoning equivalences, and in effect displaces conflict over this matter to the group as a whole, such that it is less apt to erupt into overt conflict behavior.

Several characteristics of primitive societies make ritualization of trade an especially appropriate mechanism for regulating exchange conflict. First, they lack authorities with power to enforce coercive sanctions for either prescriptions or proscriptions of certain kinds of behavior. This is especially true of non-local trade. Second, there are no trading specialists: trading conflict is not focused on a small number of individuals, and it is more likely than in more differentiated societies to be countered by crosscutting conflicts of other kinds. Therefore, it is not strongly dissociative and is less likely to require strong coercive sanctions for the mechanisms to be effective. Finally, the conflict generated by most primitive trade is likely to be less virulent than that generated by more complex societies, since primitive societies tend to be highly self-sufficient with respect to most necessities.

Southeast Asian tribal groups seem to fit this pattern remarkably well. A particularly interesting case in point is Radcliffe-Brown's description of the Andaman Islanders, since it was an example used by Mauss. The people are hunter-gatherers who live in an environment with abundant resources. They have three main kinds of portable, exchangeable property: (a) canoes, which belong to the man who builds them; (b) weapons, tools, baskets, and other small items which each individual makes for himself or herself; and (c) food. All are owned by individuals (Radcliffe-Brown 1964:41-42).

Canoes are generally not exchanged (Radcliffe-Brown 1964: 43). Moreover, given the abundance of the environment and the lack of division of labor, one would not expect to find widespread economic exchange of food. Although Radcliffe-Brown says that food is ideally shared generously and that food is widely distributed in the camp, he is very vague about how it is done.

Only with respect to distribution of a pig is he slightly more explicit—a development which is not surprising, since it might be expected that kills of large animals would be sporadic and that distribution would be more strictly regulated. In any event, if an older man makes the kill, he keeps what he needs and distributes the rest to his friends; a younger man's kill, however, is distributed by one of the elders, apparently according to some kind of rules (Radcliffe-Brown 1964:43). It might be noted that marine resources make kills of even large animals less critical then they would be in other societies.

Gifts, however, are given frequently and in great quantity. Radcliffe-Brown gives most attention to large meetings lasting several days between different local groups, which, he says, have the object of creating a 'friendly feeling' between individuals and groups. Sometimes they are given to bring a quarrel to an end. A major feature of these gatherings is large-scale exchange of gifts consisting of weapons, baskets, nets, white clay, red ochre, and other small items (Radcliffe-Brown 1964:84). Ideally, a gift should be matched by a return gift of equal value. Of the exchanges, Radcliffe-Brown says:

> It requires a good deal of tact on the part of everyone concerned to avoid the unpleasantness that may arise if a man thinks that he has not received things as valuable as he has given, or if he fancies that he has not received quite the same amount of attention as has been accorded to others (1964:42).

And later:

> Although the natives themselves regarded the objects thus given as being presents, yet when a man gave a present to another he expected that he would receive something of equal value in return, and would be very angry if the return present did not come up to his expectations (1964:83).

Yet, Radcliffe-Brown says, no one could refuse a gift, and "there was a sort of amiable rivalry as to who could give away the greatest number of valuable gifts" (1964:84). The description begins to lend a ritual air to the proceedings—a feeling which is verified by the fact that the time not spent in giving gifts was spent hunting, feasting, and dancing (1964:84). As if to leave no doubt about the ritual character of the gatherings, Radcliffe-Brown adds that, although they sometimes serve an economic function, for the most part the things which were exchanged were those which the people could and did supply themselves (1964:82-83). Thus, it seems that the exchange was part of a large ritual; far from creating solidarity in itself, it seems to have had considerable potential for disrupting the proceedings and producing a good deal of ill will.

Other examples are readily found; I will mention two from recent books, both of which are interesting because of the authors' explicit acceptance of the proposition that exchange promotes solidarity. In his book on the Semai, Denton (1968:48-50) says that direct, two-way exchange (balanced reciprocity) is taboo, only sharing (or generalized reciprocity) being proper. Calculating the amount of a gift is also taboo, although it is done by some people; the sanction for selfishness is refusal to engage in further generalized exchange. As with the Andaman Islanders, kills of pigs (and presumably other large animals) are handled very systematically—in fact, more systematically among the Semai, as might be expected from the fact that animal protein is not so abundant. When a man makes a kill, he takes the animal back to camp, where two men other than the hunter meticulously divide up the meat and distribute it to all families (Denton 1968:48-49). The entire complex of customs seems calculated to minimize conflict arising from exchange, which is taboo except under certain closely regulated circumstances.

One brief final example comes from Ben Wallace's (1970:33) book on the Gaddang, a group in Northern Luzon, who have a peace pact institution similar to that of the Kalinga. After a trading partnership is gradually established and becomes regularized de facto, the partners may decide to formalize the relationship by an elaborate ritual by which they become siblings. Formalization, Wallace says, makes the partnership a "dependable source of friendship and trade" (Wallace 1970: 32-33). What seems interesting here is the statement that formalization, i.e., ritual, makes the relationship dependable, but the de facto exchange of goods does not; moreover, there are similar ritual sibling relationships involving no exchange (Wallace 1970:33). It seems, then, that the Gaddang can have 'dependable' relationships without economic exchange, but such exchange does not in itself make the relationship dependable.

b. Peasant Societies

In modern peasant societies, the circumstances are very different. There is much heavier reliance on trade for necessities, and trade is very commonly in the hands of trading specialists, thus producing much more intense and potentially more destructive conflict. In such societies, ritualization is usually maintained in a weaker but more flexible form, i.e., bargaining. In addition, either spatial or social distance (or both) are added, in some cases along with displacement.

In peasant societies much trade occurs in markets which are physically and socially removed from the peasant communities. The trade is thus localized in such a way that coercive sanctions are effective for some kinds of proscribed behavior (e.g., violent behavior). Moreover, the traders, by virtue of their social and spatial distance from the peasants, are removed from the sphere of expectations of fair dealing which the villagers expect among themselves. This change in expectations constitutes a mechanism of displacement by which hostilities are directed toward the market rather than individual traders, and by which the market town is seen as a place to be cheated and a place of questionable morality.

In addition, trade in peasant societies is often characterized by a special form of social distance: it is often largely in the hands of ethnic minorities. Ethnic differences have many of the same, although weaker, properties of spatial distance. Interaction usually occurs in only limited spheres of social life—notably economic. (The classic definition of plural societies embodied the idea that the segments came together only in the market place.) Marriage and, therefore, kinship relations are usually limited (as are friendships, common religious activities, and recreational activities) and trading relations are thus socially separated from other spheres of day-to-day life.

This social distance has two contradictory effects. On the

one hand, as we have seen, by socially separating the traders it focuses the conflict on them and diminishes the possibilities of its being offset by crosscutting conflicts. On the other hand, it insulates most community social relations from an important source of conflict and, as with the spatial separation brought about by markets, helps relieve the trader from the expectations of fair dealing and generosity which the peasants have among themselves. This change of expectations, as does the market place, constitutes a mechanism for displacement of the exchange-generated conflict by focusing some of the tension on inter-ethnic group relations rather than on the parties to an individual transaction. Such displacement helps explain the remarkable hostility often encountered by minority trading groups. It also helps explain why traders who are the object of such hostility are not readily replaced by traders from the majority group: the latter are destroyed by the conflict inherent in their commercial activities or by the uneconomic behavior required of them if they are to avoid conflict.

The possiblity of traders' ventures failing because of the conflict they generate suggests an interesting alternate social solution to the problem of managing commercial conflict: it may simply be allowed to destroy the traders, thus making trading enterprises unstable, with many people circulating through them. Several ethnographic cases (though not necessarily in Southeast Asia) come to mind. Arensbergs' (1968:142-143; 155-159) portrayal of Irish townsmen seems to fit these conditions; the traders are of rural origin and are set up in business by their rural kinsmen, to whom they are then in debt. Trade, however, generates considerable hostility, and the trading enterprises are generally short-lived. Swift's account of the fate of Malays who entered trade during the emergency suggests a similar resolution (Swift 1965:72-75), as does the history of early American general store owners (Carson 1965:24-29).

My own work among the Mon people of Thailand (Foster 1974) provides an example of several of these mechanisms. Even three or four decades ago, Thai villages were primarily self-sufficient communities with subsistence economies. Trade has increased dramatically, however, bringing the peasants into frequent contact with merchants, some of whom even settle in the villages. As the peasants became more heavily dependent on goods acquired through trade (i.e., as they were obligated to purchase more necessities, and a major portion of their resources became committed to the market), it became increasingly important that they buy on terms as favorable as possible.

These circumstances created a dangerous situation. It was only exacerbated by the traditional social organization, which had no clearly defined role for merchants, and which stressed generosity, fair dealing, and lack of profit in personal transactions. It was especially dangerous to any villager who entered trade. On the one hand, he was unable to run a viable enterprise if he abided by local social obligations; on the other hand, his social position and that of his kinsmen was threatened by the full repertoire of formal and informal sanctions for those who depart from traditional obligations.

Although local people were severely threatened if they took up commerce, outsiders were less so for a number of reasons. First, especially if they were members of another ethnic group, they had a degree of social distance from villagers which freed them from traditional obligations and, at the same time, from the informal social sanctions against departing from customary behavior. Second, their ethnic group identification provided a ready target for displacement of commercial stress; in the peasants' eyes, they acted the way they did because they were ethnically different, not because they were traders—although many people did tell me it was impossible for a trader not to be crooked if he were to make any profit. Third, the ethnic difference freed the peasants from traditional rules of etiquette sufficiently to allow a special form of ritualization: bargaining.

An interesting concomitant of these developments which lends some support to my interpretation concerns the dynamics of ethnic relations. Although Mon farmers—the majority of Mons—are rapidly being assimilated by the Thais, the Mon traders are not. They maintain the Mon language and other customs, and they identify themselves as Mon (see Foster 1974; 1975).

c. Modern Societies

Although peasants rely more heavily on trade than do

primitives, and the trade-generated conflict is more intense, peasants are still relatively self-sufficient in comparison with people in modern, industrial societies. In the latter, most persons are dependent on trade for nearly all of the material necessities of life; the intensity and destructiveness of conflict reach extremely high levels requiring still more efficient mechanisms of control.

In modern societies the characteristic regulatory mechanism is removal of the conflict from the sphere of interaction altogether. Goods are sold at fixed prices which are not set by the parties who actually conduct the transaction; rather, prices are established by impersonal forces of the market or by literally distant and inaccessible management (e.g., business management or economic managers in a socialist economy), and the conflict is displaced to the institutional structure of the society itself.

Our own society provides a ready example. We conduct our transactions with the A&P company through the checkout clerk, who is often as ready as the customers to talk about how awful the prices are. Real management is spatially and socially distant and inaccessible, and direct, face-to-face overt conflict behavior is next to impossible. Few options for overt conflict remain: political activities and consumerism are ineffective or at best slow, and destruction of property is risky and, in any case, ethically unacceptable to most people. In any event, prices are fixed to a large degree by The Market, we believe, and are not fully under the control of even the management.

Exceptions to this pattern are instructive. The bane of small grocery business is the management of credit, where personal relationships with the customers place owners in a position similar to that of a peasant trader. In a different vein, some transactions are too large and hostile to be accommodated by the system of fixed prices and inaccessible management, and the traders are the targets of a great deal of subtle conflict behavior. The best example is probably used car sales. Attempts have been made to establish fixed prices (blue books, etc., which are used widely in sales), but prices cannot be fixed due to the size of the expenditure and the manipulability of quality. Bargaining therefore re-enters, and used car salesmen are stereotyped as crooks. Similar conditions exist for new car

Table 1: Mechanisms for Controlling Exchange Conflict

	Primitive Societies		Peasant Societies	Modern Societies
	Exchange between local groups	Exchange within local groups		
Prescription of exchange behavior	Ritualization: embedded in ritual	Ritualization: embedded in ritual	Ritualization: bargaining	Ritualization: bargaining only in large, difficult transactions
Displacement of conflict from parties to the exchange	Not applicable	Generalized reciprocity; conflict displaced to society	Minority traders or market places; conflict displaced to 'the city' or to ethnic group relations	Fixed prices set by remote, inaccessible mechanism; conflict displaced to institutional basis of society
Distance	Membership in different local groups limits frequency and kind of interaction	Not applicable	Ethnic difference and location in market towns limits range of conditions in which interaction occurs	No interaction with target for realistic conflict

sales, real estate, and other large items.

Summary and Conclusions

My argument is summarized in Table 1. Two comments seem necessary in conclusion. First, although I spoke a great deal earlier about the problem of order, I have not directly approached the mechanisms of positive solidarity, as Durkheim would have called them. Although I cannot discuss this issue at length here, a few words are necessary. It is no accident that Durkheim's discussion (and my own) seems to focus strongly on negative solidarity. I would argue that this stems from the sociological character of the arguments; positive solidarity is a cultural matter, not social, but for cultural mechanisms to be effective, social mechanisms must provide the prerequisite negative solidarity. Positive solidarity rests on affective dimensions of social action, which are closely related to sociopolitical myth, ritual, and indoctrination. In themselves, such mechanisms are sufficient to hold society together only in circumstances where social conflict is relatively weak, e.g., in most intertribal trade, as discussed earlier, or in trade for nonnecessities, where ritualization is sufficiently strong without coercive sanctions.

Second, although I have said that the problem of order can be most usefully formulated in terms of variability of social stability and unity, I have spoken so far only of mechanisms for alleviating conflict and for preventing it from disrupting the society. I cannot address myself in detail to the issue of how and under what conditions these mechanisms fail and overt conflict occurs, but a few words must be said about the consequences of their failure.

The extreme forms of overt conflict which follow the failure of the respective mechanisms are quite different. Failure of ritualization characteristically results in individual conflict or, in the most extreme cases, destruction of the ritual institutions which encompassed the exchange. Individual conflict is unlikely to have profound social consequences, but destruction of institutions may entail, literally, the destruction of the society. This is so, since, by the nature of the societies, the conflict is unorganized and once the old ways are destroyed, little remains which might provide the foundations of a new order. Simple societies have been destroyed many times by the introduction of new sources of wealth (e.g., western trade, wage labor, or new technology).

Breakdown of the minority trading mechanisms provides large-scale, intergroup conflict which, in extreme cases, can take the form of genocide. Persecution of minorities who are active in commerce has been known for centuries in the Western World and has become an important fact in the Third World today. Trading minorities are especially vulnerable to the machinations of politicians who wish to invent enemies for purposes of mobilizing political support. Even weakening or withdrawal of protection by the police power of the state may be sufficient to precipitate widespread violence against minority traders. Destruction or expulsion of the trading minority may lead to severe economic dislocations and to long-term social change, but the society is less vulnerable than simpler tribal societies.

Breakdown of the mechanisms for removing conflict from the level of interaction in modern societies leads to revolution, in which the institutional order is destroyed. Unlike primitive societies, however, the scale and complexity of modern societies requires that the conflict be highly organized to have a chance of success, and such organization provides a potential basis for reconstruction. Conflict in modern societies is, therefore, most likely to result in fundamental, but productive, social change.

From Stage to Development in Prehistoric Thailand:
An Exploration of the Origins of Growth,
Exchange, and Variability in Southeast Asia

by

Jean Kennedy

In the explication of the Southeast Asian prehistoric period, we should keep the present salient features of the area in mind. Among these, I would single out diversity—economic, linguistic, social, cultural and ethnic—as the most important. The mosaic of mainland Southeast Asian variability, especially ethnic and economic, is characterized by complex interdependence rather than discreteness. In this paper, the rise and maintenance of variability and interdependence are explored in terms of exchange.

Behind the innovations that lead to progress and growth, whether academic, social or economic, there lies ultimately a willingness to go out on a limb, by radical deviation from an established order. Growth is then dependent on the degree to which the limb becomes the route of exchange between the new and experimental, and the established mode; growth may involve transformation and accumulation as well as replacement. I shall return to these points later.

Though I have drawn data from recent published work on prehistoric north and northeast Thailand, I think my suggestions have wider relevance in Southeast Asia. Rather than discuss the problem of internal versus exogenous generation of prehistoric change in this area, I choose to disregard the possibility of external forces of change, for which I see no convincing evidence, and treat the prehistoric data as they stand. It can be shown, I think, that variability is already exhibited in the prehistoric period. A modification of the frameworks proposed to encompass the Thai data shows that interdependence and exchange can also be taken into account.

I shall argue that the prehistoric articulation of regional variants into a mosaic of interdependence may be the background against which the later, external influences, especially Indian and Chinese, should be seen. In this context, I shall discuss Wheatley's (1975) paper on the development of trade in Southeast Asia in the early historic period, which he sees as generated from the outside.

Some preliminary comments are necessary on, first, the nature of the frameworks set up to encompass the prehistoric evidence, second, the conceptions of trade and exchange in prehistoric studies, and third, the problem of making sense of socio-cultural developments in prehistory.

Prehistoric Southeast Asia as a whole is as yet little understood. While enough is known to call into serious question the very influential chronological framework set forth by Heine-Geldern (1932), which was based largely on ethnological data (Solheim 1969), the evidence of solid, well-conceived prehistoric research in the area is still very thin. It is therefore not surprising to find that most efforts have been directed towards the establishment of adequate temporal and spatial frameworks, which are prerequisite to further, more detailed studies. One cannot produce nomothetic or explanatory syntheses in a near vacuum.

It is, further, not surprising that much of the analysis of recent archaeological data, especially that relating to mainland Southeast Asia, has been cast in terms of stage models (e.g., Gorman n.d.; Higham 1972; Solheim 1969); most of these are complex stadial models in the sense of Groube (1967:4). While such sequential or developmental frameworks may meet the needs of brevity and efficiency in the initial descriptive synthesis of regional data, they are based on a series of static units, emphasizing the nature of the units themselves, and their order in time. If, as seems likely, we are justified, first, in assuming that we have, in prehistoric mainland Southeast Asia, developments that are "self-maintaining, self-transforming, self-transcending, directional in time and therefore irreversible" (Julian Huxley, cited by Groube 1967:10), and second, that the rate of change throughout is not constant, but is rather marked by sharp fluctuations, our attention should be directed to the "points of change rather than the platforms of conservatism," the strophes rather than the intervening stadia (Groube 1967:22). The application of stadial models prejudices at the outset any attempt to examine the nature of the progression from one unit to the next.

Stadial models, whether simply chronological, developmental, or a mixture of both, not only obscure fluctuations in the rate of change, but also lead to a serious confusion in the interpretation of variability. The modern interdependence of diverse patterns, good examples of which are found in northern Luzon (J. Peterson in press, and this volume) and Sarawak (Harrison, unpublished) as well as in mainland Southeast Asia, is not accounted for adequately. If minority economic modes are regarded as surviving isolates (Heine-Geldern 1932), diversity is explained, but full dependence of these modes on the dominant mode, rather than interdependence of the two modes, is strongly implied. Thus, the time-depth of variability is crucial to our understanding of the modern pattern. Stadial models tend to carry chronological implications, whether this is intended or not, and in this form they accord very poorly with Southeast Asian prehistoric evidence (Hutterer 1976; W. Peterson 1973), which shows a distinct lack of neat periods even at the level of local sequences.

I shall attempt to show that change in Southeast Asia has been much more complex than the simple progressions implied in the current models, that its essence is accumulation rather than replacement (Groube 1965; W. Peterson 1973).

Exchange in prehistory has been considered largely in terms of trade. Further, studies of prehistoric trade have tended to concentrate on the dispersal of resources, whether natural products or distinctive artifact types, beyond the boundaries of their locus of natural occurrence or of manufacture. The underlying assumptions are simple, direct, and unshakeable: that such objects do not move themselves but are moved by the agency of man; that man stands in relation to such objects not as an individual but as a member of society. Further, one suspects, it is assumed that it is not in the nature of man as a member of society to create—or to give—something for nothing; whereby production or procurement is not random or accidental, but purposeful. If one can posit the transfer of objects from one locus of procurement or production to another, it is probable that something is going in the reverse direction, whether identifiable or not. The complement of such a flow of items 'a', specific to context 'A', into context 'B' might consist in the elegant balance of a return flow of items 'b', specific to context 'B', into context 'A', both sets of items being readily identifiable. Such a neat balance of identifiable goods might be an archaeologist's dream, but it seldom comes true. The return flow to context 'A' might be the satisfaction of fulfilling societal obligations towards 'B', or the engendering of an obligation in 'B' with an indefinite prospect of return. Such transactions, with unilateral passage of material goods, might fall within a definition of trade, but they are not necessarily distinguishable from similar transfers brought about by threat, coercion, or force, with a return flow of ill-will.

The point is simply that neither trade nor exchange is to be defined easily in archaeological contexts. It is necessary, also, to distinguish between conceptions of trade as a mechanism for the dispersal of goods and as a form of exchange. The former conception may lie close to archaeological data. However, if our intention is the understanding of the dynamics of human groups, we should be interested in trade conceived as exchange; for it is only by consideration of the nature and consequences of exchange that we can move from the spatial patterns of artifacts and resources to the interactions of groups of people. Chang's pragmatic statement that, archaeologically, "Trade may be characterized as an essential form of the movement through space of natural resources, raw and processed..." (1975:211) might be rephrased thus: trade is one form of the movement between social groups of their resources, procured and manufactured.

The consideration of systems of exchange of goods and services between groups of people plunges us into territory hotly disputed by anthropologists, economists, and others in various disciplinary combinations. The shrewd archaeologist stands slightly to one side of the various lines of battle, in order to benefit from both sides of each dispute. If all is confusion, it is possible to take refuge in the specificity of archaeological data, pushing aside the protective cover of distributional charts only when the dust clears.

From such refuges, much has been gained.

Highly sophisticated distributional analyses have been made possible by the application of new physical and chemical techniques. It is often possible to trace a natural resource or raw material to a definite and specific source. Refinements such as catchment analysis clarify the study of spatial relationships between sites of occupation and of manufacture, and resource areas. Statistical analyses of artifact assemblages place characterization of consistent cultural forms on a much firmer footing, so that intrusive items may be more readily identified.

Procurement, production, consumption and exchange lead into the domain of economics. It is worth noting that the conception of trade in archaeological studies, which focuses on the spatial relations of natural resources, is paralleled by the conception of economic prehistory (e.g., Higgs 1972), which focuses on the study of evidences of procurement, production, and consumption. The focal points in the latter conception are the selection of a specific repertoire of natural resources and the means by which they are controlled and used. Thus, 'economic behavior' in archaeological expression is often a euphemism for provisioning, just as trade often means simply dispersal. Both these simplified conceptions lie close to the data. The interest in economic behavior lies again in the provisioning of society, not of individuals, and in the recognition that provisioning is moderated by socio-cultural forces. It is frustrating to find that the closer one stays to the data in hand, the further one is removed from consideration of the issues that stimulated interest in those data.

Recent refinements in handling the data of archaeology aside, there has been a resurgence of interest among archaeologists in matters explicitly social, particularly in social and political organization and in the evolution or development of society. It is no great surprise to find a current vogue in archaeology for models of social and political organization drawn from the cultural evolutionists. In particular, discussion of political and economic aspects of tribal society has come to be seen as a fruitful exercise. This is a welcome shift from the facile and often naive conceptions of tribalism that used to be proffered as meat on the meager archaeological bones. Archaeologists are among those who have benefited greatly from the accumulation of solid ethnography of the last few decades.

As sophistication in considering socio-cultural aspects of prehistoric groups has increased, so also has the intractability of the problems encountered. Thus, Renfrew's discussion of both the Aegean early Bronze Age (1972) and the late Neolithic of Wessex (1973) rests on concepts derived from the ethnological characterization of the chiefdom, especially in the terms of Sahlins (1968) and Service (1962). Insofar as such models of the chiefdom lead to consideration of the nature of the articulation of production, distribution, power and authority, the exercise is helpful and provocative. But the application of an ideal type, such as that of a chiefdom, to a particular set of archaeological phenomena does not in itself generate an explanation: it can, at best, merely point the way. Explanation can arise only from the evaluation of postulates derived from the application of the model to the data, which will, at some point, necessitate a measure of fit between the model and the data, through transformation of one into the terms of the other. This is a very tall order, because of of the disparity of the data sets involved, and the expression of one set as an ideal type.

In discussing Neolithic Wessex, Renfrew sets forth a list of features characteristic of chiefdoms (1973:543) which exemplifies part of the problem by its manner of expression. While a form of society set up as an ideal type is bound to involve a static model, many of the characteristics Renfrew identifies are expressed as comparatives: thus, greater population density and greater productivity, increase in the total number [of members] of society and increase in the size of residential groups, more clearly defined territorial boundaries and a more integrated society with a greater number of sociocentric statuses, and so on. Greater, increase, more— in comparison with what? The strong temporal bias of archaeological data is at odds with static formulations. Dynamic models are needed if processual explanations are to be sought, and it is no secret that such models are hard to come by in the realm of ethnology. Thus, while Renfrew is able to clarify to his satisfaction the nature of the late Neolithic field monuments of Wessex, suggesting a reason for the disparity between these and the somewhat unimpressive artifact assemblage, in terms of postulated economic and political modes of social organization, we are left as much in the dark as before about the developments that result in chiefdoms and the construction of very large monuments.

A related problem obtains in Wheatley's recent discussion of the role of Indian merchants in sea trade with Southeast Asia, from about the beginning of the Christian era. This contact he sees as a central force in the transformation of tribal society into urban polity. He suggests that

> the entrepreneurial activities of Indian traders induced the emergence of dysfunctional partial structures which inhibited the fulfillment of some of the social needs of the relatively segmentary societies and chiefdoms characteristic of Southeast Asia in the late centuries B.C. (Wheatley 1975:238).

It is assumed that Southeast Asia at this period

> was occupied exclusively by societies whose most advanced level of political organization was the chiefdom and among whom the instrumental exchanges characteristic of a reciprocative mode of integration predominated (1975:228).

It is further suggested that the 'ecumene' of such a group would be somewhat restricted, as to the course of a single river valley. The dysfunctions to which Wheatley refers have to do with the role of the leader of such a group, the main beneficiary of the new trade, now in a position of 'cultural brokerage', but without tribally derived sanctions for innovations or for the assertion of a new kind of authority. Thus, in brief, the eventual adoption of a novel political structure, based on divine kingship, is accounted for, as is the transformation from a reciprocal to a redistributive economic mode.

I think it can be suggested that the stage is already set, the transformations of political and distributive modes already well under way indigenously, long before the period for which Wheatley is able to provide his excellent documentation of mutually beneficial interaction.

Wheatley's argument can be summarized in general terms as the engendering of a disequilibrium by exogenous forces, followed by systemic change. Where Renfrew applies a static socio-political model to a set of archaeological data, and thus cannot account for prior development, Wheatley takes roughly the same model as a prior condition, and appears to explain subsequent development. However, it is questionable that he has in fact shown how the systemic transformation might take place. For it is central to the political model of tribalism that he espouses, whether that of a chiefdom or a segmentary society, that the leadership role, whatever form it takes, is generated by the society, that political authority is socially sanctioned, and that its nature cannot be changed from the top without prior transformation of the social sanctions that maintain it.

In discussing two contrasted types of leadership (characterized as big-man and chief) in Melanesia and Polynesia, Sahlins (1963) has made clear the limits of expansion of political authority in the segmentary tribe and chiefdom. The authority of the Melanesian big-man rests on personal power, based on a loyal following; he amasses, in Malinowski's phrase, a 'fund of power', which rests on his ability to control and intensify domestic production within his faction, and is dispensed in return for renown within a wider circle. But because of its ultimate dependence on a loyal following, the renown or political power of a big-man is internally constrained: factional loyalty hangs by a slender thread, easily broken. Thus, leadership of this form is inherently unstable, because authority over followers can be intensified only so far.

Unlike the Melanesian big-man, the Polynesian chief is installed in an inherently powerful office by his position in a ranked system of lineages. Power and authority reside more in the office and rank of chief than in the ability of the aspiring individual to gather a following. The office of chief carries with it the economic obligations to the chief of the constituent households. The economic role of the chief is redistributive. But here also, there are constraints on the economic and political leverage of the chief: extension of political power by increasing the flow of wealth to the chiefly apparatus would either overtax domestic production or decrease the redistributive return of goods to the community. "In either case, the well developed chiefdom creates for itself the dampening paradox of stoking rebellion by funding its authority" (Sahlins 1963:298). Behind both types of leadership lies the system of more or less autonomous domestic production.

If political and economic change are to be explained, it is

the social sanctions of power and authority that must undergo modification, otherwise there will be merely rebellion rather than revolution. More specifically, the assertion by a leader of divine status has no meaning without wholesale conversion of society, or at least of some productive segments of it, to a concept of kingly divinity. A shift from reciprocity to redistribution necessitates some change in the interrelationships of units of production and in division of labor. None of these changes is likely to be brought about simply by dictate from the top. Such far-reaching transformation could be brought about in a relatively short time by massive colonization or by conquest, but not, in the absence of other factors, by the kind of piecemeal contact envisaged by Wheatley.

There is further cause for doubt in Wheatley's exposition. He characterizes the indigenous Southeast Asian mode of exchange as based predominantly on reciprocity. The spurt of Indian commercial interest in western Southeast Asia at the beginning of the Christian era seems to have taken place without the need for conquest, colonization, or even coercion on a large scale. Such intrusions are not mentioned in early sources; nor do later, better documented events in that part of Southeast Asia under Indian influence suggest anything but the peaceful pursuit of mutual interest.

How, then, do the interests of profitable commerce come to be served? What are the commodities involved? For the latter question, there is as yet no clear answer, though there is certainly no lack of possibilities. It seems likely, however, that, whatever the items sought by Indian or other merchants, they were by no means all of coastal provenance. Thus, one is led to postulate not only internal trade, such that a diversity of products found its way to the coast, but also perhaps some mechanism whereby goods came to be accumulated in specific coastal loci. That the existence of such loci might be a stimulus to the development of mutually beneficial exogenous trade seems obvious. It is doubtful that such a network could be brought about by external stimulation alone. Further, given the later mention in Chinese sources of indigenous Southeast Asian seafaring traders, early indigenous trading networks may well have involved movements by water, both coastal and riverine (see Wheatley 1975:231).

I suggest, then, that the expansion of trade about the beginning of the Christian era is a continuation of an already well-established Southeast Asian pattern, extended by the interactions of Southeast Asian and Indian coastal traders.

In support of this idea, I would like to substitute for Wheatley's static tribal society a brief consideration of some archaeological evidence drawn from the systematic excavation of prehistoric and early historic sites in Thailand. Though these sites are few, a pattern is beginning to emerge.

There are three phases of concern, which correspond to three broad ecological zones. These zones are drawn as follows. The first includes the northwest and central uplands, from the Petchabun mountains in the east to the eastern catchment area of the Salween River in the west. This zone intergrades with the second, the rolling piedmont country of the Khorat plateau, just to the east of the Petchabun mountains. The third zone comprises the eastern lowlands of the central Khorat plateau, which drain directly east to the Mekong River. The first two zones are marked by considerable diversity (Bayard 1971; Higham 1972).

The best documented site for the earliest phase is Spirit Cave, which lies in a karst formation in the upland zone. Gorman has described the Spirit Cave assemblage as representative of an early, widespread technocomplex based on broad-spectrum hunting and gathering, which he labels Hoabinhian. The Spirit Cave assemblage includes lithic material and diverse plant and animal remains; it persists from late Pleistocene times until about the seventh millennium B.C. At the end of the sequence, there appears an intrusive complex which includes pottery (Gorman 1970; 1971).

In the second zone, the western Khorat plateau, lies Non Nok Tha, an open burial mound for which there is a long sequence spanning three periods. The early period is characterized by stone tools, cord-marked pottery and inhumation burial. A single cast, socketed copper tool derives from a burial of this period. The middle period is marked by the appearance of a sophisticated bronze metallurgy, but otherwise, in ceramic and burial style, it represents broadly a continuation of the early period. A discontinuous late period is marked by cremation burial and iron tools. There is evidence for rice in the form of inclusions in pottery, for hunting of a range of mammals including wild bovids, and a strong suggestion of stock raising, of Bibos, and perhaps pig (Higham 1975) from the beginning of the sequence (Bayard 1970). Though the dating of the site, in particular as it relates to the bronze, is considered controversial by some, I consider a fourth millennium B.C. date the best estimate for the early period. In fact, Non Nok Tha is one of the few sites anywhere for which the excavator has presented all the available dates, consistent or not, rather than merely a selection. The late period begins about the end of the first millennium A.D., after a long break in the sequence (Bayard 1970; 1971; in press).

There is a possibility that wet rice agriculture accompanies the appearance of the cremation burials and iron at the start of the late period. However, hunting does not cease entirely, though there is a decrease in the proportion of large mammal species. Indeed, seasonal hunting persists in the area to the present day (Bayard 1970; Higham 1975).

In the eastern-draining lowlands of the Khorat plateau, in Roi Et province, a later series of sites has been excavated by Higham and Parker (1970). Higham dates the first phase of settlement in this area to the first millennium B.C., possibly earlier. He has argued that, in much of this area, techniques of water control—necessitated by permeable soil and low, unreliable rainfall—would have been prerequisites of rice agriculture, which, in his view, these sites represent. His ecological argument—that expansion into the Roi Et area was dependent on water control, and can perhaps be correlated with the development of iron technology and the domesticated water buffalo—might be extended to the occupation of the Chao Phraya alluvial lowland (Higham in press a; in press b). Early pottery from all the Roi Et sites tested contains rice chaff as temper. At Bo Phan Khan, exploitation of salt deposits dates back to the late second century A.D. At Ban Tha Nen, an early habitation period dating to the later half of the first millennium B.C. is succeeded by a period characterized by iron smelting and then by a late occupation period. Don Tha Pan, another occupation site, dates from about the same time (Higham 1972; in press a; Higham and Parker 1970).

There are many other sites that might be fitted into this pattern. Several general points about the pattern should be made. First, it has been very difficult to interrelate sites of both early and late Metal Age on the basis of ceramic sequences. This obtains between the Roi Et sites and Chan Sen (Bronson 1973; Bronson and Dales 1972; Higham 1972 and in press a) and other sites of about the same age, such as Pimai (Parker 1971), Tha Muang (Watson 1968), and the Lopburi Artillery Camp site (Bayard 1970). At an earlier period, the same problem obtains to some extent among the Phu Wiang sites (Higham 1972; Higham and Parker 1970), Non Nok Tha, Kok Charoen (Bayard 1970; 1971; Solheim, Parker and Bayard 1966; Watson 1968), as well as Ban Chiang, Om Kaew, Kok Khon and other recently tested sites in the northeast. However, for all these sites it can be said that the pottery has a general family resemblance. At sites such as Non Nok Tha where there are long sequences, the first major ceramic discontinuity falls late in the first millennium A.D., after the rise of the Indianized centers of historic times.

A second point is that, in the later two phases, the sites mentioned seem to represent the first occupation of the areas. There are no clear parallels to Spirit Cave in the area of Non Nok Tha, nor are there parallels of either site in the Roi Et zone. Further, the earliest sites known in the alluvial valleys of the upland zone postdate the Roi Et sites (Bayard, Marsh and Bayard 1974:72). Recent surveys and test excavations by Bayard, Marsh and D. Bayard (1974) in the Pa Mong reservoir area (which lies in the piedmont zone on the west of the Khorat plateau, northwest of Non Nok Tha and west of Ban Chiang) have located both cave and open sites, with Hoabinhian-like assemblages which include cord-marked pottery. Though these sites are as yet undated, it is suggested that they are likely to be later than 5000 B.C. (Bayard, Marsh and Bayard 1974:73). This is interesting in view of the apparently very late dates for the survival of Hoabinhian industries in cave sites of the Malay Peninsula (Dunn 1964; 1966; cf. Gorman n.d.; 1971). Similarly, on the lowlands of the Khorat plateau, one of four tested rock shelters, yielding a lithic assemblage, is dated by C_{14} to about A.D. 500 (Solheim 1968b).

I have summarized the archaeological data in terms of a rough sequence, each phase marked by a shift in ecological zone and a major innovation in mode of production. This outline has

much in common with the stage frameworks mentioned earlier
(Gorman n.d.; Higham 1972; Solheim 1969). However, my
interest in such a framework is not in the opening of each phase,
the innovation that defines it, but in its closure. Thus, at Non
Nok Tha, the general pattern suggestive of rice growing, hunting,
and stock raising persists well after the establishment of the
later iron period sites of Roi Et. For the Hoabinhian phase, one
can make a similar argument of persistence, with the possibility
of a relatively late expansion into the piedmont zone as well.

In sum, the establishment of the new subsistence patterns,
here represented by Non Nok Tha and later by the Roi Et sites,
did not lead to the termination of the preceding patterns. Rather,
the patterns come into coexistence. Thus, the overall pattern is
of increasing diversity over the whole area.

In further consideration of this point, let it be said that
what follows is speculative and certainly exceeds the available
archaeological evidence. In choosing to emphasize exchange, I
am well aware that my discussion ignores a great many
important problems. I will refrain, therefore, from glorifying a
fragmentary exposition by attempting to phrase it as a coherent
model.

I suggest that, at the pioneer stage of each phase, there is
no reason to assume the cessation of communication between the
innovating group and groups representative of the previous phase,
for two reasons. First, a minor point, such innovations may
lead to lessening of competition for the same resources. Second,
there is good reason to suppose that it is precisely in the pioneer
phase that exchange across phase boundaries is established by
the extension of pre-existing networks of reciprocity. However,
the reciprocal relationship is now assymetric in the following
sense: while the exchange system pertaining to the established
mode of production of the parent group would be able to absorb
new products, it would not be dependent on them. On the other
hand, the pioneer group, whether occupying a marginal zone or
specializing within the zone of the parent group, might well be
dependent on a continued supply of some products not available in
the marginal zone, or lost by the concentration of efforts on a
segment only of the resources of the parent group. In other
words, the pioneer group offers supplements in exchange for
necessary complements. By virtue of this exchange, the overall

spectrum is broadened. This extension can be stated in terms
either of the ecological marginality of the pioneer group, or of
pioneer niche specialization within the original zone; the result
is much the same.

As the pioneer mode becomes established, the assymetric
dependence of the new on the old will tend to shift, but there is
no a priori reason to suppose that exchanges will cease; indeed,
the dependent relation might shift to the older mode.
Innovations, especially technological ones, will come to be
reflected in the old pattern. Hence, overall, the spectrum is not
only broadened and diversified; it also has a long-term tendency
to shift. A series of such steps carries with it the articulation
of different modes of production by a proliferating network of
exchanges. Early wet rice agriculture and modified broad-
spectrum hunting and gathering thus need not be seen as
contrastive isolates, but rather as the accumulated result of an
additive pattern.

Systems of exchange, in maintaining links between old and
new forms, not only foster innovation by decreasing the risks of
specialization or nonconformity; they also, by their areal
extension and persistence, are the bridge that leads to growth
rather than to simple substitution of the new for the old. The
increase in diversity and differentiation of productive modes is
conducive not only to further economic specialization, but also
to the development of intra- and inter-group controls and to the
rise of central-place exchange. In such developments, perhaps,
lies the origin of the ethnic mosiac of modern Southeast Asia.

I suggest that it was the outcome of such a course of
development, extending to coastal and riverine indigenous
traders, that stimulated the florescence of Indian trade at the
beginning of the Christian era. The transformations wrought in
the structure of relationships between domestic production and
distribution and the changes in the division of labor brought about
by increasing specialization are internally generated.

In the absence of anything more than a suggestive pattern
in the archaeological evidence, I will sum up instead with a
congruent ethnographic statement of symbiotic articulation of
mountain and valley people. I have discussed economic
exchange as a major force in interregional growth,

diversification and articulation. The following quotation is from Leach's (1954) exposition of ritual communality, crosscutting ethnic, linguistic, and ecological boundaries, in the Kachin Hills area of northern Burma—although his reference is to a much later time. Perhaps the origins of the 'ritual language' perceived by Leach are traceable to the growth and diversification of "that very large part of culture which is concerned with practical economic action" in the prehistoric period.

> I set out my problem as being a study of how particular structures can assume a variety of cultural interpretations and how different structures can be represented by the same set of cultural symbols.
>
> What we have found is roughly this. The population of the Kachin Hills Area is not culturally uniform; one would not expect it to be so for the ecology varies. But if we neglect that very large part of culture which is concerned with practical economic action—that is the whole of what Malinowski might have considered to be the apparatus for the satisfaction of basic human needs—we are still left with something, that something which in this book I have dealt with under the heading of ritual action. And as concerns these ritual aspects of culture the population of the Kachin Hills Area is relatively uniform. The people may speak different languages, wear different kinds of clothes, live in different kinds of houses, but they understand one another's ritual. Ritual acts are ways of 'saying things' about social status, and the 'language' in which these things are said is common to the whole Kachin Hills Area. (Leach 1954:279).

Acknowledgement

I thank Peter Bellwood, Alice Dewey, George Lovelace, Charles Streck and Dave Tuggle for help in the preparation and revision of this paper. While their critical comments have done much to clarify and improve both the ideas and their expression, all responsibility is mine.

I also thank the Center for South and Southeast Asian Studies, The University of Michigan, Ann Arbor, and the Travel Fund of the Graduate Student Organization, University of Hawaii, for making possible my attendance at the conference.

Exchange at the Upstream and Downstream Ends:

Notes toward a Functional Model of the

Coastal State in Southeast Asia

by

Bennet Bronson

At the heart of this essay is a speculative model, presented without the detailed supporting evidence that would be needed to establish it as a probable explanation for any particular sequence of past events. While I believe the model is potentially useful for explaining a number of otherwise puzzling findings by historians and archaeologists, it must for now remain no more than a working hypothesis. Hard data through which it can be tested do not yet exist.

For the sake of brevity I have assumed an acquaintance with several concepts bearing on the relationships among early political, economic, and geographical systems: van Leur's (1955) characterization of pre-capitalist or peddling trade and its distinction from the commercial methods inaugurated in sixteenth and seventeenth century Europe; Lane's (1966) emphasis on the primacy of political costs in early international commerce; Polanyi's (1957) separation of marketized and non-market modes of exchange; and the formal models of economically-generated settlement patterns developed by modern geographers (e.g., Haggett 1965). The most influential of these for present purposes are the ideas of van Leur as amplified and extended by Steensgaard (1974). The reader may note that the following pages contain a number of unacknowledged and unrecognized borrowings.

The proposed model is designed to improve our understanding of the history of a single key subregion: that part of Southeast Asia traditionally dominated by what van Leur (1955: 104-107) calls 'Sumatran' states, the thinly-populated coastlines of the large insular and peninsular land masses of Malaysia, the Philippines, and western Indonesia. With the exception of Java, which resembles the Southeast Asian mainland both politically and demographically, the insular-peninsular region presents a seeming anomaly in the general pattern of early political and economic development. It is known from documentary and inscriptional evidence to have contained a number of advanced political units in early times. True states seem to be as old there as in any part of Southeast Asia except perhaps Burma and North Vietnam. This is not surprising in view of the area's strategic location with respect to communications routes connecting regions notable for their early development of high levels of socio-economic complexity.

Yet these early littoral states were and continued to be unimpressive from several points of view. Despite their political power and seeming cultural importance, well documented by Wolters (1967), they left few archaeological traces of themselves (Bronson and Wisseman 1974 in press). Their hinterlands were infertile which limited cultivation. Their populations, judging by the present carrying capacity of those hinterlands, were not large. Their historically known successors—Malacca, Brunei, Palembang, Jambi, Banjermasin—were unusually dependent on commerce for obtaining even such necessities as clothing and food; their economic production was specialized and, one suspects, small. One is thus not surprised to find that states of this sort tended to be impermanent. Aside from Śrīvijaya (if indeed that term does not refer to a series of political units), no state in the subregion mentioned in Chinese sources and none of the known archaeological sites of the classical period can be shown to have lasted longer than one or two hundred years. The northern mainland and Java contrast strikingly in this respect. In Thailand, for instance, many or even the majority of the larger settlements of the pre-Thai period are multi-component sites, containing evidence of several distinct cultural periods (Bronson and Dales 1972). Many of the mainland and Javanese polities named in Chinese chronicles and local inscriptions—Champa, Angkor, Pyu, Funan, Ho-ling, perhaps Dvāravatī— unquestionably survived for a minimum of several centuries.

We therefore have some reason for thinking that events taking place in the southern coastal regions followed a rather different course from events in the North and in Java during the period of early Southeast Asian state development, between the first and fifteenth centuries A.D. This fits well enough with observations made in later times: van Leur's above-mentioned distinction between the 'Sumatran' and inland types of kingdoms in the mid-second millennium, as well as the impression of several specialists on the recent period (e.g., Geertz 1963a: 7-8) that the trade-oriented, coastal or pasisir societies constitute a sociocultural type distinct from the inland, agriculture-oriented societies of central Java and the drainage basins of the Irrawaddy, the Chao Phraya, and the Tonlé Sap.

Although the situation is interesting, we lack at present the data to come to grips with it. Archaeological field work in the southern coastal region is still uncommon; because of this, as well as unusual transportation difficulties and a general scarcity of easily-noticed monumental architecture, no urban or quasi-urban site earlier than 1200 A.D. has been discovered anywhere south of the Thai-Malaysian border (discussed in Bronson and Wisseman in press, and Bronson et al. 1973; for a possible exception see McKinnon 1973). Detailed historical information is is equally hard to come by in spite of the pioneering efforts of such specialists as Wolters (1967; 1970), Wheatley (1961), and Wang (1958). And a possible alternative approach, the use of analogy derived from studies of more recent political and economic patterns, is rendered difficult because there are so few economic historians and economic anthropologists specializing in Southeast Asia. A small number of systematic studies on limited aspects of the pre-modern and non-colonial economic situation do exist: Cushman (1975) on the eighteenth and nineteenth century junk trade between China and Thailand; Volker (1954; 1959) on the sixteenth and seventeenth century traffic in porcelain between East and Southeast Asia; Dunn (1975) on ecological and economic relationships of aborigine groups in West Malaysia; Ellen and Glover (1974) on pottery trade in the Moluccas; Macknight (1973) on Macassan trepang trade and commercial institutions; and of course the unsystematic but provocative intuitions of van Leur himself. However, these studies are too few and too preliminary to give us confidence that any post-sixteenth century pattern can be extrapolated into an earlier period. We still have nothing for Southeast Asia that approaches the precision and generality of the work done on Chinese and Japanese economic history or of the syntheses of traditional Melanesian economic systems produced by Harding (1967), Sahlins (1972) and Brookfield and Hart (1971:243-362).

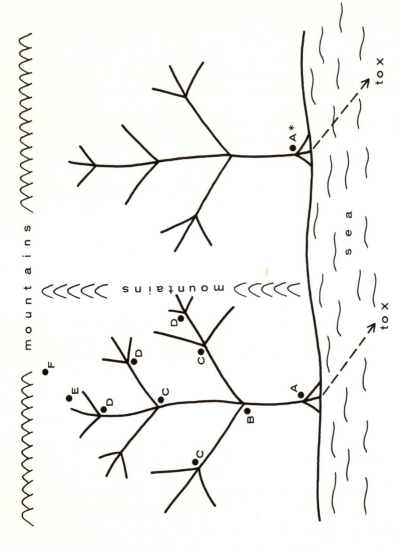

Figure 1: Abstract Model for Exchange between a Drainage Basin Center and an Overseas Power

These obstacles to inductive understanding form the justification for proposing a model based entirely on abstract, a priori considerations. As will be shown later, enough empirical data do exist to give the model a certain historical plausibility. But for the moment it seems best to present it in as schematic a fashion as possible.

The model focuses on a single hypothetical class of ancient exchange networks, one which involves the control of a drainage basin opening to the sea by a center located at or near the mouth of that basin's major river. A diagram of such a system is illustrated in Figure 1. It contains these elements:

A, the center at the river mouth;

B and C, second- and third-order centers located upstream and at primary and secondary river juntions;

D, the most distant upstream center to participate in the A-based system of market exchange and the initial concentration point for products originating in more remote parts of the watershed;

E and F, the ultimate producers of these products and perhaps centers on a separate exchange system based on non-market institutions, involving goods only part of which come from or go to the marketized system centered on A;

X, an overseas center which serves as the main consumer of goods exported from A and the principal supplier of its imports; and

A*, another river-mouth center some distance along the coast, controlling a hinterland similar to that of A.

This system is assumed to operate under several constraints. (1) The interfluvial countryside of the drainage basin is sufficiently marshy, forested, or mountainous to confine all movements of goods to water routes, rendering the economic pattern closely congruent with the dendritic pattern formed by the main stream and its tributaries. (2) X, the overseas center, is the economic superior of A, possessing a larger population

and a more productive and technologically advanced economy.
(3) The basin does not contain enough concentrated cultivable
land to permit the development of a true peasant society, where
wealth is extracted by an elite directly from a land-bound
farming population and where revenues derived from trade are
consequently of less than central importance.

Actual examples of places with many of these physical
characteristics will occur to any Southeast Asian specialist.
They include most of the modern subdivisions of Sumatra and
Borneo as well as several pre-modern states in the island region
and the mainland. My concern here, however, is less with
physical description than with exploring the hypothetical political
and economic functioning of any such system.

For one thing, it seems probable on a priori grounds that
relations between A and D will be rather more egalitarian and
less consistently coercive than is usual in relations between
high- and low-order centers in an ordinary state. This follows
from the assumptions that A needs a steady flow of exportable
goods from D and that it cannot easily assure this through direct
political measures. If D were one of a small number of
specialized centers with spatially concentrated productive
facilities and an immobilized work force, then A might find
coercion feasible. However, when (as must generally be the
case) D is a simple concentration point for forest-gathered and
swidden-grown goods produced by populations which are
inherently dispersed and mobile, any coercive solution will
require an impractical expenditure of capital and military
manpower. Non-political solutions must therefore be sought,
among which the most obvious is to develop a trading system
offering manufactured or maritime products capable of inducing
D to enter the regional economy voluntarily. For A, the most
satisfactory sort of inward-bound trade items are those which it
can produce itself but which D cannot make because of
limitations imposed by scale factors of production, because of
technological incapacity, or because necessary raw materials
are lacking. It is pointed out later that centers in A's position
sometimes show a disproportionately high development of
industries producing finished manufactured goods.

D itself can obtain outward-bound goods from its own
hinterland (from E) through a variety of mechanisms, most of

them again non-coercive. D may be ethnically allied to this hinterland population or may be peopled by ethnic groups centered downstream at C or B. In any case, quasi-kinship institutions combined with clientship and trade-partner relationships, some perhaps verging on debt-peonage, should characterize most exchange transactions upstream from D. That these will for long remain perfectly reciprocal, free of bargaining and other attempts to establish asymmetries of economic advantage, is improbable. However, it is at and above this point in the drainage basin that non-market structures can be expected to dominate trade, if for no other reason than that D is militarily vulnerable and its customers liable to disappear if dissatisfied.

B and C may relate to A rather differently, since coercion becomes more practicable further downstream. A center like B or C is fixed to a given location (a major river junction), contains a larger and more concentrated population than a D-level center, and is physically more accessible, all of which alters A's chances of success in trying political methods of assuring the flow of trade material. We may expect that B- and C-level centers will sometimes by administered by or even colonized from A; they may well be bound to A through instruments of indirect rule, such as oaths of fealty, regular tribute, and assertions by A of rights to select or confirm local leaders. Collection and onward transmission of goods originating further upstream are likely to be in the hands of representatives of A, who may be the local government or may inhabit autonomous enclaves. As far upstream as the C level, either viceroys or garrisoned trading posts would seem to be possible solutions from an economic standpoint.

If B is a producer rather than a collector and distributor of goods produced elsewhere, its relations with A may shift. It might even hope to attain equivalent status and so become A's direct rival, provided that it has a number of C- and D-level centers under its own control and a productive population in its immediate vicinity. Competition between coequal upstream and downstream centers is attested historically in such areas as nineteenth century Magindanao (Ileto 1971:1-33) and sixteenth century Burma. Several of the great inland kingdoms of the mainland and Java may conceivably represent instances where such competition was long ago resolved in favor of an upstream center whose productivity and population size were sufficient to overcome the locational advantage enjoyed by a former coastal capital.

The relationship of X to A bears a superficial resemblance to that of A to B, both being relations of political and economic inequality. But there are critically important differences. For one thing, while A and B need each other almost equally, no such symmetry exists in the needs of X and A. X is essential from A's standpoint. It produces the major portion of governmental revenues in the form of export and import duties, state trading profits, and whatever service and protection fees can be extracted from traders en route to X from more distant centers. Further, X supplies goods which may themselves serve as political instruments, as emblems of rank or legitimation, and as gifts through which the loyalty of subordinate centers can be maintained.

A, on the other hand, may not loom large in X's scheme of things. The revenue-raising measures of A-level centers are likely to become a dangerous nuisance to the traders of X, while the products of such centers can probably be obtained from a variety of sources. As in the case of exporters of tropical products in the present world economy, in the time of A's florescence a number of competing centers are likely to have existed in the same region, each possessing a hinterland capable of supplying X with the same kinds of goods. The situation encourages X's traders to bargain vigorously, periodically moving their custom from one A-level center to another without regard to the acute economic and political hardships suffered by a center temporarily deprived of foreign trade.

X may even consider that A overprices the modest services it performs in protecting commerce and in concentrating and processing export items, and may therefore make efforts to bypass it so as to deal directly with centers at the level of B or C. The experience of the European capitalist traders of the seventeenth and eighteenth centuries shows that even in preindustrial economies it can be advantageous for overseas powers to push their trading posts quite far into the hinterland, balancing the extra military expense with savings on the otherwise unreasonable exactions of would-be monopolists on the A-level. While one may doubt that many outsiders possessed sufficient resources to attempt such a solution in precapitalist times (the great Tamil merchant communities may be an exception—e.g., Indrapala 1971), the fact remains that X is far from helpless even in A's immediate neighborhood. The determined attempts of X to evade what the rulers of A may regard as their legitimate perquisites, and perhaps the chief support of their domestic authority, must often have given rise to disproportionately drastic reactions. Such reactions might range from naval buildups and intensified diplomatic activity to all-out war with other A-level states.

The natural enemy of A, after all, is not X but A*, another coastal center distant by a few days' travel. A* probably has access to the same variety of potential exports in its own hinterland and may be as capable as A of providing the services needed to attract traders from X. We can imagine that either center might manage to supply all the requirements of X by intensifying production in its own hinterland if it were not for X's interest in maintaining several competing sources of supply. The situation where a number of centers, each producing well below capacity, are forced to take shares in a regional export trade is not satisfactory from the standpoint of the rulers of either A or A*. While the wealth may thus be spread over several centers, this is achieved at the cost of a boom-and-bust regional economy where each mini-state periodically experiences grave crises as the buyers' favor shifts from port to port. The political consequences of these crises makes it certain that preventing them will be a constant concern to local governments. Yet, assuming that diplomatic representations to X and attempts to form regional cartels are both unsuccessful, the rulers of A have few remedies. They can resign themselves to a ruinous price war. They can try to exclude X's traders from from other ports through an increase in piracy and official naval activity, in effect through declaring a blockade. Or, as a seemingly less expensive alternative, they can attempt the direct neutralization of their competitors.

This may in fact be one of the few cases where wars of conquest and even extermination make apparent economic sense. For an inland kingdom focused on the control and exploitation of a hierarchically-organized peasantry, conquering a similar kingdom must usually be an enterprise of low marginal untility, with military and administrative costs which will in the short run greatly exceed any anticipated gain to national revenues. The intended victim may or may not help with military costs by submitting after the capture of its capital (which in a traditional agricultural state will contain only a small proportion of its elite and commoner population); it will in any case prove costly to administer. Extracting surplus from numerous individual landholders, the heart of administrative endeavor in any agricultural polity, must have a low margin of profit over outlay even in normal circumstances, where the extractors are an experienced and legitimate local elite. Under the circumstances of conquest, the labor and capital needed to reestablish regular state revenues must often be prohibitive, so that the would-be conqueror will prefer to loot and return home.

The cost-benefit ratio is far more favorable for a coastal kingdom contemplating a career of conquest of its peers. The revenues of neighboring coastal kingdoms derive from fees and duties levied on a small number of wealthy and vulnerable taxpayers; collecting these will require little added administrative expense. The process of conquest itself will be simplified, for only one center—the capital located at the river's mouth—need ever be seized. Moreover, the intending conqueror may expect to increase his income substantially beyond the previous combined incomes of his victims, for he then will have monopolistic control over all sources of the goods desired by the traders of X.

He may even find that he can entirely eliminate the administrative costs of conquest by adopting policies which foreshadow those of Jan Pieterzoon Coen. While one is naturally reluctant to suggest that genocide could anywhere have been a regular instrument of state policy in ancient Southeast Asia, a case could be made for believing that some governments did occasionally implement related policies. The surprising incidence of recorded population transfers after victorious wars is a case in point, as is the otherwise inexplicable emptiness of such fertile areas as the Deli Plain at the time of first European contact.

Even if the hypothesis of total war is rejected as too drastic, it remains plausible that the system under consideration will be unusually mutable. Wars between coastal centers should be frequent, perhaps more frequent than in any other pattern of regional socioeconomic organization except the parallel one which involves competition for control over inland caravan routes. Not only are the stakes high but the investment necessary to enter the game is minimal, for the aspirant to coastal hegemony needs little more than personal magnetism and enough early success to attract followers and encourage the defection of supporters of rival leaders. Many such states would be built on patronage and personal prestige and would therefore have little of the institutional inertia of polities with developed civil and religious bureaucracies. Most should rise and fall with unusual rapidity. Their capitals, like boom towns in other systems, should be capable of reaching impressive heights of prosperity and then of vanishing almost overnight.

Up to this point, little has been presented except naked speculation without either supporting data or suggestions as to how it all might be proved true or false. Nothing can be done about the paucity of facts. As I have said, only a handful of relevant studies are yet in existence, and none of them provide sufficient information to reconstruct the interplay of politics and economics in the history of any particular ancient coastal state. However, certain of the hypotheses presented above can be tested in principle through archaeological experiment, and others can be rendered plausible through adducing historical facts. The remainder of the essay is devoted to discussing how this might be done.

We should expect, for instance, that archaeological sites at the B and C levels will yield a wide range of artifacts identical with those found at A, including artifacts originating in X. On the other hand, such sites should rarely contain evidence of actual colonies of overseas merchants, whose presence upstream of an A-level center would indicate that A is anomalously impotent and that the overseas merchants represent an improbably well-organized and well-capitalized venture.

Sites at the D level can be expected to show little evidence of cultural connections with A except for a limited range of putative trade goods. The wide diffusion of Chinese ceramics and Javanese bronzes in inland portions of insular Southeast Asia demonstrates that in fact a number of foreign-made trade goods did historically penetrate through intermediate-level sites into the remote hinterlands of many river basins. However, it seems intrinsically probable that communities in A's position would have sought to produce as many of these goods as possible themselves, assuming they could muster the resources and skills necessary for medium-volume production through techniques which the inland peoples could not duplicate. That some coastal centers did succeed in this is shown by the existence of a number of surviving salt- and fish product-trading systems, as well as by historical evidence for very extensive iron-wroking and textile manufacture in Palembang (Jaspan 1975) and perhaps by archaelogical evidence for iron-working at Santubong (Harrisson and O'Connor 1969).

Sites beyond the D level should contain many of the same trade goods that reach as far as D but with a different distribution. Between A and D, each successively more remote node of the system can show almost any proportion of A-derived artifacts, ranging from assemblages virtually identical with that of A to assemblages largely local in content—a marketized network is capable of moving either large or small volumes of goods over very substantial distances. Beyond D, however, the proportions of objects from A should begin to decrease in a regular, linear fashion. This conclusion follows from the fact that, by definition, trade outward from D to E and F will be conducted by inter-village reciprocity and other non-market institutions. As Renfrew, Dixon and Cann (1968:328) have suggested with regard to the distribution of obsidian in Neolithic sites in the Middle East, non-market exchange systems (where small quantities of goods are passed onward through a succession of independent settlements) may often produce a distribution pattern showing a steady linear decrease in frequency over distance.

Sites in the position of A should exhibit, as indicated above, manufacturing activities considerably in excess of local needs and should be the only sites in their drainage basins to house organized groups of foreign merchants. Both these characterisitics are of a kind which one might hope to recover by archaeological means. Whether the most directly relevant traits of a trading port, the installations for materials handling and storage, will be archaeologically visible seems less probable. Historically, Southeast Asian shipping has not required permanent wharves, and wooden warehouses in tropical regions—particularly those built on piles—can be expected to leave no trace.

More indirect evidence for A-level functions may be provided by the presence of monumental construction, which in a coastal, trade-oriented state should be mostly concentrated in the capital. A sparing use of politico-religious monuments seems a logical feature of a society where hinterland populations are dispersed and where the segment of that population whose loyalty is critical—the elite who reside in A and in upstream centers of communication—is sufficiently small to be controlled through the distribution of benefits. In such a social system, as distinguished from one with a developed peasantry and a numerous sacrally sanctioned elite, monumental construction would seem to have little utility beyond maintaining the status of A's rulers vis-à-vis their counterparts in other coastal centers. The presence of a number of monuments in a B-level center might show either that it was for a time in a position to challenge the dominance of A, or indeed that this trade-based model is not applicable. If an inland area contains a graduated series of monumental sites, with major structures in central places, smaller structures in secondary places, and so forth, we may perhaps conclude that it once contained a kingdom of the classic inland kind. A hierarchical distribution of monuments is almost prima facie evidence for the existence of a peasant-based society.

However, the most salient of all predicted characterisitics of sites at the A-level, and of trade-centered coastal states in general, is their impermanence. This expectation is to a degree confimed by numerous examples in the history of southern Southeast Asia. Indeed, river-mouth city states, some spectacular in their heyday but all evanescent, seem the general rule everywhere south of Thailand and outside of Java. Their high mortality rate is shown by the short time that their names appear in the Chinese histories reviewed by Wheatley (1961), Wolters (1967) and Wang (1958). Their insubstantial character, when compared with the capitals and hinterlands of inland states, is demonstrated by the difficulty of finding them archaeologically. Even Śrīvijaya, the most prominent of them all, has left so few physical remains that its approximate location is still in serious doubt. It is clear on the face of it that we are dealing with a social and economic system quite different from those we consider normal in the heartlands of other civilizations. An explanation like the one offered above seems indicated.

The explanation is still, however, in a very tentative state.

It will not be overly convincing or useful until it is refined to include numerous parameters, among them estimates of the size of settlements and systems, of transport times and costs, of profits and state revenues, and of the quantities and kinds of goods involved in trade. Such data do exist in scattered sources; with them in hand perhaps even simulation models could be developed. Furthermore, it will be necessary in the future to assemble detailed local histories which focus on the interplay among social, economic, and political factors. The absence of case studies, from either the modern or pre-modern period, is perhaps the chief limitation on what can be accomplished through the kind of thinking attempted here.

One broad theme which has not been discussed is the applicability of the river-basin model to economic systems outside Southeast Asia. Its physical parameters, after all, would seem to fit parts of West Africa and northern Europe; with slight alterations they could be applied to parts of Central Asia as well. However, while I lack a specialist's knowledge of those regions, I am not optimistic that such a model can be applied cross-culturally with any great profit. The determining conditions of the Southeast Asian coastal systems include not only a river-interrupted coastline but a relatively unusual, almost neo-colonial, pattern of export trade. It is not clear to me that such conditions were closely duplicated elsewhere in the world.

II.

CONTRIBUTIONS TO THE ETHNOGRAPHY

OF EXCHANGE IN SOUTHEAST ASIA

Ecotones and Exchange
in Northern Luzon

by

Jean Treloggen Peterson

Anthropologists have examined prehistoric exchange of items of material culture and of ideas, but the potential of the exchange of critical food items has been largely ignored. Among contemporary populations of hunters and adjacent farmers such food exchanges appear to be common.[1] Only Turnbull (1965) and J. Peterson (in press a) have fully reported this type of exchange. Within Southeast Asia such relations are known to exist between agricultural populations and Negrito groups throughout the Philippines and the Malay Peninsula. These relationships are similar wherever they occur, and appear to persist in spite of extreme environmental change (Peterson and Peterson, in press; J. Peterson, in press a). Characteristically, Negrito hunters maintain a low labor intensive system dependent, in part, on food exchanges with their sedentary neighbors.

On the northeast coast of Luzon, Agta hunter-gatherers and Palanan farmers carry on extensive exchange of this sort. In addition, each population has beneficial effects on the environment exploited by the other. This exchange and the environmental modifications I shall describe have probable significance for prehistory. I shall first summarize my data on contemporary exchange and the effects of human populations on their environment. I shall conclude with a model which discusses the importance of these contemporary behaviors for an interpretation of prehistory.

The Environment and People

The Palanan Bay watershed (see Map 1) on the northeast coast of Luzon is isolated and environmentally inhospitable.

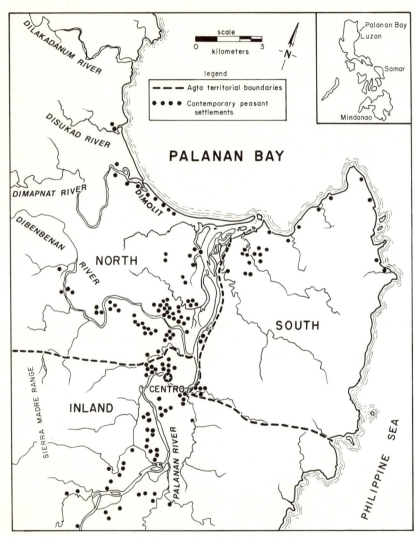

Map 1. Palanan Bay, Northeastern Luzon.

A trading launch comes annually from Manila, and contact with the Cagayan Valley is limited to a six-day hike or to the charter of light planes from across the mountains. Air travel is prohibitively expensive for Palanan residents. The area is characterized by rugged coastlines, forested hillsides, and narrow river valleys. The mean monthly dry season temperature is 82 degrees and rainfall exceeds 100 inches annually (Spencer and Wernstedt 1967:54, 423). The rainy season, from September to January, is often characterized by constant, unbroken cloud cover and incessant rain, further limiting internal mobility and eliminating external contact. Thirty-two percent of all typhoons reaching the Philippines strike the northeast coast of Luzon. Disease as well takes its toll on life in Palanan. Malaria, tuberculosis, and bronchitis in particular claim many lives and debilitate many residents of the area.

Archaeological excavation (W. Peterson 1974, and in press) indicates the existence of seasonal occupation of relatively substantial structures along the coast between 550 and 3500 B.P., and survey suggests the existence of a classic Neolithic culture of unknown date on the coast and up the Palanan River. Early Spanish records report two 'pagan' populations in the area, the Agta and the Irraya (Keesing 1962:258). The present-day inhabitants refer to the inland mountainous area to the west as Irraya and use the same term to describe the swiddening people inhabiting that area.

Presently, two ethnically and physically distinct populations occupy Palanan. About 10,000 farmers (Palanan) live in the flatland areas along the Palanan and Disukad Rivers and adjacent coastal strips (see Map 1). Palanan settlement in modern times until World War II was confined to the lower Palanan River valley around Centro. During the Japanese occupation in that area, many Palanan moved up and down the coast and up the river valleys leading to the present-day distribution. This pioneering endeavor continues as the farming populations seek new lands. The 800 Agta Negritos, referred to in the literature as Dumagat or Aeta, live largely by hunting and fishing in areas fringing peasant settlements. Agta and Palanan speak mutually intelligible languages which Hedland and Wolfenden (1967:596) categorize as Austronesian.

Subsistence in Palanan

The Palanan farmers produce mostly corn, roots (especially yams and manioc), and small amounts of rice on an average land holding of five to ten hectares per household. Land is inherited, or a pioneer may clear a forested area for permanent cultivation. An average farmer produces just under forty cavans (2.12 bushels) of corn, just over eight cavans of rice, and a variety of roots. Other domestic flora is minimally cultivated. Fruits and vegetables raised include pineapple, eggplant, tomatoes, two types of squash, and beans. Perennials and tree crops are somewhat more common and include jackfruit, papaya, coconut, and banana.

As compared to the rest of the Philippines, few domestic animals are raised in Palanan. Typically, a family might own four carabao (water buffalo), a pig, and about two dozen chickens. While all of these animals may be eaten, they rarely are. Carabao are primarily draft animals; only carabao too old or ill to work are killed, and the mayor's consent is required for legal butchering. Owners of pigs and chickens regard them less as a food source than as an investment. They are rarely killed to provide daily food. Chickens and, occasionally, pigs may be butchered to provide meat for life crisis events such as weddings, funerals, and death anniversary ceremonies. Hens are kept for their eggs and roosters for weekly cock fights. All domestic animals are primarily raised to be butchered and sold for cash in emergencies, such as critical need for medical care or house repairs.

Agta production activities are markedly different from those of the farmers. The Agta produce minimal domestic vegetable foods. Cultivation is confined to small swidden plots, usually on hillsides, which are planted predominantly by the elderly. Draft animals are rarely used; most planting is done with dibble sticks, and the plots abandoned after two or three years. Some Agta have never planted, 12 percent (n=52) were not planting in 1968, 1969, or both,[2] and 25 percent planted exclusively roots. These latter cultivate not more than .5 hectare, often less than .25 hectare, and sometimes fewer than half a dozen plants. Only 50 percent of Palanan Agta regularly plant at all, and 38 percent usually, but not always, plant.

Only 56 percent (n=52) of Agta plant a few vegetables and 46 percent claim tree crops, usually only one or a few coconut palms or banana plants. Collecting wild vegetables accounts for some vegetable intake in roughly 15 percent of Agta meals.

Some Agta (37 percent) own domestic food animals which are raised for sale to peasants. Agta have a powerful aversion to domestic meat and refuse to eat it. Wild game and fish account for the vast majority of Agta food production. For the Palanan area as a whole, Agta per-family production of boar totals 12 kilos per month, just under three kilos per month of deer, and just over 43 kilos per month of fish. Other foods— wild fruit, grasses, roots and tubers, monkeys, snakes, birds—are hunted and collected incidentally. Fresh and marine shellfish are collected regularly, and commonly marine species are stockpiled in tide pools. Tops of wild roots are replanted to propagate for collection later.

There are significant areal differences in these production figures. Agta recognize three distinct bounded territories within Palanan. The three territories offer the same types of resources, but there is considerable variation in the concentration of resources from territory to territory. The resources of each territory may be tapped only by its residents and their visiting kinsmen from other territories; marital alliances are managed to provide optimal access to resources for extended families. The regional variation is illustrated in Table 2. These boundaries, like the ethnic boundary between Agta and Palanans, represent a means of channeling exchange and interaction. Seasonally Agta exploit kin ties in other areas in order to equalize naturally occurring variation in resources within territories, and between the rainy and dry seasons.

Agta-Palanan Interdependence

The Agta have limited carbohydrate, and the Palanan have limited protein foods; through trade each supplies the other with needed foods. The extent and nature of their interdependence as expressed through food production is illustrated in Figure 2.

Food exchange represents only a part of Agta-Palanan economic interdependence. Access to cleared land and Agta

Table 2: Agta Food Production

	Agta Resource Territory		
Resource	North	South	Inland
Boar	<6 kg/week	0	2.5 kg/week
Deer	>1 kg/week	0	>1.5 kg/week
Fish	<5 kg/week	>12 kg/week	<11 kg/week
Corn[a]	26.66%	2.4%	34.1%
Camote[a]	<44%	>80%	>100%
Trade ratio[b]	.207	1.28	.36

a) Production/Consumption percent. These figures indicate the percent of corn or <u>camote</u> consumed by Agta which they produce. The remainder is obtained in trade.

b) This figure represents the mean amount of fish traded over the mean amount of corn traded, and provides an indication of the favorability of trade. A higher value indicates trade more lucrative for Agta. The figure for the southern territory is somewhat deceptive as it includes exchanges in town; local exchanges in this area are much less lucrative for the Agta.

labor are other important dimensions of exchanges between the two populations. As noted, Agta swidden small plots of land which they then leave as they move on to other forests or abandon cultivation altogether for a year or more. They retain the right to return to that land at their discretion. Many Palanan, on the other hand, are eager to acquire abandoned Agta land to cultivate permanently. By acquiring cleared Agta land they save themselves a significant amount of labor. They estimate 175 to 200 man hours of labor expended for each hectare of forest land cleared in Palanan, labor which has already been expended when they obtain cleared land. Agta, who prefer to remain on the forested fringes of peasant settlement where game is abundant, often have little interest in returning

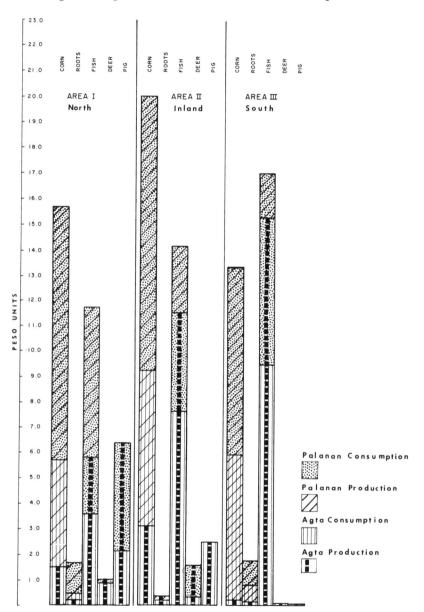

Figure 2: Agta-Palanan Food Production Interdependence

to abandoned plots. Palanan either purchase Agta land, or,
where tenser relations prevail between the two populations,
usurp it. In most cases where land is purchased Agta retain
rights to any permanent crops they may have planted on the land.
Where land-grabbing occurs, the politically and legally more
sophisticated peasants encounter few obstacles. Unable because
of ignorance or illiteracy to exercise their legal rights, and
having relatively little interest in permanently held land, the
Agta prefer to move on and avoid unpleasant confrontations when
their land is taken. In effect Agra are creating a niche into
which Palanan may easily move.

It is difficult on the pioneering peripheries of the Palanan
area to assemble a sufficient number of persons for clearing,
planting, and harvesting. Particularly in these areas Palanan
are dependent on Agta labor. Agta are reluctant to assume long-
term agricultural work which seriously inhibits their hunting and
fishing activities, but they will work a few days at a time when
the labor need is critical. In exchange for their work they
receive food and/or wages. This arrangement provides Palanan
with the labor force they critically need at certain times.

Other incidental goods and services are provided to each
other by these two populations. Palanan give Agta shelter in
typhoons and medicine when they are ill. Agta serve as
messengers and as guides to Palanan crossing the mountains.
Some Palanan rely on Agta to collect tree resin (almasiga) which
they in turn sell to the Tagalog trader once a year. Most
Palanan rely on Agta for provision of sundry forest products
such as trees for house posts, bamboo for building, rattan for
construction and repair of houses and farm implements, and
herbal medicines. Palanan provide non-critical 'luxury' items
such as clothing and cooking pots to Agta friends. These gifts
and exchanges of goods integrate Agta and Palanan into an
external trade network extending far beyond their own area.
These factory goods are obtained through two local variety
(sari-sari) stores and from the Tagalog trader who comes once a
year. Older residents recall visits by small Chinese trading
vessels.

The medium for most of these transactions between Agta
and Palanan is the ibay (special friend) relationship, a term
used by both Palanan and Agta. An ibay relationship involves

one Agta, usually married and male, and one peasant, also usually married and male. The two friends, or partners, recognize a mutual commitment regularly to provide goods and services to each other. The Agta provides protein foods to his partner in exchange for carbohydrate foods. The extent of this commitment is reflected in the fact that peasant ibay plant 10 to 30 percent in excess of their own consumption needs in anticipation of Agta requests for trade. In shortfall years a portion of this food would be utilized to feed his own family. Agta, on the other hand, place the protein needs of their ibay as high priority in distributing the protein they produce. Approximately two-thirds of the peasant population are dependent on Agta for 30 to 50 percent or more of their protein food. Others exchange more sporadically. Nearly all Agta obtain 70 to 100 percent of their carbohydrate foods from Palanan. One-third of the peasants and nearly 100 percent of the Agta acknowledge an ibay relationship, and another one-third of the peasants trade regularly.

While non-ibay exchanges of protein for carbohydrates do occur, the ibay relationship is unique in that it demands a commitment for regular exchanges, it allows for extension of credit, and it commits the partners to other economic transactions as needed. For example, an Agta who has been unable to obtain protein may, nonetheless, ask his ibay for sufficient carbohydrate foods to see him through days or even weeks, with the implicit understanding that he will provide protein when he is able. Conversely, a Palanan can ask that his ibay supply him with a specified amount of game for a life crisis event or to feed field workers during planting or harvest. Ibay may also depend on each other in crises, such as illness, and peasants may rely on their ibay to work as field laborers when the occasion demands it. There are social, political, and religious implications to this relationship as well (J. Peterson 1976).

Effectively, Palanan and Agta are specialized relative to each other. Increase by Palanan in the production of domestic animals would require labor intensification. They would have to either construct and maintain fences to keep animals out of their fields, and/or produce food to practice controlled feeding. It is probably cheaper to provide food for Agta in exchange for meat or fish. Agta labor is a bonus in this system of exchange.

Agta expenditure of protein for carbohydrate costs them little, if any, additional labor for the fish or game, and saves considerably as compared to the time and labor investment in procuring and processing non-domestic carbohydrate foods.

This combination of specialization within a population and exchange between populations allows particularly effective utilization of land and labor resources. I should note that the same principle applies to many exchanges which occur among Agta. It may, as well, effectively increase carrying capacity without increasing labor output, although it intensifies land use. I have suggested (J. Peterson, in press c) that it represents a kind of dual technology 'double-cropping' (Barth 1959:8-9).

Expansion of the Ecotone

A second feature of relations between hunters and farmers has to do with the effect of each on the physical environment of the other. The hunting-gathering Negritos of Southeast Asia have have been regarded as militarily weak and technologically inferior populations, forced by the advance of more sophisticated indigenous peoples to a meager subsistence on the margins of economically preferable land (Blair and Robertson 1903-1909 (43):114-115; Reed 1904:14, 23; Beyer, Steiger, and Benitez 1926:8; Cole 1945:5; Spencer 1954:4; Kroeber 1919:18; see J. Peterson in press b for a fuller discussion of these sources). I have indicated that Agta create a ready niche for peasant expansion, but this expansion may offer benefits to Agta as well. Using historical and ethnographic data from the Philippines I have explored the ecological alternatives to earlier interpretations (in press b). The 'marginal' areas which are described in the literature on Southeast Asian hunters actually manifest significant assets. Contrary to earlier impressions, these regions are not necessarily remote from cultivated areas. Their actual nearness to farmlands offers the potential of trade with peasants and the additional advantage that game is attracted to cultivated fields. Cultivators create, as a by-product of their planting activities, environments which are optimal for game, and hunter-gatherers provide a check on wild game populations which might otherwise destroy domestic crops. Game is attracted not only to the crops themselves, but also to the 'edge' between forest and fields, or forest and grassland—the area which ecologists have identified as the ecotone. Ecotones characteristically exhibit higher densities of non-mobile game which require more than one vegetation type, such as boar or deer (Dasmann 1964:75; Allen 1954:72-74; Odum 1959:278-81). This effect is most pronounced "where man has greatly modified natural communities, so that a patchwork of small community areas and numerous ecotones result" (Odum 1959:280-81; see also Leopold 1933:131-32 on the 'law of interspersion'). I propose that the expansion of cultivation throughout prehistory, far from destroying the potential for hunting, has in some cases enhanced it by creating more 'edge'. There is historical and ethnographic evidence from the Philippines to support this proposition. This material indicates that game and forests existed in abundance at the time of European contact and were diminished as a result of the presence and activities of Europeans. Further, it demonstrates that game abounded specifically on ecotones.

That the quantity of game has diminished since contact times is indisputable. Diminution of game has, however, apparently been the result largely of contact and external trade, rather than of indigenous farming expansion which purportedly forced the hunter-gatherers into 'marginal' or inferior areas. Spanish trade and tributes markedly diminished forests, and vast quantities of deer hides were shipped to Japan [Blair and Robertson 1903-09 (18):98-99; (12):188]. Conceivably, the peasant-hunter relationship described in historical sources as the medium for collection of Spanish tributes was comparable to the contemporary ibay relationship [Blair and Robertson 1903-09 (42):295].

The picture offered by historical records is one of a super-abundance of game and vast forests at the time of contact, and diminution of these resources not by indigenous farming peoples, but rather through colonization and trade. I might also mention that historical accounts suggest, as do World War II recollections of living Agta, that hunters are a people entirely capable of military defence against lowlanders in spite of technological limitations [Blair and Robertson 1903-09 (38):27; (40):303, 304; (14):131; (24):232 f.n.; (36):239]. If, as these various accounts indicate, the combined activities of cultivation and hunting had so slightly affected these resources [see Blair and Robertson 1903-09 (37):295], a case can scarcely be made for cultivators destroying optimal hunting ground and forcing hunters into inferior areas. I propose that, in fact, the reverse may have occurred: as cultivation spread in any given area it may well have enlarged the optimal hunting territory. My data from Palanan support this conclusion.

As noted, the peasant settlement area in Palanan has expanded since World War II. Both before and after expansion Agta frequentation and hunting ground has been on the immediate peripheries of peasant settlement. Far from depriving the Agta of valuable resources, farming expansion has actually increased the optimal hunting area because it has increased the amount of 'edge', the ecotone. I have estimated the linear extent of the ecotone of the earlier nucleated settlement as ten miles, while the linear extent of the present-day ecotone is around 30 miles. Thus, peasant expansion has approximately tripled the linear extent of the optimal hunting area.

Detailed studies of game counts on ecotones are inadequate to demonstrate the extent of the effect of expansion on game and hunting. Such studies are virtually lacking for the tropics. Temperate climate studies of game birds and white tail deer, however, would indicate that we might anticipate that expansion of the ecotone would positively affect boar and deer populations. Ecological data of this sort must be collected for the tropics.

Those hunting areas which are preferred by Palanan Agta as offering superior hunting are immediately on the peripheries of cultivated areas or are by-products of horticultural or agricultural activity; that is, they are secondary forest areas. Relatively little hunting is done away from the 'edge'. Their hunting activity is lucrative; it effectively feeds two populations. 'Edges' that have cultivated fields as one of their components are even more attractive. Many kinds of game are specifically attracted to cultivated fields. Productivity of these fields may be lowered by foraging game, and fields are occasionally decimated, particularly by pigs. Agta hunt game in cultivated fields, especially corn, camote, and cassava fields. Traps are regularly set on the edges of these fields and in abandoned swidden plots. In this respect, swiddening may offer a special advantage. Swidden fields are small and non-contiguous, thus creating 'edges' within an 'edge'. Since it is the diversity of 'edges' that attract game, swidden fields are also optimal because of the diversity of domestic plant life within them.

The data from Palanan, then, offer evidence of the contemporary value of 'edges' for hunters, of the particular value of 'edges' with a cultivated component, and of the fact that as a cultivating activity expands it actually increases the amount of optimal hunting area. This relationship between the activities of cultivators, the environmental modifications such activity produces, and the concomitant creation of optimal hunting zones certainly existed in the past as well. From the viewpoint of the prehistorian, it follows that as the practice of cultivation developed and expanded in local areas within Southeast Asia and elsewhere, it may have created greater potential for the maintenance of a hunting way of life among any adjacent hunting populations or for the cultivators themselves, because it created more 'edge'. At the very least it must have compensated for the reduction in overall home range. Certainly continuing indigenous expansion by itself could lead to destruction of this system. As 'edges' of expanding areas abut on other 'edges', overall 'edge' would be reduced. The pre-contact system, I believe, was relatively stable and afforded ample game for hunters, in spite of cultivation and burning of forests both for planting and for game drives by hunters.

Conclusions and Implications for Prehistory

These interpretations of hunter-farmer exchange and mutual modification of the environment offer far-reaching implications for the interpretation of prehistory. In prehistoric times the activities of cultivators and hunters may well have been mutually supportive, each creating and maintaining an optimal niche for the other, with food and labor exchanges enhancing relations. This is a far cry from the usual interpretations which view technologically more sophisticated populations as necessarily displacing and replacing hunting populations.

Given the assumption that certain processes occur repeatedly throughout time, as evidenced, for example, by convergent evolution, the synchronic variation exhibited by the Agta and their relations with farmers have diachronic implications.

Figure 3: A Model of Exchange and Ecotone Expansion

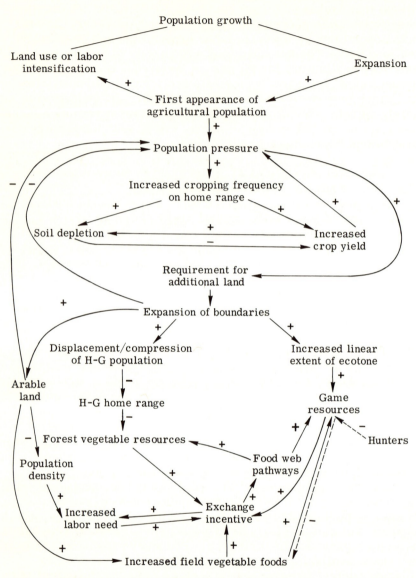

[The portions of this model dealing with agricultural expansion and exchange were developed earlier by W. Peterson (Peterson and Peterson in press).]

Warren Peterson and I have suggested (Peterson and Peterson in press) that exchange across hunter-agriculturalist boundaries constitutes an improvement in the efficiency of energy flow for both populations by lowering labor expenditure and broadening the food web. The extended food web results in an increase in resource availability for all groups involved. Exchange creates a food web which transcends ethnic and territorial boundaries and which provides greater resource variety and an improved safety margin. Exchange adaptation can also be seen as a means of surviving on reduced home range, converting potentially insufficient home range to sufficiency.

Adjacent populations of hunters and farmers offer each other double advantages. First, they modify the environment in mutually profitable ways, and second, they exchange food. I have suggested that environmental modification occurred prehistorically. I have no doubt that food exchange occurred prehistorically as well. The combined effects of the creation and exploitation of ecotones and food exchange may account, in part, for the long term co-existence in Southeast Asia of diverse technologies, contemporaneously and prehistorically. As W. Peterson and I (Peterson and Peterson in press) interpret this material, it offers one explanation for the long term persistence of technologies in the archaeological and ethnographic record. This, I might note, complements Kennedy's interpretation in this volume of prehistoric technological persistences in Southeast Asia. I should also note that the focus in this work has been boundaries or fringes, both human and environmental, rather than ideal types.

The variables operating in this system may be described in terms of Figure 3. Population pressure leads to increased cropping frequency on the existing home range of early agricultural populations and to a requirement for additional land. Increased cropping frequency increases crop yield but it eventually depletes the soil. These factors combine to induce an expansion of existing territorial boundaries, reducing immediate population pressure for that area. Boundary expansion, while it increases available arable land, displaces and compresses adjacent hunter-gatherer populations by reducing the extent of their home range. This may, in turn, negatively affect their access to forest vegetable resources, providing an incentive to exchange. As agricultural expansion decreases hunter-gatherer home range, it increases the linear extent of the ecotone, leading to an increase of some game types on the ecotone. As hunters exploit these 'edge' species, they are able to provide protein in exchanges with peasants. Other stimulae to exchange are increased cultivated foods resulting from increased arable land, and the acute labor needs of the cultivators resulting from lowered population densities. Dotted lines indicate game feeding on cultivated fields, but held in check by the activities of hunters.

Data to substantiate every aspect of this model remain to be collected. The model, however, offers new interpretations and suggests areas for future investigation. The linking of two subsistence systems in this manner may delay the need for technological change to a more labor intensive system. Where archaeological evidence suggests coexistence of two systems with different subsistence types we should consider the possibility of a linkage of this sort. Pursuit of the data essential to testing this model seems worthwhile given the potential re-interpretations of prehistory offered.

Notes

1. Such behaviors are reported, for example, for the Birhor of India (Sinha 1972:386-387; Williams 1968:128), the Paliyans of India (Gardner 1972:416-417, 441-442, 405), the !Kung Bushmen of the Kalahari (Lee 1972a:331-334; 1972b:141; 1972c:348-349), the Hadza of Africa (Woodburn 1968:50), the Malay Negritos (Skeat and Blagden 1906:50), and throughout the Philippines (Garvin 1963:32, 41, 76, 9, 80, 58, 146, 158, 163, 261; Maceda 1964a:46-48; Warren 1964:46-48; Vanoverbergh 1925:431f, 157; Schebesta 1952-57 (2): 156f; Reed 1904:44; Fox 1953:98).

2. These figures may be skewed to show more planting activity among Agta than they actually practice. This is because during the period of field work, as any time, some Agta are off hunting for periods of a year or more, not planting, and therefore not available for interview and not represented in the figures offered.

Contemporary Malay Traders
in the Gulf of Thailand

by

L. A. Peter Gosling

Throughout Southeast Asia today there are frequent glimpses of what was once a vast and complex network of indigenous interisland and coastal sea traders. Bugis craft still cluster their masts in Singapore harbor, Chinese operated tongkangs penetrate the coastal mangrove forest along the Malacca Straits for charcoal, and interisland traders stitch together the scattered islands of Eastern Indonesia and the lesser islets of the the Philippines. Not long ago it was possible to see Minangkabau traders in Colombo, and Chinese-Thai junks in Hong Kong; these are reminders that traditional sea trade networks once extended beyond the regional limits of Southeast Asia. These scattered fragments are being reduced year by year and soon will be completely replaced by transportation more suited to a transformed economy.

One surviving, but declining, traditional sea trade system is focused on the city of Kuala Trengganu in the Malaysian State of Trengganu on the east coast of the Malay Peninsula. At one time this trade system connected with those of the Java Sea, Sulu Archipelago and Vietnamese coast; currently it operates in the Gulf of Thailand, with only distant memories of longer voyages. There are passing references to the sailing vessels of Trengganu scattered in the literature (Gibson-Hill 1949; 1953), but there is no detailed study of this particular traditional trade network. The present paper is based on oral histories collected from the captains, sailors and owners of the surviving trading vessels. By now many of the informants are deceased, and this incomplete record may be a sadly inadequate monument to a complex system in decline, one which deserves more detailed treatment and a better biographer.

The oral histories were collected in Kuala Trengganu in

1955 and augmented in 1962. My colleague Tungku Shamsul Bahrein of the University of Malaysia deserves great credit for developing the excellent oral accounts of the informants. Trips on Trengganu sailing vessels and visits to the various Thai ports— where they conduct their current trade—gave great appreciation of their operations. The oral histories provide most of the material used in this paper, and quotations from the informants have been included in the text. Some of these quotations have been paraphrased or edited for clarity and irrelevant material has been eliminated where such omissions do not alter the meaning.

The current long-distance trade is carried out by large two-masted sailing schooners, or luggers, based in Kuala Trengganu. The trade is limited to ports at the head of the Gulf of Thailand— such as Ban Laem, Samut Songkhram and Bangkok—and to intermediate ports along the Thai-Malay peninsula. In the immediate post World War II period there were were also trips to Saigon and other Vietnamese ports, but these have ceased. Memory recreates the larger world of Trengganu trade two generations ago.

> We sailed to Java to bring back sugar to Singapore and here [Kuala Trengganu]. There were many [sailing ship] traders in the Java Sea, and it was hard to get cargoes, and also we were often cheated. It is said that in the old days no one would dare to cheat us, because we had a reputation of being like the Bugis [warlike], but I doubt this.
>
> We sailed to the island of Labuan, and Brunei, and my father used to sail to Sulu. We carried rice from Siam, and we returned with some kind of wood [bark] for sale in Singapore.
>
> When we sailed to Saigon, we went first to Pulau Kaki [Pulau Condor] and then turned west to get to Saigon. We would take shrimp and fish paste, and bring back rice.
>
> Once when Haji Awang was to go on the pilgrimage [to Mecca] we sailed to Penang.

> We sailed to Burma once, just to see if there was anything to trade.

> My grandfather went to Pulau Bendak [Bandanaira] many times, a very long trip. I am sure I have kinsmen there now.

The reported range of these voyages applies to the period of 1880 to 1940, but there is no way to calculate the frequency of voyages or the amount of goods traded. It appears that the Javanese sugar trade with Singapore and Bangkok, and the trade with Saigon, involved fairly frequent trips. Unlike the current trade, which depends on export of local products and import of goods for local use, it appears that this former trade involved what might be termed 'tramp' operations, in which Trengganu traders shipped sugar from Java to Singapore and Bangkok or rice from Thailand to Borneo. As the geographic range of trade has decreased, the complexity of the trading operation seems to have declined as well.

There are scattered written references to past trading patterns centered on Kuala Trengganu, but those which serve best as a cross check on contemporary oral reports are from French visitors in 1769, as detailed in John Dunmore's (1973) "French Visitors to Trengganu in the 18th Century."

> He [the Sultan] sends them [trading ships] to Cambodia, Siam, Cochinchina, China and other places north of his states. Some also make the voyage to Java, Sumatra and the Moluccas and other places in the straits.

> The inhabitants of Trongannon who own ships are forced to lend them to the King who sends them to Cambodia, Siam and other places north of his states and also to Java. They take on rice for the subsistence of his people who do not grow enough for their needs.

In addition to these reports, the French visitors also note that pepper and cloves were traded in Kuala Trengganu, reportedly brought there by Bugis trading vessels. Current informants deny that Bugis traders were important and say that cloves, pepper and other spices were brought from the Moluccas by Trengganu traders.

The mainstay of the current Trengganu trade is the shipment of solar salt from Thailand to Malaysia. Salt is produced in large salt pans or fields along the gradually shelving coastal areas at the head of the Gulf of Thailand. The production is highest during the dry first quarter of the year and ceases in the period of heavy rains. Salt fields are also found in the coastal areas of Pattani, in the far south of Thailand. In the past, more than 50,000 tons of Thai salt were brought by Trengganu traders to the east coast of Malaysia in a single year, but by 1968 the total amount of salt carried by Trengganu sailing vessels was less than 12,000 tons.

Salt is vital to the fishing industry of the villages on the east coast of Malaysia, where it is used in salting the fish catch and manufacturing belachan or shrimp paste. Without salt there is no convenient way to preserve fish for shipment to distant markets nor to store it for home use during the monsoon period when fresh fish is not available. Without salt the relatively high-value, low-bulk belachan, which provides the major source of cash income for these fishing communities, cannot be manufactured.

However, the use of salt has declined somewhat due to locational and technological changes in the fishing industry and increased transportation development. Some fishing vessels now ice their catch and market it as fresh fish. Road access has also facilitated the marketing of fresh fish, and further reduced the need for salt. This has resulted in decreased cargoes for the Trengganu traders.

Most salt currently comes from the Thai ports of Ban Laem (Baling), and Maeklong or Samut Songkhram (Metelon). In addition, Pattani is the port of origin for salt shipments in the late summer. Trengganu sailing vessels load sand as ballast for the northward trip to Thai ports. When they arrive the ballast sand is unloaded and is usually used for fill dirt at homes along the rivers on which Baling and Metelon are located. Salt is then loaded as a bulk cargo for the return trip. Almost all sailing ships return to Kuala Trengganu. There the salt is transferred directly to smaller sailing vessels which sell it in the scattered fishing villages along the east coast of Malaysia.

> Salt is good cargo. One cannot live without salt;
> it is the sea, it is our blood. One can take pride
> in this trade.

To which one crew member added:

> Even if one cannot take much money.

When the ship captains speak of past days, they remember richer cargoes.

> Once we brought rice and all sorts of foods from
> Siam, and sent to them our manufactures.

> Before my time the ships carried brass and silk,
> bird [feathers] and fine wood [aromatics]. Once
> they even carried gold, and a ship once carried
> the Bunga Emas to Siam [a golden flower paid as
> tribute to the King of Thailand].

> I have heard that we brought Siamese women to
> be brides; even a princess for the royal family.

> We carried gold from Belowai [Brunei?] and
> brought Chinese from Tamek [location not
> identified, but probably Vietnam].

The current cargoes are still varied, even if they are less impressive than the gold and girls of the past. Imports from Thailand include a wide range of foods and forest products, including onions, pickled onions, chilis, palm sugar, black beans, tamarind, pickled vegetables, dried and pickled fish, fish oil and copra. Forest products include damar powder, mangrove bark, charcoal, kerang bark, rattan, nipah thatches, shorea seed oil and coir. Manufactures include Shanghai water jars, dishes, pottery, mirrors, furniture, paper and roof tiles. In addition, clay is imported for local pottery manufacture and bat guano, dug from caves in South Thailand, is imported for use as fertilizer in rice cultivation.

Exports from Malaysia to Thailand are remnants of a once

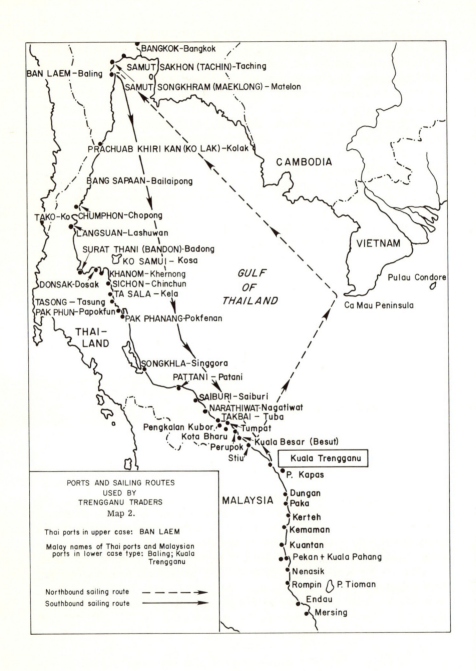

rich trade which derived from the favored place of Malayan shrimp paste in Thai cuisine and the demand for luxuries like Malayan silk and brass in local Thai trade. The major export is still belachan or shrimp paste, together with pickled shrimp sauce, tamarind, coconuts and woven reed matting. Rattan and aromatic bark from the forest are still shipped to Thailand, and some brass trays can be found in export cargoes. However, such cargoes rarely make up as much as ten percent of exports by weight, and most vessels now replace the aromatic cargoes of the past with ballast sand.

The shift from exchanges of varied cargoes to a trade based on ballast sand and salt has taken place during the last forty years. Before World War II Trengganu traders hauled entire cargoes of belachan, up to 100 tons per trip. Imports from Thailand included not only salt and the mixed cargoes detailed above, but also shiploads of rice.

> People came from all over the [east] coast of Malaya to get Thai rice in Trengganu.

> Most ships carried rice; only one in four would carry salt.

> One year I sold so much belachan in Siam that I was able to buy two new ships.

> It was a trade of the best; of our belachan for their rice.

Map 2 indicates the ports of Thailand served by the large sailing vessels engaged in international trade and the Malaysian ports served by the smaller domestic trading vessels. For each port in Thailand, the current Thai name is supplemented by the traditional Thai name, and for all ports the Malaysian name is also supplied. By far the most important port is Ban Laem, or Baling, in the northwest corner of the Gulf of Thailand, where more than seventy percent of Trengganu's salt imports originate. Both Maeklong (Matelon) and Bangkok have been important Thai ports in the past; Bandon (Badong), Pak Phanang (Pokfenan) and Songkhla (Singgora) were also very important during the period of the rice trade.

Plate 1. Salt is manufactured by the evaporation of sea water on coastal salt fields close to the small port of Ban Laem, Thailand.

Plate 2. Sand is loaded by ships' crews in Kuala Trengganu. Empty ships use sand as ballast on the trip to Thai ports and then return loaded with cargoes of salt.

The Trengganu trade system divides into two parts, international and domestic. The international system has been described in the previous paragraphs; the domestic system involves the transhipment of salt and other imports from the entrepôt of Kuala Trengganu to lesser ports and fishing villages along the east coast of Malaya between the Thai border in the north and Singapore in the south. This part of the trade system makes use of smaller ships between 18 and 40 feet in length, and from 3 to 20 tons cargo capacity. Most of these vessels are smaller versions of the perahu bedar and more than 50 of them were still in service in 1962.

At one time this trade system was entirely in the hands of the Trengganu Malays who financed, built and manned the ships, and financed the trade. In recent years, however, as the nature of the trade changed, Chinese merchants have come to own many of the vessels. The entry of the Chinese came with increasing dependence on the hauling of salt for the fish salting industry. Chinese merchants control processing and trade in salt fish and quickly perceived the advantages of a vertical organization in which they would also control salt transport. Whenever a Malay vessel came on the market, the Chinese purchased it and, as of 1962, they controlled more than half the large ships engaged in the salt trade.

Crews on all vessels, including those owned by Chinese, are made up of Trengganu Malays. The average vessel carries from three to thirteen crew members and the rule of thumb is that one crew member is required for each ten feet of hull length. Large crews traditionally included a number of young men who served as apprentices but, with the decline of trade, young men now look elsewhere for a profession and crew sizes have decreased.

Crews include one or more specialists. The captain, taikong, is in charge of the vessel. The steersman, kemudi, is the most important member of the crew after the captain. The captain may serve as steersman, and, in addition, may be the owner, nakoda.

If the captain is the owner of the vessel he often operates his own business on speculation, buying belachan in Malaysia to sell in Thailand, and buying salt and other cargo in Thailand to

Plate 3. Haji Awang, ship owner, captain and steersman, at the tiller of one of his ships.

Plate 4. While loading in Thailand, the Malay crew relaxes in front of the deck house. Coiled fishing lines, hung on the front of the deck house, are used to catch the fish which supplement seamen's diets at sea.

sell in Malaysia. The profits are split 60 percent for the owner and 40 percent for the crew, including extra shares for the steersman and the men who climb the masts. These Malay traders have Muslim contacts in many of their major ports of call in Thailand. Some of these are the descendants of Malays who settled in particular ports to serve as local trade agents, buying and selling goods on behalf of the ship captains. Muslim communities can be found in the large salt ports of Ban Laem (Baling) and Maeklong (Metelon), as well as in the Thai ports which were formerly active in the rice trade, such as Pak Phanang (Pokfenan) and Songkhla (Singgora). It was also claimed that there were Trengganu Malays settled in Brunei, Java, and even Bandanaira, as well as in Singapore, where they served as agents for the Trengganu traders. This widespread network of agents was vital to the speculative trading operations of the traditional cargo vessels.

Under Chinese ownership this pattern has changed. The Chinese now make contracts for salt delivery; the Malay captain operates the vessel to haul the salt back from Thailand, but no longer functions as broker or trader. The captain and crew are paid fixed wages. Even Malay owner-operated vessels are hired increasingly by the Chinese for salt shipping at a flat rate. The incentive to trade in other commodities has been reduced by the efficient vertical economic organization of the salt fish trade.

With the decline of speculative trading operations and the network of local agents there has been a corresponding decline in world view on the part of Trengganu traders. They wistfully speak of a past in which men were more adventurous and knew a wider world.

> None of my children will see what I have seen. It was before there were nations [regulations] and we could sail anywhere. We would buy rice in one place, cloth in another place, sugar and pots, everything you can imagine, and sell them in every other place. I would sail into towns where I had never been before and there was almost always a friend. We would stay for many days, months sometimes. Now it is like a truck, load and unload.

Journeys northward in the Gulf of Thailand involve sailing along the coast as far as Besut in northern Trengannu, and then turning out to sea northeast toward Tanjong Panjang (Ca Mau). After two or three days at sea, the ships sail northwest up the middle of the Gulf of Thailand and finally turn directly landward to their destination port (see Map 2). The west shore of the Gulf is avoided on the northward journey, for fear of running aground on the lee shore. This is particularly true during the October through March period of the northeasterly onshore or winter monsoon. More ships are lost by being blown onto shore during the monsoon than for any other reason. During the calm of the summer season, however, some ships do hazard coasting voyages, making more frequent calls at intermediate ports. Typically, on the return voyage, the ships also sail down the middle of the Gulf of Thailand, avoiding the lee shore. If they collect cargo at intermediate ports, they do so by turning sharply in a direct approach, avoiding extended travel along the coast.

The round trip voyage from Trengganu to Baling at the head of the Gulf of Thailand may take from one to two weeks in each direction and for a total single voyage travel time is generally one month. The turn-around time at each end adds another two weeks to the round trip. With a mean round trip time of five to six weeks, most ships make between five and eight voyages per year. Most of the ships stop sailing in October, with the advent of the winter monsoon, and remain safely tucked away in secluded backwaters of Kuala Trengganu harbor until the winds decline in February. Travel during the monsoon is limited not only by the dangers of storm at sea or wreck on the lee shore, but also because monsoon waves seal the river estuaries which comprise the major harbors of the Gulf of Thailand, making entrance and exit dangerous or impossible.

> It is not a safe life, nor an easy life, but it is a life. I have lost two ships, one on the coast of Siam, near Bandon, and the other at sea. At sea I lost a son. Many ships do not return. Before the Japanese War [in 1940] the largest ship ever built...a perahu pinas dogol like a cloud, like a bird...sank with all hands. Maybe it was too large a ship, and maybe it was too proud.

I sail in the monsoon. Sometimes I stop in
December, but most of the time I sail. The
really good captains can sail anytime. They
know the sea. My ship belongs to the <u>towkay</u>
[Chinese], so really I have nothing to lose but
my life.

It is not a safe life. I sometimes think I should
do something safe for a living, like being a
politician or perhaps a professor, always asking
questions. That is safe.

Navigation is simple, based primarily on piloting from
known landmarks. The use of a simple and usually inaccurate
hand compass for extended voyages out of sight of land is
common. No charts are used and successful piloting depends a
great deal on experience and judgment:

One must have a map in the heart.

Whether in the heart or the head, the 'mental' maps of the
Trengganu navigators are impressive. They can accurately
identify navigation routes by approximate bearing, and the
intervening ports by name, for the entire Gulf of Thailand. They
are able to sketch charts with remarkable accuracy, distorted
only by the use of time as a variable instead of distance. In
addition to these 'heart' maps, complex sailing directions are
passed on in the oral tradition. Hence, many current sailors
know details of the perils of the northern coast of Borneo and the
mouth of the Mekong River even though they have not made these
voyages.

Voyages are generally a relaxing experience with ample
time for contemplation and deep sleep. The steersman is the
only person who remains awake at night, and he sleeps only four
hours during the day. The rest of the crew handle the sails and
take turns preparing non-gourmet meals featuring recooked
rice, pickled vegetables and salt fish. The long reaches up the
Gulf of Thailand require little sail handling, and the dipping lug
sail is relatively easy to manage. Considerable sail handling
was required in former times, because of the complicated
maneuvering under sail necessary to navigate the mud flats and
sand bars blocking the mouths of the estuarial ports.

Plate 5. The perahu pinas gobel is distinguished by its cruiser stern and clipper bow, perhaps copied from an eighteenth century French pinasse.

Plate 6. The perahu pinas dogor under sail makes use of dipping lug sails, made of mengkuang reed matting, stiffened with battens.

Currently most ships are towed into and out of the major ports by motor launches. The crew is paid extra if they are required to load and unload cargo. Most ships could be operated by smaller crews than are currently carried.

The ships used by the Trengganu traders are of distinctive local design. Boat building is possibly the highest art form of Trengganu, as demonstrated by the varied designs of fishing and cargo craft of all sizes and shapes. In fishing boat design, function seems to be sacrificed for form; boats with sweeping elevated bows and sterns, recursive boom crutches and decorative carving are more a feast for the eye than practical examples of utilitarian fishing craft. The cargo vessels share this diversity of design, but not the artistic flair.

The usual term applied to the large cargo vessels is perahu besar (large ship) or occasionally perahu siam, indicating their major area of trade. However, many vessels are referred to by the name of their design. The oldest and most beautiful of the current cargo vessels is the perahu pinas gobel. This class of ship has a cruiser stern and clipper bow, sometimes with the suggestion of a figurehead under the bowsprit. The design is reminiscent of an eighteenth century European sailing craft. Gibson-Hill (1953) speculated that the design of the pinas gobel might be based on and named after the small two-masted French 'pinasse'. The design was reported to have been introduced either by a crew member from a French ship wrecked on the coast of Trengganu over one hundred years ago or by a British soldier who wandered into Trengganu in the middle of the nineteenth century. Gibson-Hill also reported that Trengganu shipbuilders may have acquired the design in Singapore. Given their flair for design and impressive craftsmanship, there seems little doubt that Trengganu boat-builders could easily have developed the design after seeing a European prototype—without the assistance of shipwrecked sailors or wandering soldiers.

The second major design of the large cargo vessels is the perahu pinas dogor, which has a cruiser stern but a straight bow. It is reputed to be much easier and cheaper to build than the perahu pinas gobel.

The third major design is the perahu bedar, adapted for

use in small vessels as well as large ships. It is most closely related to the classical double-ended design of fishing boats. The perahu bedar has straight bow and stern posts, is double-ended, and is much easier to build and to sail than either of the prau pinas designs with their complex crusier sterns.

> All of these boats were designed by Datok Mata, who designed them all long ago, before the British came, in the time of Sultan Zainal Abadin. The prau bedar looks very much like a boat we call prau timor or prau sulawesi. The idea for this design came from Makassar.

> The perahu bedar is really the best ship, but it is not so beautiful as the perahu pinas. I would prefer to have a perahu pinas because things must be beautiful to be enjoyed.

The older vessels were constructed of chengal (Balanocarpus heimii), a dense, rot-resistant and currently expensive wood. They were built in the 'Chinese or foreign manner', with the keel and ribs constructed first, and the side planks or plating secured to these fixed members. This construction method differs significantly from that used for the delicate, vertically pegged fishing vessels. In fishing boat construction, planks are set or shaped by heat, and joined without ribs. The adoption of alien building technology was required by the high size and strength demands of the cargo vessels as compared to those of the fine-lined, smaller fishing vessels.

The large cargo vessels range from 60 to 80 feet in length, with a beam one-quarter of the length and a depth of one-eighth of the length. Their shallow draft, from four feet when light to seven feet when loaded, permits relatively easy passage over the sandbars sealing the mouths of most of the estuarial harbors of the east coast of Malaysia and the Gulf of Thailand. Their cargo capacity ranges from 65 to 150 tons, carried in one hold, with access through two deck hatches. The deck house, where the crew lives and from which the ship is steered, is at the extreme stern; on a double-ended perahu bedar there is a platform built out over the stern to accommodate this deck house.

The two masts are raked forward, and the long bowsprit, often segmented, may project slightly downward. This forward rake of the masts and the current use of batten sails suggest a Chinese junk rigging on the hull of a European sailing sloop. However, the forward rake of the mast facilitates the use of the dipping lug sails which in turn make ship handling much easier and faster. At one time canvas sails were used and some <u>perahu pinas</u> were schooner rigged, but in recent years sails have been made of woven reed mats, and battens are required for sail stability and handling. It appears that cost is a limiting factor in the use of canvas sails.

None of the larger sailing vessels have been mechanized, although some of the smaller ships which carry salt from Kuala Trengganu to other coastal ports now have inboard engines. The low return on long haul cargo operations does not provide sufficient capital for mechanization, and it is probable that the limited cargo-carrying capacity would not justify the operating expenses of large inboard engines.

There is a romantic reaction to mechanization:

> Have you heard the sigh of the water and slap of the sails? Can you think of what it would be like to have a ship like a bus, all engine noise and smoke? The one last place there is no sound [of engine, planes, civilization] is at sea.

> I know we can make more money if we make more trips [with an engine], but the [long] time at sea is important. It is time to be with oneself.

Economic man has a different view:

> If I had enough money to buy an engine that large, I would have enough money to get into a better business.

Kuala Trengganu is the major boatbuilding center where these vessels were constructed. Some vessels were built on consignment for ship captains or shore-based owners, while others were built on speculation for sale.

The best year I had was when I built three large ships at one time. More than 45 people worked for me, and it took eight months to complete the work. I sold the three boats for $50,000 [US $17,000]. It was the best year of my life. Now all I see are rotting boats on the mud [banks].

There have been no large boats built since World War II. Most were built long ago, with some dating from the 1860's. They have been rebuilt often, with maintenance ranging from annual repairs to major replacement of old planking. No major structural or design changes have been made during the last 100 years.

It is probable that the traditional cargo vessels operated before the eighteenth century were substantially smaller than the current vessels, probably not exceeding forty feet. They were of double-ended design, like the current perahu bedar, and were based on fishing boat designs. Construction involved plating without ribs, which in turn limited the beam and cargo capacity of the vessel. Judging from their ships, it is possible that Trengganu traders were not involved in an extensive long-range trade before the eighteenth century. In the eighteenth century, both European and Chinese junk construction methods became known on the east coast of Malaya, creating a shift to ribbed ship construction and vast increases in size and cargo capacity. This was accompanied by the adoption of European design characteristics as seen in the cruiser stern and clipper bow of the pinas. The increase in cargo capacity and size enabled the Trengganu vessels to expand their range, and to probe for cargoes in distant areas. It is probable that the Gulf of Thailand trade had long been part of Trengganu trading operations, but that increased ship size enabled traders to seek new areas as far away as Java and the Moluccas. Their lack of success in maintaining these new long-range routes was probably due to competition from local sailing vessels and the expansion of colonial shipping companies in the late nineteenth century. Therefore, the flowering of the Trengganu trade in Southeast Asia may have been very brief: facilitated originally by the introduction of foreign technology in boatbuilding, it was quickly terminated by competition with even more advanced forms of foreign technology.

The decline of the prosperous sailing ship trade is due to a variety of changes in the last forty years, usually seen by the traders as increased interference by government. Both the Thai and Malaysian governments have increased the regulation of trade and imposed export and import duties. The free movement of belachan into Thailand has been curtailed several times in recent years when the Thai government has restricted imports, perhaps to encourage Thai production. Ignorance of frequently changing regulations has led to incidents in which cargoes of belachan have been seized and heavy fines imposed on traders. The rice trade has been rendered unprofitable by Thai government export taxes, Malaysian government import taxes and restrictions designed to encourage increased rice production in Malaysia. The salt trade declined when restrictions on the export of dried salted fish to Indonesia closed a profitable export market and decreased the demand for salt.

Competition from other forms of transportation has also cut into the trade of Trengganu sailing vessels. Large steam vessels, which can operate during the monsoon season, eliminated profitable trade on the Singapore to Bangkok route. The construction of a railway connecting South Thailand with the east coast of Malaya curtailed the important coasting trade which once tied the Pattani Malay communities of southern Thailand to coastal Kelantan and Trengganu. The recent expansion of highways along the east coast of Malaysia and in South Thailand has resulted in capture by trucks of much of the short-haul coastal trade which once moved by sailing ship.

Together with the loss of trade to competitors, there was a substantial reduction in the number of sailing vessels during World War II. Many were 'purchased' by the Japanese, who took some to Singapore to serve as cargo lighters and mechanized others to serve in coastal trade operations in areas where submarine warfare eliminated larger trading vessels. Some vessels and their crews were shifted to Burmese waters to supplement the local transportation system which was first sabotaged by the retreating allies and later bombed by them in the reconquest of Burma. Other vessels were commandeered to haul iron ore and other contraband cargoes in coastal trade and some were destroyed by submarines.

A submarine [American] attacked the boat.

>They shot at it and we dived overboard and dodged the bullets. When the ship sank they threw us rafts. Then they took us into the submarine for three hours. Have you ever seen the inside of a submarine? You would not believe what is there! They took us out to sea until they found another <u>perahu besar</u>. Then they put us on board the other <u>perahu besar</u> and told them to take us to shore. When we landed [in Thailand] the Siamese took all our belongings. There were others sunk during the war too...some of the biggest and the best.

As the <u>perahu besar</u> trade has been limited to fewer commodities, become more subject to government regulations and duty charges, and curtailed by competition from other forms of transportation, the traders have been forced to set low freight rates, with inadequate profit margins, in order to remain in business. When calculating their costs, many traders do not include adequate funds for replacement of their vessels; this reflects a tacit assumption that by the time it is necessary to build or buy a new vessel the trade will have disappeared. Therefore, lack of replacement capital precludes mechanization or other developmental measures. At the same time, the price of replacement vessels has increased more than 600 percent due to a rise in wood prices. Caught between rising costs and declining profit margins, the traders can only hope to play out their remaining years with some dignity, supported by now distant memories of better days.

The rate of decline has been relatively fast. In 1962 there were 27 large cargo vessels in operation, and by 1968 there were only 18 vessels still involved in hauling salt from Thailand. Each year ships which require expensive repairs are retired from service to rot slowly on the mud banks of the tidal creeks in the Trengganu estuary. This attrition has been gradual thus far, but the trade could end suddenly if a major shift occurred in competitive shipping rates or if new restrictive government regulations shattered their profit margins.

At one time there were well over 120 large cargo vessels in operation.

Plate 7. The harbor at Kuala Trengganu, the center of Malay trading operations in the Gulf of Thailand. (The narrow harbor opening poses a major problem for the entry of sailing vessels, particularly during the period of the onshore monsoon.)

Plate 8. Abandoned hulls and rotted timbers on the mud flats of Kuala Trengganu reflect a decline in the sailing ship trade due to competition and changes in market conditions.

> The harbor [at Kuala Trengganu] was so crowded with ships that you could not cross it in a small boat at night for fear of running into their anchor cables.

But sadly, times have changed:

> Once I had eight ships and four of them were large ships. Now I have only one left. One sank near Saiburi [in southern Thailand] in 1948. One disappeared with all hands in 1945, perhaps sunk by a submarine, and maybe just a storm. One blew on shore and was wrecked in Thailand. I used to be a rich man, but not any more, because I did not have insurance on the ships. It is not possible to get insurance. My father had four ships and my grandfather had five ships. We have always had ships. But now I have only one; we are down to the last person and the last ship.

Throughout Southeast Asia many traditional trading systems have been destroyed, and the surviving systems are fast disappearing. Traditional transportation operations, the technological core of trading systems, are among the first victims of modernization and development. Transportation development is easy, relatively inexpensive, and usually yields national economic benefits. However, transportation development often destroys the traditional transportation system and displaces the local entrepreneurs, transport operators and traders who play vital roles in connecting their communities to the wider world. It is paradoxical that transportation development may restrict rather than expand the horizon of the population it is designed to benefit; the Kuala Trengganu trader who once viewed a trade world which extended from Bangkok to Batavia, from Saigon to Sulawesi, now waits for the bus to Kelantan.

Traditional trade systems were often 'natural' economic exchange systems. They involved the exchange of local or regional surpluses, free of most political constraints, and encouraged a certain level of regional specialization of production which only now nation-states are attempting to recapture through the use of common markets and other forms of economic cooperation. It is unfortunate that Malays cannot consume Thai rice, that Thai cannot enjoy Malayan belachan, and that Trengganu traders no longer have a back haul cargo to offset the cost of Thai salt vital to their fishing economy. At the same time when economists in Bangkok and Kuala Lumpur are exploring common market potentials, the practitioners of a traditional and natural common market are retiring their vessels to rot in the tidal inlets of Trengganu harbor because government regulations have curtailed their trade.

There is much to be learned from the structure and operations of traditional trading systems. The mechanisms by which the Trengganu traders obtained capital for vessel construction, handled cargoes on consignment, and handled international credit and payment for cargoes acquired abroad, all demonstrate a fairly sophisticated economic organization which economists would do well to study before substituting new and perhaps less efficient forms of capital management. The information systems used by traders, their decision making process, their planning and allocative techniques are all relevant to effective development and modernization, but are ignored by contemporary planners. Therefore, the study of traditional trading systems not only can provide a retrospective view, important in understanding the evolution and operation of traditional economies and societies, but also may serve as an important element in the elusive 'blueprint for the future' so dear to development planners.

East Timor: Exchange and Political Hierarchy
at the Time of the European Discoveries[1]

by

Shepard Forman

I

The purpose of this brief paper is to raise for discussion two interrelated problems which require clarification if our understanding of the relationship between exchange, hierarchy, and early state formation is to proceed. The problems have been suggested to me by my research in East Timor, but seem to have wider application. In the first instance, I think we must exercise extreme caution in the use of ethnographic models, whether based on current field research or constructed from historical accounts, particularly in projecting backwards in time present configurations of exchange networks and political hierarchies. Historical research is demonstrating that our pictures of nineteenth century plantations and haciendas are not the colonial Latin American reality. Similarly, careful examination of historical and ethnohistorical materials is likely to show that our conceptions of political and economic order in early Southeast Asia are not necessarily accurate either. This is because European historiography and ethnography often posit their own order, their own sense of reality, on diverse and disparate data. This, however, raises the second issue at hand, namely the efficacy of utilizing native models in our reconstruction of the historical record. In brief, I will argue that native definitions of forms of exchange and hierarchy provide extremely useful data in our attempts to reconstruct actual working systems and any changes in their structure and function which might have occurred at the time of European contact. At the same time, to accept these idealized models as accurate representations of the systems themselves is to blunder in our quest for historical accuracy.

In the pages that follow, I will briefly describe: 1) the so-called 'indigenous' political and economic system in the

Map 3. The Lesser Sunda Islands.

Lesser Sunda archipelago at the time of the European
discoveries; 2) the re-ordering which took place in the course of
Dutch-Portuguese competition for commercial hegemony in the
region in the seventeenth and eighteenth centuries; 3) the relative
neglect of the Sundas following the Dutch defeat of the Portuguese
and the subsequent marginalization of the commercial economy
in Timor; and 4) the extension of the Portuguese administrative
bureaucracy in Timor in the late nineteenth century. As I
proceed, I will focus on the establishment, spread, and
dissolution of one political domain, the 'princedom' of
Letemumo, which in many ways typifies the effects of the
Portuguese presence in Timor. Throughout, I hope to reveal
some of the systemic adjustments which occured in the
adaptation of the Portuguese program of pacification to the
'indigenous' model of exchange and to suggest how this model
was manipulated and utilized, in turn, by 'native' authorities
operating within the expanding colonial bureaucracy.

II

Although real administrative hegemony only occurred in
the nineteenth century, Timor has been a part of the European
commercial system since the sixteenth century when the island
was effectively divided between Dutch and Portuguese traders.
Prior to that, the island appears to have played a minor,
subsidiary role in the trade networks which centered in Celebes
(Sulawesi) and skirted the Lesser Sundas of which Timor is a
part. When the Portuguese first arrived there in 1516, they
encountered ships from as far away as Luzon and Java,
suggesting that Timor was already a part, albeit hardly a
significant one, of the vast trade networks of the Javanese
principalities, in this case apparently under Celebes tutelage
through the intervention of the enterprising Muslim king of
Makassar. The extent to which Portuguese and Dutch merchant-
adventurers infiltrated and established their dominion over these
trading networks in the transshipment of goods between India,
China, and Europe is well known, as are the conflicts often
engendered by the personal ambitions of lay and Catholic settlers
in the area (Boxer 1947, 1948). What first attracted the Dutch
and Portuguese to Timor was, of course, the profitable trade in
sandalwood. However, their primary attention was focused on
Larantuka in Flores, and then on Makassar. Timor was only

occupied and used as an entrepôt at the end of the seventeenth century, when the Portuguese constructed a fort at Lifau, on the north coast (at the present-day Oe Cussi), to replace the one at Kupang which they lost a half-century earlier to the Dutch. Political division of the island along an east/west axis into two entities, eventually Dutch and Portuguese colonies, dates effectively from this time.

Some historical and ethnographic accounts suggest that at the time of the European discoveries Timor was already divided, neatly and rather conspicuously corresponding to the Dutch and Portuguese areas of concentration, into two unified political kingdoms: Servião in the west and Belu in the east (see Map 3). However, as the Portuguese historian Artura Basílio de Sá (1949) is quick to point out, belu means 'friend' in the Tetum dialect of the Austronesian languages spoken on Timor. The Portuguese turned it into a plural to designate all of the people and their territories who seemed to ally themselves in a nested series of exchange networks with Portuguese half-caste traders known as Topasses or 'Black Portuguese'.[2] The people of Servião, de Sá notes (1949:11), were more intrepid, owing to their subordination to "the promises of the Dutch East India Company." The Portuguese generalized this name to all of the groups and their territories who were part of the Dutch network. In point of fact, the Documento Sarzedas notes that by the second quarter of the eighteenth century the Belus were actually comprised of forth-six separate political domains of which only approximately twenty-one paid tribute to the Portuguese. Servião was comprised of sixteen domains of which seven participated in the Portuguese rather than the Dutch tribute system. Moreover, as de Sá writes (1949:14), "almost all of these kingdoms around the island were located along the coast, the Portuguese having hardly penetrated the interior." "The historic division of the island into two great Provinces, Belos and Servião, is, then, of Portuguese origin" (1949:11). The 'indigenous states' of Timor were a product of Portuguese and Dutch historiography, just as descriptions of unified 'realms' are a product of Anglo-American and Dutch ethnology. The precise nature of the indigenous 'kingdoms' in the precolonial period will be discussed further below.

Referring to myths among the Atoni peoples of West Timor about the exogenous origins of the Belu state, Ormerling (1957), basing his account on the writings of the Dutch ethnographers Grijzen and Vroklage, recounts a complex migration to Timor via Celebes and Flores of the <u>Sina Mutin Malaka</u> (China - White - Malacca). He notes that Larantuka is mentioned as a "temporary halt on the journey" in almost all of the versions, and Makassar in some. Although one account dates the migrations to the fourteenth and fifteenth centuries, before the arrival of the Portuguese, Ormerling recalls that "one of the narrators stated that the captain of the forefather's fleet of perahus was named Mengelains (Magalhaes)!" He notes that Vroklage believed that native knowledge of the Malay-Timor route was spread by Chinese sandalwood merchants and concludes, in the same footnote, that "Portuguese influence might equally well have been responsible" (Ormerling 1957:70). Later, in another footnote, he speculates that, in any case, "penetration of the Belunese in Timor's mountain areas only took place after the arrival of the Portuguese in the Malay archipelago" (1957:73). I will suggest below that these myths parallel closely the actual origins and migrations of the Topasses, or 'Black Portuguese', who early on became the 'supreme' rulers in Timor.

For his part, and despite his caution, Ormerling seems to accept the myths as substantiation of a unified Belu kingdom, suggesting that a unification of domains, or 'princedoms', into a singular realm took place through internal marital alliances, independent of foreign trade involvements.

Speaking authoritatively from the same sources, the Dutch administrator and ethnographer of Timor, Schulte Nordholt (1971) undertakes a structural analysis of the political system of the Atoni, addressing himself directly to the question of whether unified kingdoms in Belu and Serviāo ever existed. Noting the ambiguities in the historical accounts, Schulte Nordholt analyses in detail the myths of the Atoni and surrounding groups. He concludes that political unity was contained within individual 'princedoms', which were the centers of decision-making. These princedoms were defined linguistically and by marital alliances and warfare. Their administrative unity was marked by the presentation of harvest gifts, or tribute, to rulers who were at the center of trade; this, in turn, contributed greatly to an increase in their authority. These harvest gifts, called <u>poni pah</u>, or the 'rice baskets of the land', were clearly distinguished by the Atoni from <u>tuthais</u>, or gifts of homage to a ruler who had established a political relationship of superordination through the giving of brides (Schulte Nordholt 1971:386).[3] Schulte Nordholt (1971:359) points out that proportional shares of harvest gifts to rulers and others of rank were the same as shares in profits yielded through the trade in sandalwood. Unfortunately, the actual interrelationship between these spheres of exchange is not discussed, nor are the entailing exchange relationships between petty princedoms, except in the idiom of warfare. As Schulte Nordholt makes clear, encompassing alliances and any ultimate political unity should best be assessed through an examination of the relationship between these harvest gifts of corn and rice, bridewealth and mortuary gifts, corvee labor and other forms of tribute, and the extension of internal and foreign trade. Nonetheless, in his final symbolic analysis, it is the centrality of ritual power, provided through common myths, which gives unity to the otherwise independent (and self-contained?) princedoms. The Atoni political system is said to be

> based on ritual relationships, laid down in the rites and myths, consolidated by a network of affinal relationships, maintained by a system of tribute consisting of agricultural produce, and either strengthened or weakened by frequent wars. Hence the political system embraces all aspects of life and is the expression of the system of life, which becomes visible and assumes its form in this political system in a similar way as in the ancient Greek <u>polis</u>....
>
> In Timor, we find the unity of this "polis" in the sacral foundation of all relations. (Schulte Nordholt 1971:406-7)[4]

Gerard Francillon (1967), in an earlier and fascinating account of the origin and development of the 'kingdom' of Wehale, had reasonably questioned the historical validity of hypothesized 'central state' systems in Timor, substituting instead the suggestion that myth served to propound an ideological basis, not so much for governance as for ritual domination of the island. It seems hard, to me at least, to justify the idea of ritual dominance of an island if, in fact, it was not to support some wider politico-economic hegemony.

Francillon does note, further on, a tradition saying that 'taxes', referred to as 'food', were paid to Wehale from vassal states throughout Timor, but notes that "there is no rigorous historical evidence to show how this was done in practice" (1967:196). Notwithstanding, I wonder whether the myth of superiority of rulers of a 'central state' (based on precedence in marriage and the exchange of women) is not invoked to justify the flow of tribute and exchange of goods in loosely constructed trade networks which articulated with the Javanese and Malaccan trading states (and later the Dutch and Portuguese) without actually being politically subjugated by them.[5] In this system, chiefs who could organize labor and deliver cut sandalwood would gain in cloth, iron tools, and guns, which Francillon found stored to this day in the sacred houses of the old 'rulers' of Wehale.

The political reality in Timor at the time of the European discoveries, in so far as we can know it, appears to me to have been atomistic and centrifugal. There were no apical political kingdoms in the likeness of European models. Effective administration was contained within localized territorial groups. There is no archaeological or historical evidence of any sort of population center, let alone established centers for coastal trade. Trade was effected by means of exchange among a nested hierarchy of clan groupings and trading partners, with attributions of authority and power magnified in proportion to the degree of proximity to the external trading partner (the chief supervising the exchange of goods on the beach might well be assumed by foreign observers to be more important and powerful than his inland trading partner and indeed might well have been so in so far as he controlled the return flow of desired goods). Exogamous clans may well have been ranked in terms of chiefly and commoner, but they were not segmental and rarely, if ever, grouped according to larger 'tribal' sturctures. Warfare was localized and resulted from demographic pressures, conflict over the resources for and spoils of trade, and questions of the heart. Alliances seem to have occured between members of the same ethnolinguistic groups but not among them in response to other ethnolinguistic groups, except in so far as marital alliances might have forged partnerships in trade. These alliances came to be affected and certainly were fed upon by half-caste compradores, the so-called Topasses, or 'Black Portuguese', who operated initially out of Larantuka and later from Makassar, before engulfing Timor itself in a century of political intrigue for control over the lucrative sandalwood concessions.

The greater part of the seventeenth century in Timor was taken up by the rivalry between the descendants of Antonio de Hornay and Mattheus da Costa, both Larantuqueiros, who played Portuguese ambitions against the Dutch in their own struggles for supremacy over the island's trade. Hornay, referred to alternately in the literature as King of the Belus and, later, Captain-Major of Timor, was the son of a Dutch deserter and a native mother from Larantuka, the besieged Portuguese enclave on Flores. His own political/economic ambitions led him eventually to the apex of an exchange network in which guns, cloths, and glass beads assured him the uncrowned 'kingship' of Timor until his death in 1695, when an official nominee of the Viceroy of Goa seized the reins of power in the name of the Portuguese Crown. His own corrupt rule led to his expulsion and the ascendancy of Domingas da Costa, a bastard son of Mattheus, who found support for his own 'reign' among Dutch pretenders to the sandalwood trade. Portuguese attempts to enlist the aid of native chiefs by granting them military titles provided them with a tenuous foothold on the island which, in any case, was effectively controlled by the Hornay and da Costa families well into the eighteenth century (Boxer 1947, 1948).[6]

The extension of Portuguese colonial administration throughout East Timor in the nineteenth century devolved on the Christianized descendents of the 'Black Portuguese' community. In the process of pacification, chiefs of essentially independent, localized political domains, called sukus, were incorporated into more encompassing political entities, or 'kingdoms', which were, in effect, vast exchange and tribute systems. The 'rulers', known by the Portuguese term régulos, or 'little kings', were co-opted into the colonial system by the granting of titles (Coronel or Brigadeiro) in a 'second-line' paramilitary force and the tacit recognition of their hegemony over a territory and its people, known collectively as a reino. Allegiance among their constituency was obtained by the successive granting of lesser titles of rank to suku chiefs who then became pivots in the system of tribute and exchange. Power alignments among the régulos were effected through a system of 'royal' marriages until a hierarchy of powerful rulers, now related affinally, extended itself across the colony. Abuses were so great and Portuguese suzerainty so tenuous that the administration, after successfully putting down a revolt at the turn of the century, dissolved the régulados, 'freed' the populace from the onus of tribute payments (which they replaced with a head tax), and gerrymandered the 'kingdoms' into more manageable districts under the direct authority of colonial officers. A letter of 1882 from the Interim Governor of Timor to the Bishop of Macau pinpoints the source of the problem:

> Marital exchange is our Government's major enemy because it produces... an infinity of kin relations which comprise leagues of reaction against the orders of the Governors and the dominion of our laws. There has not yet been a single rebellion against the Portuguese flag which is not based in the alliances which result from marital exchange.... The major service that the [Catholic] Mission could provide its government is to bring an end to these pagan contracts which are also directly opposed to Catholicism.
> (Letter no. 40, August 26, 1882, official correspondence of Major Vaquinhos, encountered in the archive of the Bishop of Timor, Dili.)

Let us consider briefly a specific case. The history of the Makassae, a non-Austronesian people inhabiting the north-central coast, the mountains and high valleys of the Mate Bian and Ossu ranges in East Timor (see Map 3), provides us with a microcosm of the processes of integration which I believe have characterized the colony since the sixteenth century.[7] Despite their linguistic unity, common culture, and defined territory, the the Makassai (who currently number about 80,000 people) have never been an organized political unit in their own right. Even the complex organization of their irrigated rice terraces devolved on the 'lords of the land' of the individual sukus, discrete clan groupings which the Portuguese first incorporated into regulados and, then, administrative districts. Until pacification was finally completed at the turn of this century, the Makassae were comprised of numerous clans, agnatically organized, with some recollection of a common ancestry and a shared mythology. According to this mythology, a hermaphroditic ancestor emerged from the top of Mate Bian after a rock-wren kicked back the waters which had covered the earth. This hermaphrodite produced yet another who split into brother and sister. This brother and sister 'took care of each other' (exchanged labor in the fields for reproductive power) and gave birth to the original Makassae clans. Mythology then recounts a history of warfare and alliance in which the clans grew more distant, both spatially and sociologically, as they dispersed down the mountain sides to new garden sites, fissioning as they went. Now only the vestiges of former clan structure remain, somewhat coterminous with present-day <u>sukus</u>, but really an agglomerate of minimal agnatic descent groups. Present 'lords of the land' of each of the <u>sukus</u> are ranked according to their genealogical proximity to the original clans.

An ideology of exchange of productive labor for reproductive power symbolized in a complex, interlocking set of marital and mortuary rituals is the basis for a history of alliance among Makassae clans, among whom a stated preference for MBD marriage for the eldest son prevails. Wife-givers, hailed as superior, face wife-takers in an overlapping network of affinal relationships which are marked by life-long (and post-mortum) exchanges (Forman and Nau Naha, in press). These assymetrical exchanges, while obviously moving real goods between categories of persons, are also highly charged symbolically. Bridewealth, consisting of buffalos, horses, and swords (the forces of production), is presented to wife-givers whose counter-presentations consist of cooked rice and pork ('the rest of the woman,' her sperm and blood) and <u>ikat</u> woven cloths (in which her children will be clothed, a mark of their humanness and sociality). These marital exchanges, known generally as <u>barlaque</u> and specifically in Makassae as <u>tufurae gi ira</u>, are the linchpin of traditional Makassae social organization.

Secondary exchanges, known only by the Portuguese term <u>contrato</u> (literally, 'contract') and clearly lacking in symbolic significance, have been superimposed on these basic, primary exchanges. They represent the hierarchization of Makassae society which accompanied the process of pacification in which 'noble' clans emerged in association with the 'kingdoms', or <u>regulados</u>, which were extensions of the Portuguese bureaucracy into the countryside. In these secondary exchanges, which occur only among 'lords of the land' and other families of rank, coral beads accompany the bride to her husband's house in exchange for an additional payment of animals and, occasionally, gold ornaments. These coral-colored glass beads come from abroad, exist in limited supply, and have obviously filtered down from the the 'elite' sector of Timorese society. While they evidently preceded the Portuguese in Timor, their present distribution is limited to chiefly families and remnants of the nineteenth century 'dynasties' which the Portuguese established through their system of military entitlements. Initially, the beads undoubtedly accompanied other trade goods as a means of linking up internal exchange nexuses with the international trade in sandalwood. Later, they became the symbols of status and rank and a critical focal point in the upward flow of tribute through 'lords of the land' who became wife-givers to 'commoner' clans, thereby ensuring the mobilization of buffalo, horses, and other gifts which they, in turn, passed on through a nested hierarchy of political domains which culminated in the personage of the régulo.

The incorporation of the Makassae into the Portuguese colonial system took place in the last decade of the nineteenth century through the extension eastward of the 'princedom' of Letemumo, itself affinally related to the 'royal' house of Oralan, the seat of the 'kingdom' of Vemasse. According to the heirs to the 'princedom' of Letemumo, their ancestors accmpanied the Portuguese from Larantuka to Oe Cussi, the enclave in Dutch Timor, from where they moved to Vemasse in the expectation that the capital of the Portuguese colony would be established there. When the Portuguese established their capital at Dili instead, in 1769, the family remained in Vemasse as a primary link in the colonial establishment. A century later, their loyalty was rewarded when Dom Domingos da Costa Freitas, a Galoli speaker known by the native name of Gali Kai, was made a Coronel-Brigadeiro of the Segunda Linha and régulo of Vemasse. Along with the epaulette and sceptre of office, the régulo was entitled to the tribute of the inhabitants of his reino, ample incentive to expand his domain under the aegis of the Portuguese colonial office. In 1899, Gali Kai's son, Dom Francisco da Costa Freitas, a native 'aide-de-camp' of the Governor, was named a Coronel in the Segunda Linha and head of the reino of Baucau, which incorporated the Makassae of the north coast. His son-in-law, Tomas de Costa Soares, was made Coronel Regente of Vemasse and elevated to régulo of Letemumo on the intercession of his brother-in-law, Dom Francisco, in 1899. Although the regulados were officially dissolved around the turn

of the century, Dom Francisco retained the prestige and aura of
office until his death in 1922, whereupon it was assumed by Dom
Tomas who ruled over the houses of Oralan and Letemumuo, now
united in the 'kingdom' of Vemasse until his death in 1929. At
its height, around 1900, the power and authority of Vemasse
extended throughout the eastern part of Portuguese Timor over
territories inhabited by at least four different ethno-linguistic
groups numbering several hundred thousand people. The
'kingdom' was integrated at the elite level through the careful
placement of the daughters of Vemasse in marriage to suku
heads who were then clearly elevated in status, accepting the
rank of tenente coronel and the headship of a localized region
known as a juridisçao. In this way, a network of affinal ties
among so-called 'ruling families' became the bulwark of the
system, clearly threatening the authority of the Portuguese
colonial administration. [8]

The people themselves were incorporated into this system
through a nested hierarchy of domains in which local 'lords of
the land' were given lesser titles of military rank and insignias
of office in successive campaigns of pacification. The
responsibility for most of the Makassae rested with the
'princedom' of Letemumo which reached out across the coastal
valleys and upland toward Mate Bian, which, according to
informants 'ran red with blood' until the last years of the
nineteenth century. A system of telescoping authority developed
in which the head of the important river valley of Uai Mutu swore
his allegiance to the régulo of Letemumo, in exchange for the
rank of coronel, and then sought the support of his kinsmen
further inland. They, in turn, paid homage for the privileged
rank of tenente coronel. Sa Uai, the head of the clan of Laumana
on the crest of Mate Bian, was one of the last to swear his
allegiance to Letemumo. In a ceremony still remembered by
many, he received 100 coral-colored glass beads from the
régulo of Vemasse and, in his presence, cut his hair from the
traditional shoulder-length of the warrior. He was offered the
rank of major in the second-line force and, at his investiture,
presented the régulo with ten buffalo collected from his
clansmen. A belt buckle, an ancient Portuguese flag, and the
glass beads are enshrined in the sacred house of Sa Uai,
evidence of his importance in the new political order. In the
native ideology, Laumana became a suku daburo, one of those
clans which offered tribute in the form of food (and could be

trusted to cook for their 'ruler'). It received its orders from
Coronel Braga of Uai Mutu, the suku betana of the river valley
which acclaimed the supreme leadership of the régulo of
Vemasse and through whom the tribute from the mountains
flowed toward the coast.

Significantly, tribute in the form of food, livestock, and
labor did not seem too heavy a price to pay to bask in the glory
of the colonial regime. The régulos were respected and honored
by the inhabitants of their reinos, and their names and their heirs
are venerated to this day. Undoubtedly, the dovetailing of the
system of military entitlements and 'royal' marriages with the
primary exchanges of bridewealth and dowry payments
contributed greatly to popular acceptance. The acquiescence of
the Makassae in the subsequent system of direct taxation has not
been so ready. By breaking up the regulados and replacing them
with administrative districts and posts in which colonial officers
dealt legalistically with suku chiefs with whom they have no
social ties, the Portuguese ultimately alienated the native
population. As one old informant falsely remembers:

> When the Holandeses were here, we paid them
> cloths for what we wanted. The Holandeses didn't
> tax us. We only sent them cloth. The Holandeses
> were good. The Portuguese only demand money
> for taxes.

III

I do not present the case of the Makassae as a model of the
political system of Timor in pre-historical times. Rather, I am
suggesting that the history of the Makassae provides some
possible insights into the processes of political integration both
before and during the Portuguese presence. The dovetailing of
the asymmetrical alliance system of the Makassae with the
distribution of rank and title in the Portuguese colonial
administration points up a critical fact in the intersect between
exchange and political hierarchy which might have some general
applicability in ranked systems characterized by directed
external trade. It raises the question of the relationship between
native apprehension of hierarchy and alienation of product. In
the case of the Makassae, it suggests that the native exchange

ideology afforded a sense of legitimacy to the form of hierarchy which became attached to it. The importance for the native population lay not so much in the material nature of the tribute paid, although that may have been burdensome, as in their understanding of the structure of the social network through which tribute moved. The question can hardly be reduced to economics. Reciprocity, redistribution, tribute, taxes, quartering, and corvee labor all have their cultural definitions, and each has its specific linguistic referent. These definitions, their meanings to the population so engaged, are to some extent recoverable. The attempt to recover them must be made if we are to understand how and why production is geared up for particular kinds of hierarchical exchanges.

A critical, unresolved question in anthropology and history exists in regard to the development of political hierarchies and the evolution of the state. Trade has long been considered a central component of this question. I believe we must also focus our attentions on native conceptions of exchange and hierarchy. What are the symbolic qualities which legitimize rank and hierarchy and justify different exchange transactions? This goes beyond merely asking what entitles a chief to tribute, although that is certainly a part of the question. The real question, it seems to me, is what is exchange? What forms does it take, and what meanings are attached to it? Harvest gifts to local chiefs and tribute to foreign masters might be differentially conceived, but as forms of exchange they are not mutually exclusive. Taxes paid in money to an indifferent colonial administration are not part of the same idiom. The 'whys' of these broader issues are fundamental to our discussions of the relationship between exchange and hierarchy.

Notes

1. This is a somewhat revised version of a paper presented to the conference on Trade in Ancient Southeast Asia: The Role of Economic Exchange in Cultural and Social Development, session on 'Ethnographic Models', Ann Arbor, Michigan, March 22-24, 1976. The paper is preliminary and seeks more to raise some questions than to prove a point. Additional historical research on the subject is scheduled for the summer, 1977, on a grant from the Horace H. Rackham Graduate School at the University of Michigan.

2. Boxer (1948:175) says the name Topasses was derived either from the Hindustani topi, meaning hat, which was a distinctive feature of Christianity; or, more likely, from the Dravidian word for interpreter, tuppasi.

3. This internal/external aspect of political 'unity' is further marked by the Atoni distinction between musu fui (wild enemy) and musu aem (tame enemy), in referring to wars between political communities and internal wars.

4. For a compatible symbolic analysis of contemporary Atoni political structure, see Cunningham (1965).

5. This would be close to Glover's (1972) interpretation of 'ephemeral' kingdoms in Timor, whose growth and decline depended on changing patterns of trade. See also an unpublished manuscript of Claudine Berthe-Friedberg.

6. For a discussion of the relationship between Hornay and Francisco Vierra de Figueiredo, a Portuguese merchant-adventurer in Makassar, see Boxer 1967.

7. Fieldwork among the Makassae was carried out from August 1973 to October 1974 under a grant from the National Science Foundation.

8. Informants' accounts offer fascinating sidelights into Portuguese attempts to manipulate these alliances 'in order to keep the peace'. Particularly piquant are tales of the romantic involvements of several Portuguese governors with Timorese 'princesses'.

Trading Patterns of Philippine Chinese:

Strategies of Sojourning Middlemen

by

John T. Omohundro

Discussion of trade networks in Southeast Asia cannot proceed very far without introducing the Chinese, who directly, as traders, or indirectly, through their products, have participated in exchange in the 'South Seas' for two thousand years (Yü 1967:172ff). In this paper I shall describe some aspects of Chinese commerce and immigration to the Philippines over the last one hundred years, pointing to some rather stable patterns as I perceive them in the biographies of Iloilo City merchants alive in the early 1970's.

The paper is divided into three loosely related sections. First, I define and historically bracket a particular style of immigration and trade termed 'sojourning'. Second, I explore the degree to which Chinese social and commercial networks overlap and reinforce one another in the pursuit of wealth in capital-intensive enterprises amidst foreign surroundings. Finally, I argue that ethnic differences per se, such as those between Filipinos and Chinese, may facilitate trade between ethnic groups and may contribute to the perpetuation of these differences.

The Sojourners

Sojourning is defined here as a form of immigration wherein bachelors are dispatched through customary channels to distant sources of employment with the understanding that they will remit large portions of their income for consumption and investment in the home community (Kung 1962). It is basically an export of people and an import of remittances. Sojourning involves periodic returns to the hometown, and, for the Chinese, establishing organizations as bases in the overseas local for receiving, placing, and dispatching migrants and their money.

The sojourning pattern is found centuries back in Asia within China, between China and Southeast Asia, and within Southeast Asia (for example, the Minangkabaus, Ibans, and Javanese).[1]

It is not always easy to distinguish sojourning from the whole constellation of activities which are usually designated 'trade', 'tributary relations', 'piracy', and so on. Trade and tribute are of course related, as exchanges of goods between home and alien areas; however, the sojourning Chinese sometimes functioned as laborers or middlemen among alien buyers and sellers, without involving goods and capital from China. From a certain perspective, namely from an interest in the direction of the flow of wealth, the sojourners from China were more like pirates. The host countries perceived this, as I shall show below. An amusing anecdote, indulging no doubt in some mythologizing, reveals the intertwined destinies of pirates and sojourners in the life of a certain Mr. Ong.

> My father lived in a village by the shore of a small bay in Fukien where bandits and pirates used to hide. One time a pirate who was befriended by my father gave him a bamboo pillow. Sometime later my father discovered that the pillow contained money. He took the money to Fuchow City to buy-and-sell, but lost it playing mah jong and returned penniless to his village and wife. Later, when times were hard, my father consulted a temple fortuneteller and was counseled to seek his fortune in Southeast Asia. It was then he came to Luzon, bringing my mother and me.

The sojourning pattern has a long history in China. Bachelor migrations, remittances, hometown associations in distant cities, and guilds of traveling merchants have been developing in South China for centuries (Shiba 1970; Morse 1932). Chinese sojourning (immigration without capital) to the Philippines before the Spanish galleon trade was probably very slight: the non-Muslim Filipinos did not initiate interregional or intercultural trade, and there was no call for Chinese labor. There may have been colonies of Chinese traders (pirates?) residing in the Philippines under the protection of datus and sultans. The first Spanish who came to the Manila area found a thriving Chinese group residing there (Wickberg 1965:4). The Spanish colonial peace therefore may not be the key variable for increasing the size and permanency of Chinese trader settlements. The boost the Spanish gave inter-island trade as well as China-Philippines trade through the galleon voyages is much more important. The arrival of the British and the subsequent growth of the Philippine economy in the eighteenth and nineteenth centuries first made Chinese sojourning possible and profitable. By that time immigrants to the Philippines scene could arrive broke, even indentured, and parley local economic opportunities into capital.

The line between Chinese sojourning, that is, capitalizing on the local economy, and actually colonizing, or breaking new ground, appears thin. For example, Chinese entrepreneurs in West Java in the eighteenth century manipulated their local political connections and tried their hand at the Dutch cultivation system by leasing the labor of villages from local authorities and compelling peasants to grow sugar cane (Steinberg 1971:50). Also, entire independent kongsi of Chinese entrepreneurs and miners moved into West Borneo frontiers, paying taxes to local sultans for the mineral rights to gold there (Steinberg 1971:51). A similar action may be seen in Antique Province, Philippines, to the west of Iloilo City. A poor and mountainous province of low population density, Antique had a subsistence rice economy until British and Chinese merchants began stimulating the peasants to grow sugar and building brown sugar mills. Chinese from the Iloilo City area were also speculators in Antique mining claims, some of which were actively worked. As mining and sugar interests increased in the last century, the Chinese who had pioneered their development moved into the province's capital of San Jose, established a merchant community of kinsmen and hometown-mates (t'ung-hsiang), and began to serve the new economic interests with restaurants, service stations, trucking lines, and so forth. A single surname predominates in the San Jose Chinese community, the name of Pe, descendants in one way way or another of the original mining and sugar pioneers. This example strikes me as one of colonizing, 'creating your own market', rather than the more conventional sojourning. Nevertheless, in recruitment and connections to China through remittances and return trips, the Pe's of Antique resemble the sojourners in most respects.

The old pattern of sojourning within China was converted in the last century to sojourning in the Philippines very smoothly, with steamships criss-crossing the South China Sea, making possible a new category of Chinese 'passenger' rather than only the Chinese 'sailor'. Organizations in South China and the Philippine cities made possible both a concentration of people and capital, and their mobility over long distances. Organizations such as revolving credit associations for accumulating capital were successfully exported by Southern Chinese to some areas of Southeast Asia (Wu 1974) but not to the Philippines. There, capital was accumulated through lineage associations, trade guilds (such as variety store or lumber store associations), chambers of commerce, and personalistic networks of kinsmen, affines, and hometown-mates. Simply to have these connections is not the key variable, however; I have discussed elsewhere (Omohundro 1974) the specific Chinese business practices of loans, distributorships, partnerships, inter alia, which were exercised through these connections. One practice, the cabacillo-agent relationship, will be discussed in detail below.

The volume of remittances the Southeast Asian Chinese channeled back to hometowns in China was undoubtedly large (Barnett 1943), but the ability to remit money (disregarding how leaky that channel might have been) is but one aspect of the capital and labor mobility developed in China and useful overseas. In Iloilo City over one hundred years ago, Chinese exchange agencies (ch'ien chuang) were working to move money to and from China and, most importantly for commerce, to move money among merchants in the Philippine Islands. These agencies appear to have been branches of and modeled after mainland banking systems developed in the southern cities (Jones 1972).

Labor in Philippine Chinese commerce, composed mostly of young immigrant apprentices or older business failures, was also mobilized. Employees in Chinese concerns became ensconced in a paternalistic family enterprise, but they could be and were extricated and grafted onto another kinsman's or town-mate's operation elsewhere in the Philippines. The employee population was therefore connected closely to the Chinese merchants on the whole, but highly mobile as to locale and occupation. Residence histories from 96 businessmen in Iloilo

City show that, in the course of a man's Philippine residence and business experience, two or three movements about the Philippines before settling down as a married merchant with family constitute a very common pattern. A large minority of Chinese moved more than five times, not counting the many dislocations of the Japanese Occupation. Once married and established as a self-employed merchant, a Chinese became very sedentary, moving only when failure struck. Before the 1930's when a large influx of Chinese women made Chinese family life possible in the Philippines, the ratio of mobile bachelors to sedentary family men was much higher and the composition of any one Chinese urban community even less fixed in time.

This mobility of capital and labor increases Chinese responsiveness to market fluctuations, allowing them to bail out quickly from failures and capitalize fully on fleeting opportunities.

The exploitative strategy of the sojourning Philippine Chinese (Omohundro 1976) bears comparison with that of the migrant workers in the Virgin Islands (Dirks 1975). Both groups have been concerned with minimization of expenditure, rapid utilization of resources, and avoiding social encumbrances with local peoples. For this reason both groups worked long and hard, lived in hovels, avoided entangling marital alliances with locals, and saved as much as possible. Each was involved in their own way in what the American camp song terms, "two pence to spend and two pence to lend and two pence to send home to my wife, poor wife." An important difference between these two sojourning groups is illustrated by this lyric: the Chinese were merchants, needing capital in order to function as sojourners; so they needed the full six pence. Virgin Island migrants earned by their manual labor only, and therefore did not need to and did not want to lend two pence. Community organization among Virgin Islanders was minimal and little effort was expended on defence against blocking tactics by natives. The Philippine Chinese on the other hand benefitted from the importation from China of a complex community organization, because this aided capital accumulation and defense.

Yet, free of the restraints of their home areas, both

Table 3: Regional Origin of Fukienese Immigrants
in Iloilo City, Dumaguete, Dagupan, and Davao[a]

County of origin	Percent from each county (hsien)			
	Iloilo City	Dumaguete	Dagupan	Davao
Cnin-ch'iang	59.0%	8.5%	90.5%	6.4%
Nan-an	23.4	5.1	5.8	81.6
Ho-shan[b]	7.0	69.5	0.7	3.5
Tung-an	0.2	5.1	- -	0.6
Lung-chi	- -	- -	1.5	4.4
An-chi	0.7	3.4	- -	0.3
Hui-an	3.0	- -	0.7	0.6
Other hsien	1.5	8.5	0.7	2.6
Total percent	94.8	100.1	99.9	100.0
N	554	59	137	343

Table 4: Regional Origin of Cantonese
Immigrants in Iloilo City and Davao[a]

County of origin	Percent from each county (hsien)	
	Iloilo City	Davao
Tai-shan	56.0%	77.3%
Kai-ping	34.0	11.9
Hsin-hui	2.0	3.6
Chung-shan	1.0	3.6
Shun-te	1.0	2.1
Other hsien	6.0[c]	1.5
Total percent	100.0	100.0
N	109	194

a. Data from Iloila City Chinese Cemetery gathered in 1972 by this writer. Data on Dumaguete, Dagupan, and Davao gathered by Doeppers (1971).

b. Combined with the total from Hsia-men (Amoy City), which is a separate district within Ho-shan.

c. The other hsien recorded from tombstones in Iloilo Cemetery was Nan-hai.

Virgin Islanders and Chinese have had similar single-minded extractive strategies. This is reflected in the perception of indigenous peoples toward the two sojourners. The Virgin Island migrants are called <u>Garot</u>, apparently an ethnic epithet derived from the name and behavior of a gluttonous bird. The Filipinos have commonly called the Chinese <u>Intsik</u> <u>Baboy</u>, 'Chinese Pig', which strikes me as the appropriate animal symbol representing the Chinese 1) disregard for slovenly living conditions, 2) willingness to scavenge, that is, take on the ignominious tasks, and 3) sleek fat growth with potential rewards to their patrons.[2]

Commerce and Social Networks

There is accumulating evidence that recruitment to sojourner enclaves like the urban Philippine Chinese is quite selective, in several respects. Only certain South Chinese villages sent sojourners (Chen 1940). Only certain kinds of men and boys were likely to be sent, namely young bachelors 11 to 25 years old. The target of individual immigration was also very selective. Iloilo's immigrants came from quite specific areas in Fukien and Kwantung and have done so for a long time. The composition of the Iloilo community in terms of regional origin has not fluctuated much since the mid-nineteenth century. For example, Iloilo City has always consisted of 50 to 60 percent Chin-ch'iang county (<u>hsien</u>) immigrants (see Wickberg 1965), but other provincial towns differ quite strikingly in their composition (see Table 3). Iloilo's Cantonese population, though representing the same proportion of Chinese in Iloilo as in other Philippine cities (10 to 20 percent), are not from the same areas as Davao's Cantonese (see Table 4).

Each Philippine city's Chinese community has been stable in its special regional composition primarily because immigration follows social channels. Each regional group in a Chinese enclave attracts a proportionate number of its own kin and town-mates. The reason why there are regional differences between towns to start with is harder to pinpoint. Differences could be due to each town's small size. Random factors could provide each town with a different starter population (Doeppers 1971). Another provocative possibility will be explored below.

Table 5: Surnames of Fukienese Immigrants to Iloilo and
Degree of Concentration by Home Township within Home Hsien[a]

Surname of Immigrant[b]	Number in Iloilo	Chin-ch'iang Hsien[c] % From each township	Nan-an Hsien % From each township	Hui-an Hsien % From each township	Ho-shan Hsien % From each township
UY	56	22% T'ang Hsi 22% Chuan-chou	(scattered)	100% Wu-mei	(scattered)
YU	26	(scattered)	83% Ho-k'eng	(scattered)	(scattered)
TAN	49	(scattered)	(scattered)	- -	100% Hsia-men
YAP	11	(scattered)	(scattered)	- -	83% Hsia-men
CHU	9	77% Liu Hou	- -	- -	- -
HUAN	6	83% Ch'en-chu	- -	- -	- -
SY	30	53% Fang k'eng	(scattered)	- -	(scattered)
ANG	19	41% Ying-lin	70% Tuo Ya	- -	- -
PO	21	(scattered)	31% Mei T'uan	- -	- -
ONG	42	47% Yu-chan	23% K'uei Feng	- -	- -
SO	6	80% Hu-mei	(scattered)	- -	- -
LIM	34	28% Hou Hai 28% Wu Tuan	67% Chi-tung	- -	- -
SUN	10	- -	- -	71% Chuang Nei	100% Hsia-men
CHENG	21	60% Hsin-shih	87% Shang Ts'ao	- -	(scattered)

a. Data gathered from Iloilo Chinese Cemetery, 1972.
b. Surnames are given in Fukienese dialect; surnames not listed were either too few to count reliably or had no common township of origin.
c. Township names are written in Mandarin Chinese.

Because immigrants proceed to locales where they have contacts to help them, each Philippine Chinese community consists not only of certain Fukienese counties, but certain townships and villages are disproportionately represented. Table 5 shows the clustering of Iloilo's immigrants according to townships of origin. On the township and village level, surname groups are important social groups, so village-mates who followed one another to Iloilo predictably share membership in the few surname groups represented. The counties of Chin-ch'iang and Nanan, most heavily represented in Iloilo, have the highest degree of overlapping of townships with surnames. Similarly, those surnames which overlap with certain townships of origin are the most numerous in Iloilo. There are about 35 Fukienese surnames in Iloilo, of which eight are carried by 60 percent of the population.

Clearly, then, the recruitment procedure was highly selective and stable through time. There was also some nonrandom clustering when sojourners arrived in the Philippines. The Spanish era data on residence patterns show this (Doeppers 1975). This residential clustering has been obscured by re-shuffling of stores and families in the American era. But it can still be detected in the slight clustering of Tan's in textiles on one street, Cantonese in another block, Yu's and Yap's in textiles along another street, and, across the way, a group of Chua's in hardware. On the edge of the city and in neighboring suburbs of Molo and Jaro, some family and village-mate clusters of general stores are still evident. In Iloilo, residences cluster more by social group (for example, by surname or friendship group) than by merchandise line, though in Manila it appears that social group and merchandise line may overlap more extensively on some streets (Doeppers 1975). Immigrants from different provinces are in noticeably different merchandise lines, but within provincial groups, within the Cantonese and Fukienese groups, there is very little specialization by township or village. Who is apprenticed to whom and which economic opportunities knock seem to be more important determinants of merchandise line at the subprovincial level.

The consequences of a stable and nonrandom distribution of sojourning immigrants from certain South Chinese regions may be to produce small but perceptible ethnic differences in the

Figure 4: A Cabacillo-Agent Network:
The History of Mr. Lo

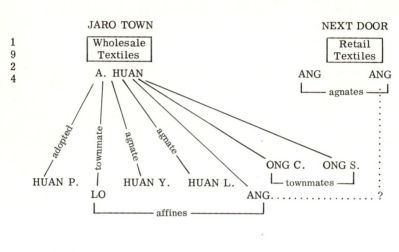
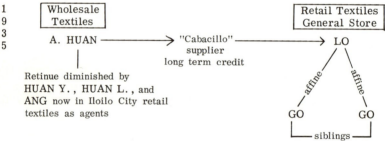
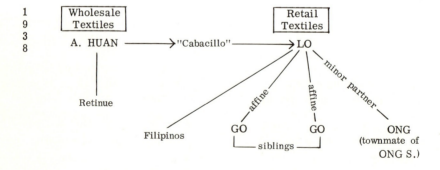

Figure 4 (continued)

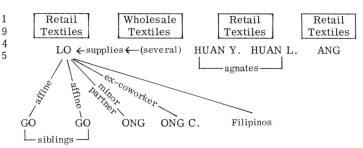

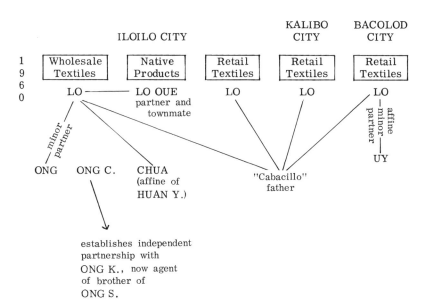

Chinese 'seeded' into various Philippine cities. Variations in
local urban environments, isolation from China, and increased
communication among cities have blurred some of these cultural
differences, no doubt. On the other hand, the Philippine Chinese
themselves recognize differences among Chinese urban enclaves.
What evidence is there that differences in regional composition
may mean cultural differences?

G. William Skinner (1964:31-43) has shown that standard
marketing areas in Szechwan are well delineated economic units,
with their own local elites elaborating their special regional
ethnicity. The standard marketing area is 'a culture-bearing
unit', its boundaries coinciding with kinship groups, marriage
endogamy, secret societies, temple communities, folklore,
weights and measures, etc. Clearly, marketing structures
reinforced social integration. Unlike the bureaucratic
structure, which was discrete at each level, the marketing
systems were woven into interlocking networks with the standard
market towns, intermediate and central market towns connected
both vertically and horizontally. Two things are needed to
connect Skinner's analysis with the variation in Philippine
Chinese urban enclaves: 1) evidence that Szechwan marketing
systems resemble those in Fukien and Kwangtung; and 2)
evidence that immigrants to cities like Iloilo are from the same
marketing areas in China. It may be that differences in Chinese
immigrant composition among Philippine cities were due to
efforts to perpetuate regional subcultures by continued
geographic separation in Southeast Asia.[3]

There _are_ marketing networks among Philippine Chinese,
however, even if not complete transpositions of homeland
systems. They are reinforced by numerous social and political
connections. These networks simultaneously extend vertically
from salesman to importer or from retail distributor to
manufacturer, and horizontally through space from Manila to
Iloilo or Iloilo to the countryside.

During the Spanish and American regimes, recruits to the
Philippine Chinese merchant life were tightly regulated by an
apprentice system and introduced to these marketing networks.
The apprentice system, which I have described elsewhere
(Omohundro 1976), introduced apprentices to commerce and to
sociopolitical contacts. The social connections which made the

apprenticeship system possible included agnatic, affinal, and ritual kinship, co-residence in China (hometown-mates), friendships, and classmate connections. Fellow apprentices were thus not only related to their employer, but frequently to each other; if they did not begin with mutual connections, apprenticeship itself led to them. [4]

One of the oldest and most common marketing networks which resulted from such an apprentice system and is still evident in Iloilo is the cabacillo-agent system. The cabacillo, or head, topped an expanding patron-client hierarchy of smaller merchants, or agents. He began his relationship to them by accepting them as apprentices when they were young immigrants. As they progressed in commercial responsibility and family status, the apprentices struck out as agents for the cabacillo's distribution network. Agents were often originally selected as apprentices through a variety of social connections, and came to be further connected to the cabacillo and each other through business. The cabacillo as benefactor offered many services, such as emergency help, credit, and political or legal support. The agents often became cronies, blood-brothers (kiat pai hia ti), and partners among themselves. Men who were once agents became independent, and eventually the successful became cabacillos themselves. So the business network, like a nuclear family, is dynamic and mortal. But the social ties thus evolved may be activated even after a generation or so.

Figure 4 illustrates the business biography of Mr. Lo, a successful Iloilo textile merchant. In 1924 the fifteen-year-old Mr. Lo was apprenticed by prior arrangement in China to A. Huan's large textile store in Jaro, a town contiguous with Iloilo. A. Huan, originally from an area near Lo's native place in Chin-ch'iang county, had five other apprentices besides an adopted adult son. The diagram shows the complex interrelationships of the apprentices to A. Huan, to each other, and even to neighboring textile stores. All but two of these men or their descendents are living and doing business in Iloilo today (1972); most are still in textiles and dry goods and remain close socially though they are friendly competitors commercially. The diagram will show that some also have become involved in each other's business lives.

By 1935 Lo had married in China, been promoted through

Table 6: Distribution of Chinese Businesses
in Iloilo City and Province, 1972[a]

Iloilo Provincial Towns	Number of Ethnic Chinese Business Establishments
Estancia	18
Passi	13
Pototan	8
Sara	6
Balasan	6
Janiuay	6
Dueñas	5
Calinog	5
Dingle	3
Barotoc Nuevo	2
Tigbanan	2
Others[b]	10
Total	84
Iloilo City Municipalities	
Iloilo City proper	483
La Paz	28
Molo	18
Jaro	15
Total	544

a. The survey was conducted by this writer, counting all Chinese regardless of citizenship. No data are available for Gigantes Islands, Guimaras Island, or other Iloilo provincial towns not mentioned in this table.

b. Including one establishment each in Banate, Barotoc Viejo, Cabatuan, Carles, Ajuy, Jordan, Nuevo Valencia, Lambunao, Oton, and Leon.

the ranks in A. Huan's store, and been established as a dry goods merchant, with savings as well as abundant assistance from A. Huan. This is the typical cabacillo-agent relationship. Lo was selling retail; A. Huan was the distributor and initial backer. Lo chose to remain in Jaro, while his cronies from the store had become agents for A. Huan in Iloilo City. Even before advancing beyond the agent role, Lo had taken two affines as apprentices.

In the late pre-war years, Lo's business was still expanding within the cabacillo-agent network. He took as a minor partner and full-time accountant, a town-mate of his old cronies.

In the boom years after the Second World War, Lo reached the point where he could strike out totally independently, for A. Huan had retired and cabacillo-roles are not inherited. Lo moved into the larger market of Iloilo City, hired another old crony, and dealt with distributors on a more impersonal, contractual basis. His main competitors in big-line textiles were his stockroom chums from the apprentice years. They all carefully managed their businesses to avoid direct competition.

By the 1960s, Lo himself had become a patron, or cabacillo, to clan brothers and his own sons; in turn, their businesses were so independent as to resemble those of typical agents. Some employees left, entwined in their own complex social-commercial webs, like Ong C. Others came in, like apprentice Chua, accepted because of his affinal link to old cronies.

Mr. Lo's biography is unusual only because he was so successful. The failure rate of businesses (and hence of their proprietors) in post-war years has run as high as 11 percent in a seven-year period, and one-quarter of the merchant community is losing ground rather than prospering (Omohundro 1974:316ff). But Lo's sequence of business network stages is similar to many successful merchants. It is clear that Philippine Chinese business networks are simultaneously dense and multi-stranded social networks of a long-standing ethnic tradition.

The economic hub and center of Chinese cultural activity

Table 7: Degree of Interrelatedness of
Iloilo Chinese Merchant Families, 1972[a]

Links to Consanguineal Kinsmen	N. of Families	N. of Links Between Persons
No links	20	-
Links with no intervening kinsman[b]	30	36
Links with 1 intervening kinsman[c]	22	35
Links with 2 intervening kinsmen[d]	17	32
Links with 3 intervening kinsmen[e]	7	13
Links with 4 intervening kinsmen[f]	3	4
Subtotal	89	120
Links to Affinal Kinsmen[g]		
No links	20	-
Links with 1 intervening kinsman[h]	14	20
Links with 2 intervening kinsmen[i]	14	20
Links with 3 intervening kinsmen[j]	9	14
Links with 4 intervening kinsmen[k]	3	6
Subtotal	60	60
Total N. of links between 67 families	149	180

a. Determined by the number of genealogical links within the prescribed distance to other Iloilo merchant families, from a sample of 67 families.

b. e.g., father : son; brother : sister.

c. e.g., grandfather : grandson.

d. e.g., Ego : first cousin.

e. e.g., Ego : Ego : first cousin's son.

f. e.g., Ego : father's first cousin's son.

g. Individuals related to a member of a business family through only one link of marriage; usually the last link.

h. e.g., wife's brother.

i. e.g., father's sister's husband.

j. e.g., father's brother's daughter's husband.

k. e.g., father's brother's son's daughter's husband.

on Panay Island, Iloilo City is also the center of most social-commercial networks. The present-day cabacillos live in Iloilo City close to the supply and the agents are dispersed among the further markets or lower links in the distribution chain. The bare bones of this complex network are shown in Table 6. I have not yet determined the full extent of these merchants' interconnections. But if connections within Iloilo City provide any clue, then Table 7 presents strong evidence for a high density of Chinese social networks, offering many resources for business dealings. On the average, Iloilo Chinese merchant families are related by close consanguineal or affinal ties to 2.7 other business families in town. Table 7 has restricted the counting of links to consanguineal and affinal kinsmen of only certain types, and only 67 of the possible 500 business families have been counted. If one were also to count links to ritual godparents, old cronies, hometown-mates, and such, the density of connections among Iloilo businessmen would be much greater.

How many commercial arrangements overlap these social ones? Tabulations from 95 businessmens' biographies in Iloilo (Omohundro 1974) reveal that one-half of a merchant's lifetime commercial connections have had some social relationship to him as well. These social relations include not only kinship but ritual kin (bloodbrother or godparent), classmate, t'ung-hsiang (hometown-mate), and so forth. In other words, Chinese business networks are intermediate in degree of proscription, social relationships being used as frequently as impersonal, contractual relationships for conducting business.

I see in these tables and in biographies like Mr. Lo's a broad dispersal of Chinese throughout the province linked by their business and social biographies. When we recall the high selectivity of regional origin of these immigrants, the evidence mounts for the hypothesis that regional marketing and social networks in South China have served as conduits and models for Chinese establishment in the Philippines. [5]

The Importance of Being Earnestly Different

Above and in an earlier article (1976) I have accounted for ethnic Chinese success in business in the Philippines by emphasizing substantive cultural differences between Chinese and Filipinos. The sojourning pattern, immigrant associations, credit arrangements, competitive strategies, the Chinese family, and the apprentice system, as Chinese cultural patterns, all confer commercial advantages upon the immigrant merchants. We might also consider whether simply being different from the Filipino majority, simply being distinguishable as an ethnic group, also facilitiates Chinese commerce.

Brian Foster (1974; and this volume) has proposed a number of reasons why the very presence of difference helps Mons in their commercial activities in Thailand. Like the Mons, the Philippine Chinese benefit from the fact that indigenes do not think highly of commerce, either as an activity or as a measure of the man. Like the Mons, the Chinese are removed from some of the political and kinship pressures which threaten the commercial activities of the wider society. Like the Mons, the Philippine Chinese advertise their ethnic distinctiveness and consequently shift the stress inherent in face-to-face commercial transactions to the ethnic group level.

I perceive the usefulness of these ethnic differences to be as follows.

1. A shift to commercial transactions across ethnic lines increases the chance of decision-making by both parties on more purely economic, goal-oriented and impersonal bases. When dealing with 'the others', there are fewer extenuating circumstances to interfere with goals of profitabliity, liquidity, and so forth. For example, Iloilo Chinese commercial and labor dealings with Filipinos are rarely complicated by other social relationships between transacting parties.[6] Chinese employers, in particular, vary rarely accept invitations to be the godparents (compadres) of their Filipino employees, claiming that such a tie interferes with business. On the other hand, they accept so many outside invitations, for public relations' sake, that they lose count of them.

2. In transactions across ethnic lines, there is the mutual expectation of negative reciprocity. Parties to the transaction can conclude the deal without destroying the relationship by saying, "What do you expect when dealing with a Filipino (Chinese)?" When mutual expectations are at least consonant, even if not comradely, then commercial transactions can

be regularized. When expectations are confused, commercial transactions are quite uncertain. This can be illustrated by dealings among Chinese in Iloilo City.

As consumers, Iloilo Chinese purchase nearly everything wholesale from each other. The 'friendly discount' between businessmen is still a valuable aid to minimizing family expenses and preserving liquid capital. But unlike a straight business deal between Chinese, such as between supplier and retailer, the 'friendly discount' is open to considerable latitude of interpretation and manipulation. Simply because all Iloilo Chinese know each other, there is a general 'friendly discount' for any Chinese who requests it for personal use from another Chinese store. The closer the friendship or kinship to the shopkeeper, however, the greater the discount, to the point that goods may be sold at cost or at a loss to close relatives and friends. The profit motive is held in such high regard among Chinese merchants that they disbelieve one another's claims of selling at cost or at a loss. Everyone expects the other fellow to make some small profit from all transactions. But one also expects great protestations by the seller of sacrifice on behalf of friends, kin, and town-mates. Therefore, merchants are confused as to whether transactions among themselves are being conducted on generalized, balanced, or negative reciprocal terms (Sahlins 1965), given their allegiance to the profit motive and their uncertainty of their exact relationship at any time to others in the community. Some merchants get compensation by identifying themselves as altruistic. Others seek to make a profit, but hide that fact. There is suspicion and quite a bit of hypocrisy among merchants on this account, for they are far less certain of the divisions among them than of the division between them and the Filipinos.

3. In commercial transactions across ethnic lines, each party exploits certain aspects of the stereotypes which the other holds for him. In fact, one might find that each group purposely developed their ethnic personae for complementary business dealings. Barth (1969) claims that an important aspect of ethnic group boundary maintenance in a polyethnic situation includes reinforcement of proper ethnic behavior by the other groups in contact. A Chinese is rewarded, therefore, undoubtedly commercially, for acting in a way the Filipino interprets as normal for Chinese. If to act like a Filipino merchant conferred

economic advantage, we might expect mestizos and Chinese who integrate well in Filipino society to do better business with Filipino customers. This is not the case in Iloilo City. Of course, there are many features of the Chinese persona that Filipinos despise, but they obviously respect Chinese business acumen, and actually prefer to do business with them.

4. An ethnic difference between parties in a commercial transaction may facilitate trade by 'differentiating the reward structures' of each side so that they are complementary rather than identical. Ethnic groups maintain their boundaries in part by supporting a certain set of values, or reward structures, that individuals can use for self-ascription and self-evaluation. In the language of the social psychology of bargaining, Filipinos and Chinese may differ enough in their payoff matrices (Rubin and Brown 1975) by virtue of membership in different ethnic groups, that trade can be rewarding for both. These payoff matrices are composed of as many motivational factors as the researcher wishes to insert: guilt, benevolence, a sense of justice and equity, the desire to avoid being duped, and so on. I conducted very little social psychological inquiry in Iloilo City, so this aspect of Filipino-Chinese trade remains untested. But the Filipinos, Chinese, and I all recognized and discussed differences in values among us. For example, the Chinese is prepared to work long hours, be obsequious to customers, and make a small per-unit profit. The Filipino (ignoring differences among them, here) is prepared to pay for increased leisure and for dominance in the bargaining situation. It is possible with such reward structures that each party profits and so seeks to preserve their differences.

5. The post-war history of Chinese businesses in Iloilo City bear out another of Foster's contentions, that a series of phenomena may be applied to reduce tensions inherent in face-to-face commercial deals. The pronounced ethnic differences between Chinese and Filipinos have diminished in the last generation as local-born Chinese children come of age to assume business control. Their facility in Filipino language and culture is used in trade relationships. When these younger Chinese affix their trade relationship to a social or kin relationship, it is more and more frequently one from the Filipino cultural repertory. The consequence of this trend is that an ethnic Chinese's categorization as a lumber salesman, sugar broker,

or plastics manufacturer begins to account for as much of his behavior as his Chinese ethnic status. This "ad hoc categorization by occupational requirements" (Foster 1974:446) is increasingly evident to Iloilo Chinese themselves. As families seek to diversify to increase security or accomodate a growing family, they may be heard openly evaluating the 'style' of a particular enterprise, anticipating that it will demand different relationships with both Filipino customers and Chinese suppliers. Fifty years ago, informants claim, almost all businesses of any size did "a little bit of this, a little bit of that." Now the trade networks are more specialized, the skills involved are more diverse; as the prominence of Chinese ethnic traits decreases, the prominence of their 'merchant' traits increases, proliferating categories and uncovering new commonalities. The importers of Japanese moterbikes, for example, are now more likely to behave like their counterparts in Cebu than like their cousins in glassware across town.

The tensions of face-to-face trade in the marketplace are also being displaced by insulating the trader from the responsibility for the terms of the exchange (Foster 1974:446). The Philippine government in post-War years has demanded far greater adherence to 'fixed price' transactions. This is particularly useful for the Chinese at the retail level: store merchandise today bristles with price tags announcing "Fixed Price/₱5.00," and so on. The local government rigidly enforces this practice. Animosity toward Chinese businessmen is not directed at their prices now, but at their treatment of Filipino employees (greatly increased at government demand since World War II) and at their hoarding practices. Iloilo Chinese insulate themselves from Filipinos by employing Filipino salesclerks on a scale unprecedented in the past (Omohundro 1974:135f). Movement up the distribution network, to manufacturing for example, also insulates, but in Iloilo industrial development is very small and this strategy involves emigration to Cebu or Manila.

To conclude, it is provocative to speculate that the history of Chinese commerce in the Philippines from pre-Hispanic times until now has been a progression through all of Foster's levels of commercial transactions. First, ritualized trade relations ('tribute') and outright piracy predominated in the early days of commerce between Chinese junks and local coastal polities.

Then under the Spanish feudal hegemony, the Chinese were legislated into ghettos (parians) and certain economic functions (Philippines-China trade, craftsmen, and so forth). Finally, ethnic categorization is now giving way to ad hoc categorization as a trading class. Further, commercial tensions in the modern polyethnic trading system of the contemporary Philippines are being partially displaced to the government level.

Notes

1. Minangkabau sojourners are mentioned in Steinberg (1971:17); the bejalai (expedition) of the Ibans is discussed in Freedman (1961); for the Javanese wong dagang or bazaar trader, see Geertz (1963:43).

2. The symbolic anthropological approach to ethnic group interaction has some exciting possibilities. Leach (1964) has already explored the significance of animal categories in verbal abuse: the entire inquiry could be extended into the domain of ethnic interaction. For example, what learned and shared perceptions of one another's cultural peculiarities are reflected in specific epithets? In Southeast Asia, one of the most common symbols for traders emphasizes their mobility. Wisseman (this volume) quotes pre-Madjapahit Javanese inscriptions poetically comparing merchants to migratory birds. The term for bazaar merchant, wong dagang in contemporary Javanese, derives from 'tramp', or 'wanderer' (Geertz 1963b:43).

3. This speculation requires some qualifications. A standard marketing area in Szechwan, averaging only 60 sq. km., is too small an area to have contributed all of a Philippine city's Uy's or Tan's. A central marketing area, ranging between 1250 to 2340 sq. km. is a more likely unit but Skinner does not claim much cultural distinctiveness for such a unit. Nevertheless, unity at the central marketing level was provided by the elite in the town, the same personnel who ran the 'travel agencies' and brokerages moving people to the South Seas. Also, apparently not all Philippine cities' immigrants cluster in certain townships of origin as well as those in Iloilo (Doeppers, personal communication). The data is simply not consistent enough to reject or support the idea that Philippine Chinese are intentionally nonrandomly distributed.

4. Doeppers (1976) has recently determined from late nineteenth century Spanish tax records that employer-employee relationships in Cebu City were unproscribed. That is, only about 14 percent of the employees were of the same surname and same hsien as their employers. Thus, either Iloilo City

apprentices were recruited more systematically than those in Cebu, or our data are not commensurate. I suspect the latter case, in part. First, Doeppers relied on certificate surnames, which (during the American era, at least) were extremely rarely the true surname of the holder. Second, Doeppers counted only surname and hsien of origin, since those items were on the Spanish records. Biographies of contemporary Iloilo merchants such as Mr. Lo reveal the use of certain kinds of affinal links and 'friend' links, and, of course, many business relationships were built on social connections created after immigration.

5. Not treated here due to space limitations are the subjects of business connections to other cities, to other nations, and to Filipinos. Briefly, I might note that Manila is the only Philippine city to be important in many Iloilo merchants' networks. Many business, social, and associational ties extend to Chinese individuals or organizations in Manila. No other city is of much importance. Few Iloilo merchants have anything to do with other nations except for a few social connections in Hong Kong and Taiwan. Connections elsewhere in Southeast Asia are nil. The subject of business connections with Filipinos is a gargantuan one to be treated in future articles.

6. The main exceptions to this absence of social relationships are the few crucial individual ties Chinese extablish with important Filipino customers, landlords, suppliers, or legal help (Omohundro 1974:316f).

III.

EXCHANGE AND THE PREHISTORIC AND

HISTORIC DEVELOPMENT

OF SOUTHEAST ASIA

The Opening of Southeast Asia,
Trading Patterns Through the Centuries

by

John K. Whitmore

In this paper, I am taking the opportunity to suggest a general historical framework for the patterns of trade in Southeast Asia before the twentieth century. The following is thus a description of my impressions on this topic, presented in the hope that it will provide a broad view in time within which the other historical papers may be placed; my secondary purpose is to propose certain new perspectives that may be useful for the further study of trade in the Southeast Asian past.

To examine the role of economic exchange in this region, we must be aware of the ways in which international commerce has penetrated Southeast Asia and come in contact with local societies and economies. My contention is that the process by which this occurred generally intensified through the centuries, that as time went by more and more parts of the region made contact with foreign trade. While there certainly were fluctuations in this development, we must consider that those societies which at one time had taken part in this trade remained aware of and interested in it. From this point we may begin to ask about the impact of this commercial involvement on the internal situation.

My approach to the historical development of Southeast Asian trade is to examine the patterns of penetration from the outside. I am interested in the changing routes of international trade through the area, the numbers and types of shippers and traders on these routes, the amount and types of goods handled by them, and the areas of Southeast Asia directly and indirectly involved with the trade.

In talking about the 'opening' of Southeast Asia, I do not wish to imply that the area was ever 'closed' in the sense of being absolutely cut off from the outside world. Through the last milennium B.C., increasing contact took place across the region and beyond as a developing network of communication appears to have stretched from the southeast coast of China to the Bay of Bengal, along the coast of the mainland and out into the island world of Southeast Asia. Archaeological information from these centuries suggests that they were a time of dynamic advancement in various parts of Southeast Asia (Kennedy, this volume; Hutterer, this volume). Wet rice agriculture became established during these centuries, in all probability, and pottery styles seem to reflect changing times. The knowledge of bronzecasting spread across the region. This 'Dongsonian' movement, to use the term commonly applied to it, reflects the networks of communications and information being formed throughout the region. The Malayo-Polynesian expansion to its eastern and western extremities (Easter Island and Madagascar) in these same centuries indeed suggests a push outward from Southeast Asia that would lead to the sharing of common mythological elements by both of these distant areas as well as by the east coast of India and the coast of mainland Southeast Asia (Taylor 1976).

Of particular interest here are the developments surrounding the Java Sea. Unlike the region to the north and east, in what is now eastern Malaysia and the Philippines, a significant number of megalithic and bronze sites are known in southern Sumatra, throughout Java and the Lesser Sunda Islands all the way to Kutei on the central coast of east Borneo as well as out into the Moluccas (Heekeren 1958; Holt 1967). From the evidence of these sites, we might postulate growing ancestral cults and active chieftainships amidst people eager to use new knowledge and technologies for religion, war, and decoration.

Thus, I believe that, even before foreign trade had begun to penetrate Southeast Asia, indigenous populations of the region were in a loose and general contact with peoples of outside areas. While the Mauryans in northern India and the Ch'in and Han dynasties of north China were consolidating power in their respective realms and expanding it, dynamic chieftains and their peoples throughout Southeast Asia were apparently beginning to pursue means of greater political integration, following lines of development allowed and encouraged by their own cultures (Kennedy, this volume; Hall 1976b:79-92).

In this way, I would postulate an active, not a passive, Southeast Asia meeting the expanding international trade route roughly two thousand years ago.[1] With the zenith of the Roman empire on the west, the Han empire in the east, and the growth of commerce in India, the international trade route worked itself, via a series of links, through Southeast Asia towards China. Coming from the Mediterranean, this route went to the west coast of India, around to the east coast, and across the Bay of Bengal to the Malay Peninsula. In Southeast Asia, the specific points of contact were the west and east coasts of the upper Malay Peninsula connected by overland transport, and the port of Oc-eo on the western edge of the Mekong Delta (Wolters 1967, ch. 2). The commercial importance of Southeast Asia at this time lay predominantly in the fact that it sat astride this maritime route to and from China, with luxury goods moving from west to east. Only to a very limited degree was there any penetration into or contact with other parts of Southeast Asia away from the main route. Drawing on K'ang T'ai's third century report, Wolters (1967:52) has shown that some raw materials were brought to Funan from across the eastern sea by Southeast Asians. There is also the evidence of western goods found in different parts of the mainland (Wolters 1967:38, 271, n. 60, 273, n. 86). The major area of regional interaction in Southeast Asia apart from the international trade route was the area along the edge of the Java Sea in the vicinity of southern Sumatra and western Java. Already, according to Wolters' description (1967:57-70, 352), a locality somewhere around the area of the Sunda Strait had taken the opportunity to stand between the trade of the outside world and the goods of the rich Java Sea region.[2] This locality, Ko-ying in the Chinese transcription, dealt with the horsedealers of northwest India and the peninsular dependencies of Funan, exchanging local goods for western products and most likely putting the latter into trade further east in the archipelago. While outside sources provide little specific knowledge of the eastern archipelago beyond Java (Wolters 1967: 39, 56, 178), we see a small amount of goods from this region (cloves, gharuwood, sandalwood) beginning to appear in India (1967:65-8).

Wolters (1967:34-6) has demonstrated that, by the early fifth century, a major change had occurred in that section of the international trade route which crossed Southeast Asia. No longer did it take the path across the upper Malay Peninsula, but went through the Straits of Malacca to make direct contact with the northwestern edge of the Java Sea region. Initially, this trading area seems to have been in western Java.[3] Wolters (1967:162-8, 175-6, ch. 13) believes that, despite contacts between parts of Java and south China, over the next two centuries the trading center came to lie on the southeast coast of Sumatra. Increasingly thereafter, the trade of the archipelago, including western Borneo, Java, and the islands of the east, focused on the region soon to be controlled by the empire of Srivijaya around the Straits. The upper Malay Peninsula with its hinterland in the Menam and Irrawaddy river valleys was also drawn into this concentration of trade (Wheatley 1964:67-86).

The prime reason for participation in this trade continued to be the wealth that could be gained from handling the increasing flow of eastern and western goods between China and India. This trade was to a great extent in Middle Eastern aromatics and drugs in exchange for Chinese silk. Local Sumatran communities had already begun, however, to inject their own goods (pine resin and benzoin) into the flourishing international trade. These goods were identified as 'Persian' and took the place of the Middle Eastern resins, frankincense and myrrh. Wolters (1967:95-127) has done a splendid job in working out the detail of this pattern and shows how the southeastern area of Sumatra came to be a 'favoured coast' which aided the flow of international commerce with its ships and facilities while developing commercial methods of its own. Though the main thrust of indigenous trade involved Sumatran products, like the above 'Persian' goods and camphor, a variety of goods continued to come through the Java Sea area to Sumatra: cloves, nutmegs, and probably dragon's blood and other forest products (Wolters 1967:123-4, 137, 150). The Spice Islands of the eastern archipelago thus continued to put their products into foreign commerce via the Java Sea and its contact with international trade in the vicinity of the Sunda Strait. At the same time, the Java Sea area was transmitting bronze items and international goods to the eastern islands as well (Heekeren 1958:40-3)

Though little direct evidence exists, the ships which transported the goods and traders between the southeast coast of China and Ceylon and India were undoubtedly the same ones which plied the Southeast Asian seas and were manned by Malay crews. In Wolters' description (1967:ch. 14), Srivijaya emerged in the seventh century, following the burst of trade as the T'ang dynasty unified China, and put down rivals for the trade of both the international route and the Java Sea region by drawing the Malay seafarers to its wealth and power. Thus did Srivijaya gain control of both shipping and the potential piracy. At the same time, Srivijaya should also be seen as an inland power which expanded its central base and sought allies in the hinterland, thus gaining both military manpower and access to the valuable forest produce of the mountain regions. [4]

From the late seventh century to the early eleventh, Srivijaya maintained itself as the focus of trade in Southeast Asia, while the international trade grew with the increasingly heavy involvement of Arab traders (Wheatley 1961:216-32). The emphasis remained on aromatics and drugs, particularly from the Middle East, in exchange for Chinese silks,[5] and the Sumatran empire came to dominate not only the Straits of Malacca but also the upper Malay Peninsula, including Ligor and the 'Kalah' area where Arab trade was centered (Wolters 1970: 9). The area around the Java Sea, recognized as a specific region by the Chinese Buddhist pilgrim I Tsing and others, had flourished in the seventh century and continued to dominate the trade with the eastern archipelago, serving as the transmitter of information concerning the Spice Islands to the Chinese. [6] Despite the rise of political power in central Java during the following centuries, Srivijaya remained the major link between the international route and the wealth of Java and beyond. The mainland routes in the meantime either fed into the international route or moved along the coast northeast to China and west to Bengal.

The tenth and early eleventh centuries, however, saw shifting international and regional economic and political situations which began to loosen the trade route and Srivijaya's control over it. The empires of Angkor and Pagan were growing on the mainland and beginning to involve themselves in international trade. [7] Indian and Chinese traders and shippers were moving out into the sea routes for the first time in large numbers and were looking to go more directly to the sources of local goods as the Southeast Asian products themselves, especially the spices, gained a worldwide recognition (Wolters 1970:42-8). Finally, east Java had begun to take advantage of the natural wealth at the disposal of the Java Sea region and was developing its own trade (Wisseman, this volume). All this was compounded by the rise of a newly unified and increasingly prosperous China under the Sung dynasty (Wheatley 1959:5-41).

Though Srivijaya fought with Java and sought to establish itself with both the Chola power of South India to the west and the Sung to the north, the old situation was gone and no Srivijayan effort could maintain its former control. The Chola attack of 1025 shattered Srivijaya's hegemony and let loose the gathering forces (Hall and Whitmore 1976:306-7, 310). North and west Sumatra, heretofore dominated by the southern part of the island, gradually began to deal directly with the foreign traders (Wolters 1967:178f; 1970:9-10, 42-2, 47-8). The same traders also began to go to east Java for the goods of the Java Sea region and the spices of the eastern archipelago. Thus, the old interface between the international route and the Java Sea that had existed since the fifth century broke down and was replaced by an interface between Java and the eastern archipelago. Over the second half of the twelfth century, according to a well known Chinese source, the Ling Wai Tai Ta, the Javanese surpassed southeastern Sumatra in wealth and ranked behind only the Arabs (Wheatley 1961:63). [8]

North of the Straits of Malacca, the economic systems of the mainland generally linked themselves to international trade not by feeding directly into the central trade route which was shifting south to the Java Sea, but by going from the upper Malay Peninsula across the Bay of Bengal to Ceylon and South India (Hall and Whitmore 1976). In this way, these trade contacts were blocked off from the Chinese view and must be approached through South Asian sources (the same is undoubtedly true for trade developments on the west coast of Sumatra; see Hall, this volume). The confusion that exists concerning the upper Malay Peninsula in the twelfth century may be resolved by this approach. Instead of looking for political hegemony by one power or another at any particular time, we should consider the economic interests at work in Khmer, Burmese, and Ceylonese terms. In this view, the 1160's raid from Ceylon on lower Burma is best seen as an attempt to keep the way open for commerce and communications.

The pattern of trade along these various routes was also changing. While the commerce in aromatics, drugs, silks, and exotic luxury items continued, bulk goods of a more practical value were being carried in increasing quantities. Cotton goods, mainly from India, became much more important, and porcelain flowing out of China was traded all the way to the African coast. Indeed, China incurred a serious trade deficit which led to the outflow of great amounts of metals, particularly illegal copper cash (Wheatley 1959; Hall and Whitmore 1976:322-4).

Thus, from the tenth to the thirteenth centuries, a dispersion of the trade routes took place as the old system weakened and greater numbers and different types of foreign traders pursued Southeast Asian goods more directly into Southeast Asia itself. With the rise of new ports on the southeastern coast of China and the increasing commercial and military strength of the Cholas in South India, the foreign traders not only continued to transport the goods of east and west but wished to handle the 'country goods', to borrow a later term, themselves. They 'opened up' the coasts of the Philippine/north Borneo area and of north and west Sumatra in the process (Hall, this volume; Hutterer, this volume), but dealt still with intermediaries, now the Javanese, in obtaining the increased flow of spices from the eastern archipelago. These traders also began to penetrate the core areas of the lowland empires on the mainland, though they appear to have gone no further inland (Hall and Whitmore 1976:322; Chou 1967).

This pattern set the framework for the trade developments of the following years. From the thirteenth century to the fifteenth, though political changes led to a different configuration of states, trade continued in the same general way. The basic point is that Java, with its control of the spice trade, must be seen as the dominant commercial power during this time and that this dominance influenced much that was going on around it. It is no accident that the Mongols moved directly on Java in 1292 (Wolters 1970:44), and Javanese power continued over southern Sumatra and surrounding island ports through the fourteenth century, resisting even the intrusion of the newly founded Ming dynasty in China.[9] Within this context arose the northern ports of Sumatra. Instead of stressing the independent status of Samudra-Pasai and its neighboring harbors, we should see them, I believe, responding to the situation established by Javanese power and the growing north coast ports of that island.

While Java insisted on a certain power relationship between itself and the outer islands, it had no need to control the Straits ports as had been so necessary for Srivijaya. The Javanese were content with their exchange of rice and cloth for spices as well as with the shipping that went with this exchange (Meilink-Roelofsz 1962:22-6, 103-15; Wisseman, this volume). Thus, ports like Pasai on the northern and western coasts of Sumatra were relatively free to handle the forest produce of their island and the local trade (Hall, this volume). The increased piracy of the Straits area (Wolters 1970:47) would also have been a result of this loose control. In this situation, Malacca arose during the first half of the fifteenth century. It was at first part of the early Ming tributary structure, but shifted in the 1430's to the pattern of international trade (Wolters 1970:154-70). To do this, the rulers of Malacca had to come to terms with the Javanese commercial and cultural patterns. The role of Javanese merchants in Malacca through the fifteenth century was most important (Lach 1965:513-4; Meilink-Roelofsz 1962:36-8). For them, this new international port was a good market for their rice and their spices as well as a convenient intermediary for the goods of the international trade route itself. The Javanese shipping gained specifically in terms of its control over the island traffic to and from the Straits.

Despite the disintegration of the Pagan and Angkor empires through the thirteenth and fourteenth centuries, trade on the central and western mainland continued in the way that it had begun. Pegu in the Irrawaddy Delta began to take part in the commerce involving northern Sumatra and the Straits area as well as the Bay of Bengal. This port was soon followed by the formation of Ayudhya, out of the loose commercial and political matrix of the lower Menam valley, with an orientation towards China. Both these capitals, and perhaps also a Khmer capital on the Mekong river, became trading as well as political centers and handled the flow of goods from upriver areas in exchange for regional and international goods.[10] As Malacca grew into a regional and international entrepôt in the middle of the fifteenth century, Pegu developed a solid trading relationship with it. Ayudhya, on the other hand, saw Malacca as an intruder into its sphere and tended to remain uninvolved with and hostile toward its operations (Wolters 1970:154-63; Wake 1964:117-9; Lach 1965:510-1, 514, 520, 526, 538).

The stunning entry of the Portuguese onto the Southeast Asian scene as they crossed the Indian Ocean in pursuit of spices brought an end to the five hundred year development of this trading system. Of significance was not only the fall of Malacca in 1511, which once again removed the focus of trade from the Straits region, but particularly, I would stress, the immediate penetration by the Portuguese into the Spice Islands (1511-1513) (Meilink-Roelofsz 1962:153-5; Forman, this volume). With this thrust, they broke the Javanese hold on the spice trade of a millennium or more, and for the second time we see foreign traders seeking direct access to Southeast Asian goods. This pattern of foreign penetration in an attempt to get the goods at their sources is, in my mind, the major theme of the next four hundred years, to the beginning of the present century and beyond.

The Portuguese were not able to control the spice trade, and the opening of the eastern archipelago led to a variety of groups, western and eastern, competing to exploit its wealth (Schrieke 1955:47). The north coast ports of Java continued to be active through the sixteenth century and into the seventeenth when they were destroyed by the emerging inland power of Mataram (Ricklefs 1973:13-6, 21-2). Trade in the Straits area split between Acheh, which controlled the pepper and gold of Sumatra and dealt with western commerce, on the one hand, and Johore, the heir of Malacca which handled the eastern trade, on the other (Andaya 1971). The mainland ports of Pegu and Ayudhya thrived with the direct foreign contacts, and Cambodia established a Mekong port linked to the Malay population on the northern fringe of the South China Sea (Lach 1965:543, 545-7, 560; G. Wm. Skinner 1957:7-9).[11] To the east, Brunei and Sulu managed the regional and Chinese trade, while the new Spanish presence in Manila forged a link between Acapulco and Canton (Lach 1965:581, 642; Schurz 1939).

The appearance of the Dutch in the seventeenth century epitomized this trend. They eagerly reached out to all the main trading areas of Southeast and East Asia in an effort to gain a major share of the Asian trade. From their base in Batavia on the northwest coast of Java, besides seeking to keep all competitors out of the Moluccas and loosely dominating the Java Sea and Straits regions,[12] the Dutch made continuous and vigorous contact with the mainland ports and capitals of Burma,

Ayudhya, Cambodia, Laos, and Vietnam. A major competitor for them in the central and eastern mainland through the 1630s were the Japanese, before being cut off from their homeland by Tokugawa policy (G. Wm. Skinner 1967:8-9; Nguyen 1970: 188-92). Thereafter the Chinese offered the stiffest and most consistant competition. Basically, however, the indigenous political situations of these areas did not allow any long term success for the Dutch efforts, and the capital of each of the areas retained a certain amount of control over its own internal trade. Foreign penetration of these realms and their economic spheres remained limited.

European attempts to dominate Southeast Asia slackened through the eighteenth century and shifted emphasis to the age-old concern for contact and trade with China. This occurred at the same time that Chinese entrepreneurs were expanding their involvement in Southeast Asian trade. The latter were not only able to establish themselves in the various mainland ports ahead of the Dutch, but they had also begun to play a significant economic role in the provinces of the European powers themselves, Java and the Philippine Islands.[13] Various Southeast Asians also undertook active roles in the commercial exploitation of their environment, harvesting pepper, forest goods, and the produce of the sea to meet external demands (Bastin 1961; Morison 1961:90-2, 219, 288-90; Dunn 1975:118; Reber 1966:ch. 4, 205). The Europeans, especially the British, moved from the middle of the eighteenth century to the middle of the nineteenth to open China (Bassett 1964; Lamb 1970). This was done in the Opium War and succeeding military engagements and, through the first half of the nineteenth century, was accompanied by increasing pressure on the mainland capitals of Southeast Asia to open their economic systems to direct foreign contact. The Thais, long active in international commerce, came to terms in the 1850s with this European desire for economic and political access (Wyatt 1968). Other parts of Southeast Asia, Burma, Vietnam, Cambodia, Laos, Malaya, the Sulu Islands, and Acheh, all required brutal force before they 'opened up' to Western satisfaction.

Meanwhile, the Dutch and Spanish had begun to try to exploit their own domains in Java and Luzon respectively. As the nineteenth century progressed, international commercial developments began to penetrate areas of Southeast Asia beyond the capitals, becoming a third force, besides the direct European colonial presence and the Southeast Asian responses, that historians must consider. This international demand from the growing capitalist system for such produce as abaca and rice began to open Southeast Asia down to the village level, in certain localities, for these world market forces (Owen 1971, 1976; Dunn 1975:118; Wilson, this volume).

What I have attempted to describe in very brief form is my view that gradually over the past two millennia foreigners, both eastern and western, became aware of the natural wealth that Southeast Asia had to offer. They initially obtained the goods of the region from indigenous intermediaries who controlled the sources of the goods. Eventually, however, the foreigners began to desire a direct contact of their own with these sources and, following the shattering of the Srivijaya domain in the eleventh century, the Javanese system in the sixteenth, and the hold of the mainland capitals in the nineteenth, they were able to make good their wish. By the beginning of the twentieth century, the penetration and opening of Southeast Asia had reached a point where foreigners had come to dominate politically and/or economically vast portions of the region. These foreigners did not, of course, directly control all the population and territory, nor did they try to. Their aims lay in pursuing their economic and strategic interests, and they avoided, to a degree, social or cultural responsibility for the people under them.

What influence did this commercial penetration and opening of Southeast Asia have on social and cultural developments in the region? Two basic questions come to mind beyond that concerning the pattern of contact: first, what was the manner of articulation between the external routes and the existing or developing internal forms of exchange? and second, in what way did the internal situation adjust in order to handle the external contacts? Indigenous response, whether positive or negative, lies at the root of this problem, since the mere existence of the trade routes does not provide the answer. Only when the local peoples were prepared to deal with these contacts, in their own fashion, would these questions gain importance.

The papers included in this volume present a variety of different situations involving exchange in Southeast Asia, past and present. Peterson shows a natural, symbiotic form of exchange between highlanders and lowlanders, such as Kennedy and Hutterer postulate for prehistoric times. Bronson's dendritic model predicts an upriver extension of exchange in reaction to coastal contacts. Hall and Forman discuss political and economic reactions of the hinterland to maritime developments, Muslim and Portuguese respectively. Wisseman and Woodward see the kings of Java maintaining control of foreign luxury goods and integrating them into the indigenous social and cultural system. Omohundro and Wilson describe foreigners establishing themselves locally and providing the trade mechanism. As Foster argues, shifting patterns of exhange offer conflict as a potential result. The necessary adjustment, in his mind, moves from ritualization to categorization and then impersonalization. In our continued efforts to examine the history of trade in Southeast Asia, we need to be much more aware of the ramifications that economic interaction has had for the social and cultural systems of the region we study.

Notes

1. I strongly agree with Kennedy's discussion in this volume of Wheatley's postulations on tribal societies in prehistoric Southeast Asia. What we need is a much stronger sense of dynamic, not static, social, economic, and political patterns in the region before external contacts.

2. The exact location of such a trading point at this time and in following centuries is problematic given the general lack of archaeological remains. Miksic (this volume) points out the geomorphological instability of the coast lines in this area, and both Bronson's (this volume) and his papers postulate changing locations for political and economic reasons as well. Impermanence, competition, and a 'floating' nature would thus appear to have been the rule for these coastal trading centers. Wolters comes to grips with this problem in his 1975 article.

3. Wolters, with his focus on the Straits of Malacca and Sumatra, has a tendency to overlook the Javanese situation, and we find only occasional references to it scattered through the book (1967:35-6, 78, 138, 151-2, 160-2, 164-5, 206, 277, n. 53). Wisseman (this volume) notes that the inland political powers of central Java may have actively sought to suppress any north coast ports throughout the first millennium A.D.

4. K. R. Hall (1976b) examines the inland side of Srivijaya, supplementing Wolters' (1967, 1970) focus on the maritime nature of the state. Bronson (this volume) presents an upstream/downstream 'dendritic' model that may be applied to the Srivijayan situation.

5. See Woodward (this volume) for an indication of the stylistic interrelationship of silks from the eighth and ninth centuries found in Japan, Java, Central Asia, and Europe.

6. Wolters (1967:198-202) points out that the image of the island world east of Java appears as very barbaric in the Chinese sources and indeed that one Chinese term for this 'vaguely definable region', Lo-ch'a, is a transliteration of

the Sanskrit rākṣasa (demon). Another term for the area appears to have been K'un-lun which, as Taylor (1976:32-3) explains, was a term used by the Chinese for areas and peoples just beyond the known world. I suggest that the Javanese may have been screening the Eastern Archipelago, source of the valuable spices, from probing foreign eyes.

7. The study of the early economic history of mainland Southeast Asia is only in its initial stages. Hall (1975) has examined the commercial growth of the Angkorian empire in the tenth and eleventh centuries; Aung Thwin (1976: 230-1) notes the economic expansion of Pagan Burma at the same time; and Hall and Whitmore (1976:307-13) attempt to follow the commercial currents of the period.

8. Marco Polo's evidence from the end of the thirteenth century tells of a wealthy Java supplying spices directly to the many foreign traders and a number of Sumatran kingdoms dealing independently in their own local products (Benda and Larkin 1967:12-3).

9. Again, Wolters (1970) is focussing on the region of the Straits of Malacca and Sumatra with the result that his references to Java are scattered.

10. We are beginning to understand the impact of trade on the political development of mainland Southeast Asia following the collapse of Angkor and Pagan. Michael Vickery, in a personal communication (26 Sept. 1975), suggests "that wealth and power were... gradually siphoned away from Angkor to both Ayutthaya and the Lovek/Phnom Penh area" because of the trade stimulus (see Lach 1965:526, 545; Wolters 1970:56, 61, 67, 157; Kasetsiri 1973). An important element in Southeast Asian trade c. 1400 was the presence of the Ryukyuans, taking the place of private Chinese traders due to the Ming dynasty exclusion policy (Sakamaki 1964).

11. We must stress the importance of trade in the politics of the sixteenth and seventeenth century mainland and point out the significant role played by Malays around the Gulf of Siam. L. A. P. Gosling (this volume) gives a very good indication of a later manifestation of the Malay presence there (in its

declining phase). Vickery, in his personal communication, states, "...when reliable information on Cambodia is again available in the sixteenth century, Phnom Penh is an important commercial center with an international population. The eventual relative victory of Ayutthaya was due to its more favorable geographic location."

12. The Dutch presence, if not control, of the Straits region and Sumatra is very well described by Andaya (1971:especially ch. 3), and the translation by C. Skinner (1963) of the Macassar chronicle gives an indigenous view of Dutch power. Another indigenous view may be seen in the Banjar chronicle, translated by Ras (1968), where a warning against growing pepper was based on the fear of foreign intervention (331, 443).

13. For the 'sojourning' nature of the Chinese involvement, see Omohundro (this volume). A variety of works deal with the Chinese in different locations; for the Philippines, see Wickberg (1965:3-20); on Java, Lombard-Salmon (1972); for Thailand, G. Wm. Skinner (1957:ch. 1); and on Vietnam, Nguyen (1970:195-201) and Ch'en (1974). Wang (1959) gives a brief general overview.

Archaeology and Palaeogeography
in the Straits of Malacca

by

John N. Miksic

Archaeologists have found few sites of early coastal settlement in Southeast Asia. Gorman (1971) analyzed eighteen Hoabinhian sites, fifteen inland and only three coastal; he noted that few other Hoabinhian maritime sites are known, and explained the scarcity of such sites by reference to a postulated two-meter rise of the sea level in the Recent Epoch which may have destroyed most of these sites. Gorman also noted that no Hoabinhian sites have been found in alluvial plains, and that "this is unexpected" (1971:306).

Historical sources are available from the first millennium A.D. and later which yield progressively more information regarding societies of the Southeast Asian coasts and alluvial plains. References to these societies frequently occur in the context of commercial activity. These literary sources suggest that as early as the second century A.D. commerce formed an integral part of the adaptation of some Southeast Asian coastal societies.

The difficulty in locating coastal sites in Southeast Asia can be linked to considerations of the interaction of human activity and the processes of coastal formation. Closer attention to changes in the Southeast Asian land-sea boundary and to possible consequences of this geomorphological instability for coastal societies may augment future investigations of early maritime Southeast Asian culture and long-distance trade.

Interdisciplinary Studies of Coastal Adaptation

Recent workers in the Mediterranean have called attention to the classical Greek literary genre of chorography. In this type of writing Herodotus, Strabo, Pliny and others included descriptions both of various societies and of the lands in which they lived (McDonald 1972:9-10). Arguing for the combination of similar sets of observation, Kraft (1972) proposed the union of sedimentation process study, coastal geology, and archaeology as a discrete subfield of scientific research. To this group of fields others have added history and settlement pattern study (McDonald and Rapp 1972b; Vita-Finzi 1969).

An interdisciplinary study of the Mississippi River delta conducted in the 1950s (McIntire 1958, 1959; Gould and McFarlane 1959; Byrne, LeRoy and Riley 1959) combined coastal geology and archaeology. The deltaic coast of Louisiana has built seaward fifteen miles "since sea level stabilized" (Gould and McFarlane 1959). The coastal plain of Mississippi sediment thus laid down covers between 1200 (Byrne, LeRoy and Riley 1959) and 1500 (McIntire 1959) square miles. This plain is dissected by minor branches of the main river channel; major and minor rivers have built levee systems. Cheniers (banks of sand), shells and other debris heaped up by storms on former beaches also form areas of raised ground. On these cheniers (the most recently formed of which are found in environments of swamps and lagoons) American Indians lived for centuries, exploited the rich food resources of the swamps and coastal waters nearby, and left occupational debris—shells, bones, tools and potsherds.

As the shore prograded with the deposition of new sediment, the Indians shifted their settlements from time to time in order to remain in the same habitat, with access to both marine and estuarine resources. Thus older sites are on cheniers further from the present coast, and on levees abandoned by distributaries at earlier stages of delta formation. The sequence and dating of the Indians' ceramic development is independently known; thus the levees of earlier rivers which have shifted their courses, and former coasts indicated by cheniers, can be dated by the human remains found on and in them, and stages of growth of the delta can be charted.

Through geomorphological analysis of the patterns of chenier and levee development, local variations in coastal growth can also be detected. Such variation is often the result of change in river courses and loss of sediment supply to particular beaches with concurrent cessation and even reversal of coastal growth in the affected region.

A project involving more extensive interdisciplinary cooperation has been carried out in the eastern Mediterranean, on the southwest Peloponnese coast and hinterland (McDonald and Rapp 1972b; Kraft 1972; Kraft, Rapp and Aschbrenner 1975). The University of Minnesota Messenia Expedition utilized history, soil science, geography, engineering, palynology, agriculture, metallurgy, geophysics and archaeology to study human adaptation, settlement patterns, environmental change, and their inter-relationships during the Bronze Age.

A summary statement of the Messenia project relevant to the present inquiry notes that "in any country that has always looked to the sea for some of its food and for much of its trade, communications, and political security, the coastal landforms take on a special importance" (Loy and Wright 1972:43). Information from the specialized studies cited above can be used to create a general framework for the analysis of cultural and geological change and their systemic interaction. This framework will be briefly developed here, and suggestions made for its application to maritime Southeast Asia.

Model of Human-Landform Relationships

A major process of coastal formation in both the eastern Mediterranean and in Southeast Asia has been long-shore drift of sediments brought to the coast by rivers, with the effect that an initially jagged coastline has been smoothed. Bays between promontories are filled in; beach ridges form, creating lagoons which gradually become swamps and then undulating lowlands (McDonald and Rapp 1972a:240). Islands near the shore are joined to the mainland and become hills. This process has been described both by Greek chorographers and in a well-known passage of the Hikayat Marong Mahawangsa.

> King Marong Mahawangsa sailed for Rum. At that time king Marong Mahawangsa, looking to the shore, saw how Pulau Lada had already ceased to be an island, so that in the end it was to be called Bukit Lada. Pulau Djambul had shared this fate and was in the end called Bukit Djambul.

> Pulau Seri was on the point of merging with the
> land and was to bear the name of Gunung Djerai,
> because of its height. Looking also to the north-
> west he further saw that Tandjung Bara and Pulau
> Keriang, which were still surrounded by sea,
> would before long become one with the land and
> in the end bear the names Bukit Tandjung and
> Gunung Keriang, respectively. (Quoted in Ras
> 1968:193.)

Rivers emptying into these embayments deposit alluvium, form levees, and periodically alter their courses. They cut through old beach ridges to find new outlets to the sea. Their mouths move seaward with the coasts; for instance, the mouth of the Greater Meander River near Miletus, Anatolia, shifted ten miles in twenty-five centuries. Miletus, once situated on a coastal promontory, now lies inland (McDonald and Rapp 1972a).

River mouths are favored locations for human settlement. Here access to resources of both sea and land is easiest, as is control of marine transport between, on the one hand, gatherers of products of mountains, agriculturalists of the alluvium, gatherers of the shore and local fishermen, and, on the other hand, distant coastal centers of collection of a different range of products. Human activity modifies coasts through denudation of uplands and consequent increased erosion, some of the products being deposited at the river mouth and in the coastal area; through interference with natural drainage patterns by building canals, draining swamps, constructing weirs; and through harbor works and garbage deposited by the harbor population (Simmons and Herrmann 1972). Sedimentation and resulting river course and coastal change are sometimes met by human adjustments, such as attempts to maintain a stable configuration through the use of cooperative labor to dredge canals and maintain levees. When these efforts are unsuccessful, efforts may be made to adapt to the new configuration by movement of ports and riverine settlements, and construction of new canal networks.[1] When even these attempts to maintain the man-land relationship no longer suffice, new settlement patterns may develop, or sometimes political upheavals occur as symptoms of social disequilibrium.

Application of this schematic model of the human

relationship to specific instances of coastal sedimentation encounters severe difficulties. In measuring the relative importance of human agencies in altering coasts, and the speed at which coastal alteration took place during a particular period, certain things must be known. These include: the degree to which sedimentation is due to nonhuman causes, and the intensity of those human activities which affect denudation and sedimentation.

Nonhuman causes of change in sedimentation rates and coastal configurations include changes in climate, vegetation and sea level, and tectonic activity. Of these, sea level change and tectonic activity are most problematic. A relative rise in sea level at a particular place can be due to either a world-wide absolute (or eustatic) rise in the level of the ocean, a fall in the local land surface due to movement in the earth's crust (tectonic change), or a combination of both. Unfortunately, the issue of worldwide sea level change in the Recent Epoch is a subject of great debate among geologists and oceanographers, and the respective roles of tectonism, sea level and human agency in modifying coasts are, therefore, not easily differentiated.

In order to examine tectonic changes in coasts, intensive studies of local areas are needed. In the Mediterranean, for instance, Flemming (1969) studied 179 ancient cities excavated by archaeologists, and concluded that tectonic activity rather than eustatic sea level change was responsible for the submergence of some and the uplift of others. Archaeological studies of shell mounds have also been concerned with questions of sea level change (Hurt 1974; Holmes and Trickey 1974; Snow 1972).

In Southeast Asia Verstappen (1953, 1973) has postulated a Recent sea level several meters higher than at present. Haile (1969, 1971) has disagreed, preferring the theory that since the end of the Pleistocene the sea level has never been higher than at present. Such disputes can only be resolved through future research into the sequence of deposition and erosion in particular coastal areas. Archaeological investigations on coastal sites can contribute to such research.

In Southeast Asia there are several areas where rates and processes of sedimentation have been studied. These areas also hold interest for students of early Southeast Asian maritime adaptations. Thus mutual awareness of the problems and prospects of specialists in the several disciplines concerned has the potential for mutual benefit.

Several attempts at combining archaeology, history and sedimentation studies in Southeast Asia have been made and will be reviewed here. We can also correlate specialized studies in individual fields and examine their relevance for the study of Southeast Asian coastal adaptations, with particular attention to the period A.D. 200 to 1400 when, judging from literary sources, trade formed an important facet of these adaptations.

Hydraulic and Non-Hydraulic Coastal Adaptations

Archaeological research has been carried out in the Mekong Delta, the Malay Peninsula, and eastern coastal Sumatra, areas where historians and historical geographers have argued that ports and kingdoms named in written sources once existed.

Malleret's archaeological work in the Mekong Delta recovered evidence of early trade, landform modification, and settlements (Malleret 1959-63). His finds were being applied to problems of economic development when recent political events apparently halted the project.

A brief United Nations report sketched the relevance of environmental archaeology for developmental planning in the Mekong Delta (UN/ECAFE 1973). Study of previous human activity and interaction with soils, sediments, erosion and fertility, it is stated, can assist in planning future modification of the land. In the Delta, a "general picture of successive phases of exploitation of the landscape has emerged..." (UN/ECAFE 1973:3). Major components of early exploitation in the Delta involved settlement on raised beach ridges and large scale expenditure of effort and expertise on canal building. The canals, some several hundred kilometers long, radiate from ancient settlements, rather than adapting their courses to the needs of specific agricultural usage (Malleret 1959-63, I:117-24, and maps, plates 12 and 13; Paris 1931, 1941). It has therefore been proposed that the canals were primarily designed to facilitate transport and communication rather than agriculture (UN/ECAFE 1973).

Southern Thailand has received recent attention from a number of archaeologists and geologists. Archaeology here too is beginning to confirm postulated involvement of inhabitants of Southeast Asian coasts with early trade networks (Wales 1974). In south Thailand no large rivers build deltas, but silting and beach ridge formation due to wave action are processes which can be shown to affect settlement distribution. Beach ridges here reach heights of three meters and lengths of several kilometers. On these ridges modern settlements and transport routes are located, and coconuts and fruit trees grown. Between the ridges the lower land is planted with rice, or left as marsh where it is too low to be drained.[2]

The western side of the peninsula is fringed by a nearly continuous mangrove belt, but on the east mangroves are abundant only in estuaries and in the lee of islands. The rest of the east coast is sandy beach. A major geomorphological feature of the southeastern Thai coast is the Satingpra peninsula, itself a still-forming beach ridge about three meters high, with a series of lakes and lagoons eighty kilometers long on its lee side. It is claimed that early settlers in this region produced 'major works', including about two hundred reservoirs and a system of waterways which served a 'core area' of at least 804 square kilometers (Stargardt 1973a, 1973b). It has been noted that, as in the Mekong Delta, some of these waterways may have been constructed and maintained to facilitate maritime transport and communication, rather than for agricultural benefit. The stimulus for this activity is, therefore, laid to long distance trade (Stargardt 1973a).

Stargardt dates the construction of these works to the period of the similar development in the Mekong Delta or slightly later. This argument is based in part on postulated cultural connections, supported by ceramic similarities. A second part of the argument involves the assumption that western Indonesia lacked similar development and could not, therefore, have been a source for its diffusion. It is true that evidence of such landform modification on the coasts of the Straits of Malacca is lacking, and that the center of the Malay Peninsula may have formed a boundary between a realm of hydraulic expertise and another in which such expertise never developed, or only developed much later under external influence.

On the other hand, geomorphological and ecological similarities would not lead us to postulate such an abrupt dichotomy. This apparent division may, given the meager attention devoted to the subject of the history of settlement patterns and landform modification in west Malaysia and western Indonesia, be due to sampling error. A consideration of the geological, historical and archaeological evidence regarding the possible adaptations of early Straits inhabitants may delineate possibilities for research which could amplify knowledge of early Straits coastal society.

Coastal Geomorphology
and Early Straits Settlements

The coasts of the Straits of Malacca present an initial contrast with the east coast of the Malay Peninsula in that the Straits are almost totally bordered by mangroves. Wave activity in the Straits is of much lower energy than on the east coast of the Peninsula, favoring mangrove development. However, the pattern of numerous beach ridges paralleling the present coast is duplicated on a scale equal to, or in some areas of much greater magnitude than, that in southeastern peninsular Thailand.

The pattern of settlement on former beach ridges of the Straits coasts was noted in 1895. L. Wray, curator and geologist of the Perak Museum, during a search for old shell mounds on the Perak coast found a series of seven beach ridges with the low land between them used for padi. South of the Perak River another series of beach ridges included one over three kilometers long and fifteen to twenty meters wide (Sieveking 1954-55). Later Courtier (1962) noted the extension of these features to the north. [3]

In this same area Evans (1928, 1932) excavated a series of coastal sites whose dates are uncertain, but which may have been occupied at some time during the first millennium A.D. Wheatley (1961:197) also noted that a number of other unexcavated sites in this area have been revealed by aerial photography. Evans' sites were partially eroded by the sea, indicating that river course changes may have resulted in decreased sediment supply to the area and coastal retreat since the time of their occupation.

Wales (1940) correlated early settlement in northwest Malaya with coastal changes. The Bujang-Merbok estuary has been linked with the long distance trade of the late first and early second millennia by historians (Wheatley 1961; Wolters 1967). Archaeologists (Wales 1940; Lamb 1959, 1960) have recovered evidence of intensive commercial activity there in the form of huge deposits of Chinese and Middle Eastern pottery and glass, and religious activity in the form of numerous temples and associated ritual artifacts. Evidence of activity earlier than A.D. 1000 is however a matter of dispute. Data on ancient settlement and land use is lacking for this region.

Geologically the Bujang valley seems to be a former estuary, bounded on the north by the former coastal promontory of Gunung Jerai (mentioned in the Hikayat Marong Mahawangsa). This estuary has become filled with silt, perhaps because of a change in the courses of rivers which were once tributary to the Bujang. The date at which these changes occurred is unknown. The former estuary is now a large mangrove swamp laced by many minor channels.

Another site on the Straits coast of West Malaysia, at Kampong Sungai Lang, was discovered under a covering of peat (Peacock 1964). The finds, wooden planks and bronze drums, are of interest in themselves; we shall consider this site again for other evidence it can provide regarding human-coastal relations.

Turning to the vast eastern coastal plain of Sumatra, we find it variously described as 'unique' (Chambers and Sobur 1975) and 'appallingly large' (Mohr 1944). If all eastern Sumatra below one hundred meters elevation is included in the plain, it includes fifty percent of the entire island. Some historians, from Coedès (1918) to Wolters (1967), have argued that this coast was the base of major maritime powers cited in Chinese and Arab sources of the first and early second millennia A.D.

Archaeology has yet to lend definite support to these arguments. Finds from east Sumatra have included antiquities such as statuary and inscriptions attributed to the first millennium A.D., but no evidence (e.g., large ceramic deposits) to indicate the probable urban centers of those kingdoms whose numerous envoys visited Chinese imperial courts, and in whose lands Buddhist pilgrims found flourishing centers of study and worship (Bronson et al. 1973; Bronson 1975).[4]

The geological uniqueness and the (as yet unfulfilled) promises of archaeological discoveries on this coast have stimulated a number of studies aimed at reconciling the archaeological and historical evidence through consideration of coastal change. Obdeyn's (1941-43) was the first attempt. His map of the possible first millennium configuration of the coast has been modified by later scholars (Soekmono 1963; see also Dinas Purbakala 1955) and criticized (Verstappen 1973), but the general impression of all reconstructions is the same. Most recently, Chambers and Sobur (1975) combined a study of these earlier sources with their own data, and described the probable earlier configuration as a series of huge embayments, later progressively filled by silt, resulting in the present rather smooth coastline. Previous peninsulas and headlands are now inland and offshore islands have become mainland hills. Beach ridges can also be found in some areas.

Such a reconstruction implies that early coastal settlements should now be found some distance inland. When we ask how far inland, however, we face the difficult problem of charting the rate of coastal advance, which is unlikely to have been uniform in time and at all locations. If the growth of the coastal plain is due to coastal deposition of silt plus products of volcanic eruptions, local factors at specific points along the coast may have created different patterns of coastal change. The local depth of the ocean bed, river-course changes, near-shore ocean currents and wave patterns, and human activity all may have acted at various times and in various ways to alter the coastline.

It has also been argued that sedimentation may not have been the most important process in determining the growth of Sumatra's coastal plain. Verstappen states that "the width of the alluvial plain was determined by sea-level changes and crustal movements rather than by the rate of sedimentation of the rivers" (1973:56). In assessing the importance of sea-level changes, Verstappen assumes a post-Pleistocene eustatic sea level several meters higher than at present; other geologists challenge this assumption (Haile 1969, 1971; Shepard et al. 1967). Tectonic activity may have been a major factor; however, its quantitative effects on coastal change cannot be judged until more research at specific localities is conducted.

Verstappen's estimate of 2000-5000 years B.P. for the beginning of the formation of the coastal plains of north Java and east Sumatra is logical and has the merit of explaining the surprising absence of Hoabinhian sites on coasts and alluvial plains. If the sea level stabilized about 5000 years ago or has risen only very slowly since that time, earlier surfaces of alluvial plains would have been deposited at lower elevations. The present height of alluvial plain surfaces is dependent on the gradient of rivers flowing through them and the height at which their mouths join the sea. Therefore Hoabinhian sites in alluvial floodplains should now be buried under later accumulations of silt as the sea level rose and river gradients declined. This stabilization of the sea level at or near the present height may or may not have been preceded by a higher level.

Human activity as a factor in coastal change is demonstrably important, but not uniform. Hollwoger (1966) found that in north Java river delta growth during the 24 year period 1922 to 1946 was as great as during the 65 preceding years, indicating a doubling or tripling of the rate of sedimentation. Verstappen, in a comment included with the same article, agreed that the increase was "due to human interference in the natural environment" (Hollwoger 1966:355). Human interference may also result in coastal recession, as Verstappen notes (1966), through such activities as deflection of river channels. Examples are cited below. Tjia also agrees that sedimentation rates in Java and Sumatra have accelerated since 1920, "undoubtedly due to an increase in denudation rates," (Tjia et al. 1968) plus eustatic change and tectonic activity.

In general, therefore, human activity in the twentieth century has accelerated coastal change. In specific instances, however, it is necessary to consider other factors of potentially equal or greater importance and to be aware of the probability that these factors have not acted uniformly over the past

2000 years. Present linear rates of coastal growth cannot be projected back to gain an estimate of the age of any particular area of coastal plain (Verstappen 1966:355; 1973:56; Kraft, Rapp and Aschbrenner 1975:1191).

With these considerations in mind, it is possible to propose some lines of inquiry which will enable researchers to reconstruct the history of changes in a particular stretch of coastline in Sumatra or the Malay Peninsula where similar geomorphological and human factors have operated. Beach ridges, mangrove forests and former mangrove areas, and river levees are primary sources of information.

Mangrove forests that develop in former shallow bays and estuaries are sometimes later cut off from their normal semi-saline enviornment by formation of new beaches and sandspits. These mangroves die and form beds of peat which can be dated radiometrically. Such dates then indicate the approximate time when a specific area was cut off from sea water.

Research on peat formation in northern Borneo and West Malaysia has yielded data on rates of peat accumulation and dates of former coasts. A sample of peat obtained 24 kilometers north of Port Swettenham, West Malaysia, from 26.15 meters below present sea level was dated at 10,000 plus or minus 200 years B.P. (Keller and Richards 1967). The authors cite this as evidence that the Straits of Malacca have remained tectonically stable during the last 10,0000 years (1967:124). At Marudi, Brunei, a sample of peat from a bed eleven meters thick, resting on a clay base, "deposited in a mangrove environment" yielded a date of 4000 B.P. thus dating the location of the coast at that point (Muller 1975).

At Kampong Sungai Lang the drums cited by Peacock came from a mound covered by over a meter of peat. When agricultural development of the area drained the peat bed, the peat dried and contracted, exposing the top of the mound. A sample of the base of the peat was dated at 2150 B.P. (Peacock 1964). Peat beds exist in southeast Thailand, but apparently have not been dated (Moormann and Rajanasoonthon 1972).

In Sumatra peat beds are extensive. Sobur et al. (1975) note a deposit of peat seven meters thick under a southeast

Sumatran swamp. Wherever such beds exist, they can aid in dating local coastal development.

The existence of peat beds also has implications for settlement. Under indigenous cultivation techniques peat soils are unfavorable for agriculture.[5] Density of habitation in peat areas in Sumatra, therefore, is low. In the past, peat areas probably could not support dense agricultural populations.

Beach ridges are important features of parts of east Sumatra. Tjia et al. (1968) cite ridges 150 kilometers inland at Indragiri, and 21 kilometers inland at Komeringhilir, Tulangbawang. Major beach ridges are found in the north and south regions, with few in the central part of the plain (Mohr 1944). The northern ridges are more numerous and broader than in the south.[6]

As in other coastal regions of Southeast Asia beach ridges and present and former river levees are favored places for settlements (Verstappen 1973). Coconuts grow on the sandy soils of the ridges (Mohr 1944) and between the ridges are low-lying lebaks (swamps), some of which are fertile rice-growing areas while some are fishponds (Verstappen 1973:157). In the talang area north of the Mesuji river near Tulangbawang, which Verstappen believes may once have been an island, beads (batu manik) have been found, indicating possible settlement at some undetermined past time (Verstappen 1973:55; Tjia et al. 1968:21).

In some cases beach ridges give evidence of coastal recession as well as progradation. The most prominent case is found in northeast Sumatra near Belawan, where intersecting beach ridges indicate that the coast near a former river mouth has been abraded by the prevailing northwest current (Tjia et al. 1968:19). This recession may have been as great as two kilometers (Keller and Richards 1967:103). The process has also been studied in west Java (Verstappen 1966).

Ancient human settlements on beach ridges can sometimes indicate the course and rates of coastal change, as in the Mississippi delta. Beach ridges can also be dated if, as is common, they are built partly of shell debris. Such research is just beginning in south Sumatra (Chambers and Sobur 1975);

the results have not yet been published. This technique can be extended to other beach ridges and areas of marine shell deposition where human settlements may be located.

Coastal Change and Society

The earliest known instance of human activity affecting a coast in Indonesia was discovered through the collaboration of a historian and a geomorphologist (Noorduyn and Verstappen 1972). Study of a mid-fifth century A.D. Sanskrit inscription in north Java led to the interpretation of the text as a memorial to the alteration of a river course, on the levee of which the inscription was found. The goal of this labor may have been to improve drainage for farming. Former river courses in the area were charted by observing their abandoned levees. A succession of beach ridges marks former coastlines between the inscription and the sea; these are cut off by the sea at one end, indicating recession of the coast there due to the loss of sediment to the new river mouth.

Evidence for hydraulic management in Sumatra is exiguous and of no great antiquity. However, there is some indication that knowledge of some techniques of water control existed prior to introduction of European technology. Perhaps the earliest documented evidence of water management is found in Anderson's account of his "Mission to the East Coast of Sumatra in 1823" (Anderson 1971). He reports a local account of the dredging of a new course for a river near Belawan fifty years previously; perhaps this event can be connected with the coastal recession in that area noted by modern geologists. Also mentioned is the construction of a channel connecting the Sungai Aior with the Deli River. In neither case is the purpose of the work disclosed.

Effects of human activity on silting by causing denudation are not easily gauged. Mohr (1944:547) notes that the upper Musi River valley was still well forested in the 1930s; however, much of the sedimentation in the Musi River mouth area is the result of long-shore transport of sediment, and thus dependent on activities elsewhere. Other than to acknowledge that sedimentation rates have undoubtedly increased recently, a more specific judgment of the role of this activity cannot yet be given.

Ras' (1968) account of the effect of coastal change on a maritime trading center in south Borneo furnishes insights regarding consequences of such change for social structure and political processes. The kraton (court) of the sultanate was located at a river mouth at Tanjong Pura, once a promontory as its name indicates, now surrounded by alluvium. As the bay beside the promontory filled with silt, and the river mouth was transferred to another location, the kraton changed places at least three and perhaps four times, moving into "marshy areas little suited for agriculture" (Ras 1968:198). Not all changes in kraton location may have been peaceful; as the port moved further from the palace, the sultan's control may have become more tenuous, providing opportunities for usurpation.

As Ras notes, the position of the coast was important not only because the port facilities were located there, but because many of the subjects of the sultan lived on the water and in the channels of the mangrove swamps. The swamps have impressed westerners as an "inhospitable, and sometimes treacherous, coastal environment" (Sobur et al. 1975:2), but in the Southeast Asian maritime world they have long sheltered specially adapted populations whose important role in the early Southeast Asian trade has been little studied.

The environment of the mangrove swamp as a whole has been neglected by scientists, including the subject of potential human effects on mangrove. Yet the

> pantropical enonomic importance of mangroves is larger than might be surmised from the available literature.... The background of a little-known but possibly substantial role of mangrove forests in the economy of this region lends a special urgency to the need for expansion of knowledge of mangrove ecosystems (Lugo and Snedaker 1974:41).

Mangrove wood is one of the best in the world for making charcoal—thus its value to early ironworkers in coastal north Borneo (Harrisson and O'Connor 1969). The forests support abundant animal life and, in addition, 50 to 80 percent of their production flows to the nearby ocean, much of which supports fish. Human interference with local drainage patterns, e.g., through canal building, 'short-circuits' this flow of energy, bypassing mangroves and channelling run-off into narrow areas, thus leaving many nutrients in the swamp, unavailable to offshore life (Lugo and Snedaker 1974:49, 55-6).

Human activity can also be beneficial to mangroves. Anderson preserves a tradition that a low mangrove-covered island in a river called Pulau Gorab formed around an ancient shipwreck. Human debris and house pilings on tidal mudflats can provide shelter from tidal scouring and encourage mangrove colonization.

The mangrove dwellers in Southeast Asia have nearly vanished. They are at present among the poorest, lowest status and least studied social groups.[7] Yet evidence from the early period of European contact implies that they were once a powerful and influential local group among the Straits maritime trading societies. Solheim (1970) speculates that their adaptation may be several thousand years old; Pires (1944) indicates their wide distribution and fearsome reputation in the sixteenth century; and Andaya (1971) chronicles their status in the Sumatran and Johorean sultanates of the seventeenth century and the events which led to their rapid political and social eclipse. Less well known is the process by which many of the richer and more powerful sea nomads probably settled permanently on land and became Islamized Malays, leaving only the poorer and more isolated groups still practicing elements of the traditional maritime adaptation by the twentieth century.

In summary, then, two symbiotic patterns of settlement should be considered in discussing early Southeast Asian maritime adaptations: settlement on the levees and beach ridges, utilizing lower land for rice and higher land for coconuts, and seminomadism in the swamps and on the rivers. The implications of these two patterns for archaeological inquiry into Southeast Asian maritime trade remain to be explicated, but given the preceding discussion of geomorphology, several hypotheses can be constructed regarding the probable nature of coastal polities in Southeast Asia in the centuries after Christ. Locational anaylsis promises to provide a means of testing these hypotheses through examination of changes in settlement patterns and distribution of various types of artifacts among sites.

Social Complexity of the Early Straits

First, it is possible that urbanization in the sense of large concentrations of population did not exist. The urban center in Wheatley's (1971) terms of a ceremonial complex integrating commercial and social activity over a broad area, acting as a legitimator and mechanism for economic redistribution, may have been present without the separate phenomenon of centripetality which generates great population densities in small areas of which Adams (1965) gives examples. Generation of 'effective economic space' seems to have been a continued concern of Southeast Asian rulers engaged in maritime commerce, the pursuit of which was perceived by western colonists as piracy (Tarling 1963).

Wheatley demonstrates that ceremonial centers without large populations in China were effective generators of such spatial organization. Development of socio-political complexity, in terms of change from kin-based societies, linked with the growth of ceremonial centers, seems to have preceded large centralized population centers in several regions of primary urban genesis.

In Mesopotamia Adams linked growth of population centers to a process by which ceremonial complexes differentiated themselves politically from the surrounding countryside. Thus population nucleation may have been partly a result of social complexity rather than its cause. Alternatively, both phenomena may have been responding to a third source of systemic disruption. Other civilizations without cities in this sense are cited by Wheatley (1971) in Egypt and Mesoamerica.

Complexly organized societies may also have developed in the Straits, but they appear not to have developed the centripetality of most primary areas of urban genesis. This condition probably had multiple causes, among them the structure of the long distance commerce, i.e., the fiction of the tribute trade. It was probably trade which fueled the development of this complexity and whose rhythms and fluctuations directly affected Malay society (Wolters 1970). A second factor or set of factors may have been constituted by the environmental differences between two types of centers. One type of center is located in alluvial plains, surrounded by a uniform habitat suitable for supporting a large permanent population through agriculture. A second type is the ceremonial center, such as those in Java and Sumatra; these are often located in environmental zones marginal to human populations, such as on mountains or on the nearest solid ground to the coast. The agricultural potential of the surrounding area is often limited.

The settlement pattern of the eastern Sumatran coast of the first millennium A.D., then, may have included ceremonial centers where ritual specialists resided, and where the only permanent architecture of the society was erected. The few permanent pieces of architecture in Sumatra from precolonial times, e.g., at Muara Takus and perhaps in the area of Bukit Seguntang (Schnitger 1936, 1937), may be of this type of ceremonial center, since few indications of nearby contemporary settlement have been found. Soekmono (1967) notes that in eastern and central Java candi (sacred shrines) were usually far from the capital cities. The ruler's quarters occasionally may have been located at the port, and occasionally separated from it, as Ras noted.

The ports probably changed their location fairly frequently both as the result of socio-political factors and geomorphic processes. The cultural phenomenon of the mobility of the center in Cambodia and Java may have been paralleled by movement of the political center on the coasts of the Straits of Malacca, but as the result of more specifically environmental factors. The seminomadic boat dwellers who probably served as the military power and the merchant mariners of the rulers, and whose loyalty may have been reinforced by gifts of prestige objects obtained from long distance trade and local agricultural products, may have left few archaeological traces, and those may be located in former or present mangrove swamps. The exchange of products from hinterland mountains, agricultural products from dispersed settlements on beach ridges, and marine products of the swamps and off-shore waters probably formed the local focus of redistributive activity. Functional specialization of social sectors and subsistence activities may have been quite diverse.

Thus we may distinguish multiple centers in this hypothetical society, differentiated functionally.

Future excavations may or may not confirm this hypothesis.

The second point that we can make is that settlement patterns in coastal Southeast Asia may have been dispersed, but their linkage through a dendritic system such as Bronson (this volume) describes may be observable archaeologically. Human activity aimed at maintaining or altering the riverine transport system may also be demonstrable. Stargardt's characterization of the center of the Malay Peninsula as a dividing line between hydraulic societies to the east and nonhydraulic societies to the west may be correct. However, some slight evidence indicates that western Indonesians were not entirely ignorant of the technology involved. Evidence of such activity would shed further light on the early social organization and settlement of the coasts.

Research in this direction is now underway in southern Sumatra. The Proyek Pendidikan dan Penelitian Lingkungan of the Institut Pertanian, Bogor, has recently conducted intensive land-use studies in three areas of south Sumatra, one of which is the Musi-Banyuasin drainage system. Extensive data on, among other topics, geomorphology, soil chemistry, aquatic biology and forestry, and modern settlement patterns have been collected for an area of 187,000 hectares of land and estuarine waters. Even on large-scale satellite photos, patterns of irrigation and settlement created by Bugis immigrants stand out clearly: they have settled on river levees and built extensive irrigation systems.

Data of this type can be used to test the hypotheses regarding the forms of economic integration which may have existed in Sumatra in the past. In the search for ways of studying the development of complex societies the usefulness of locational analysis has been pointed out (Chorley and Haggett 1967; Renfrew 1969b; Crumley 1976). A logical next step is to test the assertions advanced in this paper through generation of specific predictions regarding probable connections between settlement patterns and economic systems of the type described above. Locational analysis may provide the conceptual framework for such an endeavor.

Recent studies of locational analysis in riverine systems (e.g., Plog and Hill 1971; Weide and Weide 1973) and in mangrove swamps (Bruder, Large and Stark 1975) have been noted with interest by archaeologists. Assuming that early first millennium sites in Sumatra can be found (by no means a dependable assumption), a history of settlement in riverine systems can be written. If the above hypotheses regarding involvement of Sumatrans in long distance trade are correct, we should see changes in the settlement pattern and in the settlement hierarchy through time. The investigation can then weigh the factors affecting site location, such as local craft specialization, raw material collection, subsistence and social systems, and changing land-forms. Ideally, it will one day be possible to compare the changes in site location patterns between separate riverine systems in the Straits, and integrate studies of sites not located directly on rivers. In this way a clearer picture of the role of trade in eastern coastal Sumatran history may emerge.

Some scholars have demonstrated an intuitive appreciation of the potential of site location analysis as a means of gaining insight into cultural processes in Indonesia. Verstappen stated that "the use of the soil and the social structure have been influenced by the natural data in this case by the beach ridges" (1953:69). John Anderson saw reflections of an earlier period of Javanese influence in Sumatra, such as the remains of a colony and fort in Deli. Bronson et al. (1973:36-8) describe the common occurrence of sites with earthworks in east Sumatra. Intensive locational analyses have not yet been attempted, however. In combination with other techniques of analysis, locational analysis may help answer some of the questions regarding Straits' history. Its ultimate value will be demonstrated by the new questions which it may inspire.

Notes

1. As examples of intensive historical, archaeological and geological study of the interaction between human activity, sedimentation and topographic change in irrigated alluvial plains, Adams (1965) and Adams and Nissen (1972) are valuable sources.

2. For description see Pendleton (1949); for aerial photos of beach ridges in the Satingpra area see Williams-Hunt (1949).

3. For further sources on beach ridges of the Malay Peninsula, see Tjia (1973:19-24) and Stauffer (1973:173-4).

4. Wolters (1975) comments on the implications of Bronson's work for interpretations of some Chinese sources relating to south Sumatran settlement and commerce.

5. Some major problems are: high acidity and a tendency to crack and contract when drained for agriculture.

6. There are several local words for beach ridges in the Straits. In the area from Tulangbawang to the Musi, *talang* is used to refer to the low ridges and plateaus in the alluvium (Verstappen 1973). Mohr notes that the same features in the Jambi area are called *kasang*. In west Malaysia *permatang* is often used.

7. For a compilation of sources regarding seminomadic adaptations in maritime Southeast Asia see Sopher (1965).

Prehistoric Trade and the Evolution of
Philippine Societies: A Reconsideration

by

Karl L. Hutterer

Limited in their research enterprise by the nature of available data, archaeologists have over the years developed a predelection for certain research topics which seem particularly congenial to their tools and interests. Among them is the problem of prehistoric trade. Many aspects of the exchange of material goods can be approached through archaeological methods of inquiry and usually can be related to factors of the natural environment as well as the structure and organization of a given society. Yet archaeologists have paid relatively little systematic attention to the problem of prehistoric trade in Southeast Asia. This is surprising for two reasons: on the one hand, the occurrence of trade is highly visible in Southeast Asian prehistory, and, on the other hand, the diverse cultural and social traditions of the region offer a superb opportunity for the comparative study of the role of economic exchange in relation to the functioning and transformation of socio-cultural systems.

I have previously concerned myself with the problem of prehistoric trade in the Philippines and its relationship to social change (Hutterer 1973a; 1973b; 1974). Based on archaeological work on the islands of Cebu and Samar, I focused on a narrow time span, the last 500 years before Spanish contact, for which there is ample demonstration for a strong trade between the Philippines and other parts of Asia. In the present paper, I have no new data to present and I cannot, therefore, engage in the testing of new propositions. Rather, I am taking this opportunity to review my earlier statements in the light of an expanded framework of inquiry. The purpose of this paper is to identify a variety of problems which need to be addressed in future archaeological work in the Philippines and to reflect on possible working hypotheses for such future research.

Recapitulation

Archaeological assemblages dating from the last period of Philippine prehistory, that is the last 500 or so years before Spanish conquest, stand out through the presence of large amounts of glazed ceramics which originated from Chinese, Siamese, and 'Annamese' kilns. These intrusive ceramic wares are evidence of a maritime trade of foreign goods which impinged on the archipelago. A number of other artifacts found in sites of that period (e.g., glass objects, ornamental articles of various precious materials, certain metal artifacts) may also be related to this foreign trade, but their place of origin is in most cases uncertain.

Because of extensive looting of archaeological sites and the subsequent dispersal of the recovered ceramics and other artifacts throughout the worldwide antiquities market, it will never be possible to estimate reliably how many pieces of ceramic ware from China and mainland Southeast Asia were traded into the Philippines. However, the figure must be in the millions, if one takes into account the number of whole pieces excavated in legitimate archaeological projects, the volume of sherds encountered in sites, and the number and sizes of looted sites. Further, if we take into account that pottery is only the archaeologically most visible manifestation of this trade and also that, according to historical sources, a variety of other items were regularly imported into the Philippines, one can appreciate how vigorous this trade must have been.

I have argued (Hutterer 1973b; 1974) that these trading interactions played a major role in the evolution of certain Philippine societies, namely those which are commonly classified as 'lowland societies'. For the sake of the succeeding discussion, I will briefly recapitulate my earlier argument.

Based on ceramic evidence alone, foreign trade contacts with the Philippines seem to have begun sometime between the tenth and the twelfth centuries A.D.[1] It is usually assumed that, at least in the early stages, the ceramic trade was primarily carried out by 'Arabs' and 'Persians' although, as far as the Philippines are concerned, there is no direct and very little indirect evidence about this point and Southeast Asian traders are equally likely to have brought the foreign goods to Philippine shores.

No quantitative investigations have been undertaken to date, but it is clear from a cursory perusal of the evidence that the overall volume of pottery imports increased through time. An apparent peak was reached during Yüan/Early Ming times (late thirteenth through fifteenth centuries), and some commercial patterns appear to have undergone changes at that time (Fox 1967): the relative importance of ceramics in the total trade volume increased vis-à-vis non-ceramic items; the quality of the trade ceramics decreased as they were specifically manufactured for export to a distant and undiscriminating market; and primary trading activities were increasingly restricted to a limited number of regional entrepôts. I have argued (Hutterer 1974) that this foreign trade constituted an extremely important element in the socio-cultural evolution of Philippine societies. It would seem that three major areas of social change were connected with foreign trade.

First, it appears that the growth of foreign maritime trade is correlated with the growth of larger nucleated settlements along the Philippine coast. This development was a response to both the opportunities and demands of the exchange interactions. From an archaeological perspective, this growth appears to be sudden and vigorous and may well represent a postitive feedback effect between the opportunities of the foreign trade on the one hand and the local response to it on the other hand. In terms of social and demographic processes, the nucleation and growth of coastal communities represents a change in settlement patterns as well as in community patterns. The pattern of settlement changed from a relatively dispersed and undifferentiated mode to one that was differentiated in terms of population density, settlement size, and settlement hierarchy. The community pattern, at least of coastal settlements, changed from a linear to a nucleated arrangement, probably entailing some amount of internal differentiation.

The change in settlement pattern involved a regrouping of population which was evidently achieved through internal migrations. There is archaeological evidence suggesting that the the growth of coastal settlements was sustained by people moving from the interior to the coast, and it is also probable that some population movement from island to island took place, especially around common interior seas. Ethnographic, historical, and possibly some archaeological data can be summoned to suggest that this population redistribution was not structured along lines of ethnic demarcation. In other words, the growing population of the coastal centers was probably derived from diverse ethnic sources.

Second, the expansion of foreign trade had an impact on economic systems within the Philippines and it stimulated changes in the articulation between different Philippine societies. As the foreign trade concentrated increasingly on a small number of port communities, a need arose for mechanisms by which, on the one hand, exotic imports could be distributed throughout the islands and, on the other hand, local export goods could be channelled into the foreign trade network. Thus, the coastal population centers became entrepôts and developed a primitive market economy. There is also good evidence that manufacturing industries for a variety of products (e.g., native pottery, metal implements) were located on the coast, indicating that the coastal economic system was based not solely on import/export business but incorporated the production and distribution of manufactured goods. Many of the goods in demand for export, primarily products of the rain forest, were not directly accessible to coastal communities or were not available in sufficient quantities to any one entrepôt to satisfy the demands of the system.

Forest products, accounting for the bulk of exported goods, constituted resources which were located outside the territorial control of lowland/coastal communities. Thus, coastal populations had to enter into exchange interactions with populations of hunters and swidden agriculturists in the upland and interior portions of the islands. This had some repercussions on the exploitative patterns and larger economic systems of these populations by favoring exploitative specialization, namely the collecting of commerically valuable forest products which could then be exchanged for manufactured goods and probably some subsistence items from the lowlands. (It should be noted here that this reconstruction relies heavily on ethnographic comparison [e.g., Conklin 1957; Dunn 1975; J. T. Peterson, this volume; Rahmann and Maceda 1962]. The continuation of the pattern into modern industrial states is significant.) Structurally, this interpretation accords well with Bronson's (this volume) dendritic model, although the prehistoric reality may have been formally somewhat less neat and more flexible than the abstract model.

Finally, foreign trade and connected developments can be linked to changes in the social structure of coastal communities themselves. Based on both ethnohistoric and archaeological evidence it can be concluded that, during the period under consideration, a pervasive system of social ranking developed within coastal societies. While there remain many questions about the nature and precise form of this rank system, Spanish observers indicated that the basis of rank was primarily economic achievement and had relatively little to do with descent. This class system provided the social basis for the emergence of a new kind of political leadership. According to ethnohistoric information and modern ethnographic parallels, it appears that the political leaders of the sixteenth century were individuals from the upper economic classes who were able to gain control over the flow of goods and services through deft manipulation of commercial and personal relationships and, thereby, achieve political influence and power. Individuals and their families would bind themselves to a leader through the creation of reciprocal social and economic obligations. The leaders of such alliance groups ('datus') often, in turn, entered into alliances with other more powerful leaders and formed political federations of a higher order. Larger settlements contained two or more levels of political leadership and exercised control over a certain amount of hinterland. It seems that the overall importance and influence of a settlement's top leader was correlated with the settlement's size and its role in the larger economy. The principal means of demonstrating economic wealth and political influence of leaders were the ostentatious display of expensive foreign trade goods and the espousal of foreign religious ideologies. [2]

Problems

The preceding reconstruction of historical events and the ensuing anthropological argument have been limited to the last 500 years of Philippine prehistory. Viewed strictly within these chronological limits, the statements made seem to be defensible. The imposed limitation, however, has deprived the discussion of some rather important perspectives and has, thereby, skewed the whole approach to the problem. It is necessary to put the problem of foreign trade in the prehistoric Philippines, and the related questions of social development, into a larger context and to raise some issues which have an indirect, but very definite, bearing on the interpretation of social processes that may have taken place during the first half of the second millennium A.D.

One of the most immediate queries concerns the date and circumstances under which Philippine societies entered into the network of maritime exchanges in Southeast Asia. Among archaeologists, the tendency has been to see the beginning of this trade fixed by the dating of the earliest Chinese porcelain found in Philippine sites. According to presently available evidence on the dating of intrusive Asiatic ceramics, the beginning of foreign trade would then be very late, no earlier than the tenth century A.D. and possibly as late as the twelfth century A.D. This view coincides with the opinion that social developments in the archipelago lagged considerably behind those elsewhere in the region. The reason for this is commonly seen in the fact that the Philippine Islands, being neither an exclusive source area of exotic goods for China, India, or West Asia nor having control over crucial routes of trade, were rather marginal to the international exchange network impinging on Southeast Asia.

Implicit in the view that foreign trade reached the Philippines late is the assumption that the main impetus came from the outside. The question of who intitiated the foreign trade interactions involves more than one-upmanship. At issue are general considerations about the nature of cultural and social processes as well as an evaluation of the developmental status of Philippine societies when they first entered into overseas trade relationships. Since there is no evidence of foreign colonization of any part of the Philippines in prehistoric times, the trade cannot be explained as the result of direct external domination of indigenous island economies. Thus, the exchange interactions must be related to aspects of the internal organization of Philippine societies. On the basis of principles of evolutionary theory it can be postulated that the content, organization, and geographical reach of a society's exchange interactions are directly related to the degree of social, economic, and political differentiation within that society (Flannery 1972; Renfrew 1969a; Wilmsen 1972).

The question of the developmental status of Philippine societies is also important because it defines the terminus a quo for evolutionary developments that may have taken place during the period of prehistoric overseas trade. The problem is complicated by the tendency to speak of Philippine societies as if they could be represented by a single classificatory level of socio-cultural development. It is clear, however, that this is not the case and that, even prehistorically, the Philippine Islands presented an ethnic mosaic of groups aligned along a broad scale of socio-cultural and economic evolution. This, in turn, provokes such questions as: Which societies articulated directly with the foreign trade? How were these groups differently articulated with the foreign trade? And how were they differentially affected by it and adapted to it?

Finally, there is the problem of defining more precisely the developmental status as well as the social and political structure of the lowland societies at the time of European contact. In my earlier papers (Hutterer 1973a; 1974), I remained vague about this, venturing only that by the sixteenth century lowland societies had evolved which took a hand in the control of trade exchange. This entails a number of implications, as we are dealing with some elements that play a role in the development of state societies.

This list of questions is anything but exhaustive, but it will suffice to point to some important areas for future research. The questions address themselves not just to particularistic concerns of Philippine cultural history, but they are way stations in the search for a better understanding of the interplay between the natural environment, the social environment, and the individual human being. The very success in answering these questions will depend on future investigators' willingness not only to search diligently for empirical evidence but to address the problems within a framework of wider regional relevance and general theoretical significance. Because of the problem orientation of past archaeological research in Southeast Asia, much of the type of data necessary to approach the problems identified here does not exist. Yet, the development of future research must begin with a re-evaluation of whatever evidence is at hand.

Reflections

A. The Antiquity of Foreign Trade.

The single-minded attention to Chinese ceramics as a data source on prehistoric trade in the Philippines has resulted in a significant bias in assessing the antiquity of maritime trade interactions. While there may have been some historical justification for this narrow approach, it is clear today that, in spite of their prominence, glazed ceramics entered the far flung trade network only relatively late and always constituted only part of a much larger range of commodities exchanged. The chronological and typological range of intrusive archaeological ceramics is similar throughout Southeast Asia. Yet, there is solid historical evidence for many areas of the region that extensive foreign trade was carried on for many hundreds of years before the first Chinese wares were loaded onto ships. Unfortunately, archaeologists have devoted very little systematic attention to this problem. At present, we do not have a comprehensive, or even a reasonably representative, list of prehistoric trade goods, nor is there an empirical framework for assigning provenances within or outside of Southeast Asia or for tracing the movement of certain goods. Among a number of categories of prehistoric artifacts to which special attention should be directed in this respect are artifacts of bronze and iron, and in the following I will, therefore, devote a brief discussion to Southeast Asian metallurgy in the context of trade and social development.

A well developed metal technology implies, among other things, a certain degree of craft specialization, a relatively differentiated economy which can afford the energy expended in the extracting, processing and distributing of metals, and a trade network that brings together ores and fuels and disposes of the finished products.[3] Southeast Asia has had a well-developed indigenous metal technology at least since the early third millennium B.C. (Solheim 1970). The early dates for bronze in the region come from northeast Thailand and Vietnam and, of course, pertain only to the mainland. However, these early metal traditions must be considered important predecessors to later developments taking place during the last pre-Christian millennium. One of these developments, associated with a larger cultural complex commonly referred to as

'Dong-son Culture', is of some interest in the prehistory of insular Southeast Asia. I am not concerned here with whether the notion of a 'Dong-son Culture' represents a viable concept. I wish only to call attention to the distribution of two classes of items which have been associated with the Dong-son complex: bronze kettledrums and ceremonial bronze axes. Both items have been found from South China through Vietnam, Thailand, Cambodia, Malaya, Indonesia, all the way to Irian Jaya (Heekeren 1958).

Pearson (1962:45) has argued that the type site at Dong-son reflects the presence of a truly stratified society and a primarily 'ceremonial and trading' center. According to him, Dong-son bronzes were traded into 'out-lying areas', where rulers and chiefs of ranked societies acquired them as religious and social status symbols. Be this as it may, the most economical explanation for the presence of the sophisticated bronze objects through so wide an area is certainly some mechanism of exchange.

While the dating of the Dong-son phenomenon is still somewhat controversial, recent C-14 dates for bronze drums found in Thailand and the Malay Peninsula have consistently clustered around a few hundred years B.C. (Anonymous 1972; Peacock 1965). This is of some interest since it coincides with the time frame for the introduction of metal in general, both bronze and iron, to the Southeast Asian islands. Thus, although no 'Dong-son' bronzes have ever been found in the Philippines, the earliest bronze and iron there date to about 500-300 B.C. This compares very closely with the date for the introduction of metals to the Indonesian Archipelago where the first appearance of metals also coincides with the spread of highly elaborated bronze objects. The implication is that metals first found their way into the Southeast Asian islands during an early surge of maritime trading activities and that the Philippines participated in this interaction, although evidently in a different way than Indonesia.

Bronze and iron are not the only items of probably foreign origin in Philippine sites of the first millennium A.D. Ornamental objects of precious or semi-precious stones not native to the islands are common, especially beads of carnelian and occasionally jade among others. The larger archaeological context also suggests that glass ornaments, appearing together with the early iron, may have been of foreign manufacture. It seems possible to enlarge this list considerably to include such items as gold ornaments, earthenware pottery, rare raw materials, condiments such as salt, and so forth.

It should be noted that earlier writings on Southeast Asian archaeology have generally assumed that the knowledge and practice of metal technology spread to the islands within the context of some kind of population movement (Beyer 1947; Hoop 1938; Solheim 1964; Marschall 1968).[4] Currently available evidence makes such an explanation neither necessary nor particularly plausible. However, the agency of trade invoked here remains as much a conjecture as earlier evaluations. Only future archaeological research, focusing specifically on this problem, will be able to shed new light on it.

B. The Status of Philippine Societies
   in the First Millennium A.D.

While it is not too difficult to make a case for an early participation of the Philippines in some kind of intra-Southeast Asian exchange network, it is far more difficult to sketch some picture of the social conditions under which such an exchange would have taken place. At issue is not only the nature and extent of inter-ethnic exchange occurring during the first millennium A.D., but also how it was embedded into the larger social context of the societies involved in it as well as the evolutionary status of these societies. In this connection it must be remembered that the Philippines, like most areas of Southeast Asia, are marked by considerable social, cultural, and economic heterogeneity. I have argued elsewhere (Hutterer 1976) that this social and cultural diversity and fragmentation is related to ecological conditions of the tropics and that it is, therefore, of great antiquity. To simplify matters, I will limit myself here to those societies which, during the early first millennium A.D., had achieved the highest degree of socio-cultural complexity in comparison to other Philippine groups. This does not imply, of course, that overseas exchange interactions were necessarily limited to these societies, although they would probably have been different in many respects from external exchanges carried on by other groups.[5]

The archaeologist treads here on extremely hazardous ground, since very little reliable evidence has been collected for this period and even less published. However, perusing the available data, it may be observed that all those artifacts which may be considered as intrusive in Philippine sites can be classified as being related to high social and economic status. There is little question that ornaments of jade or carnelian derive from extraneous sources and represent highly valued goods. While it is not clear whether any, and how much, of the prehistoric glass found in the Philippines was manufactured locally, it is likely that much of it was imported and was far more valuable than the trinkets spread by European colonizers. From whatever informal evidence I can draw on, it also appears that iron was of great social and economic value. The presence of exotica itself is not a reliable indicator of social complexity. Hunters-and-gatherers and other types of unstratified societies engage in long distance exchanges of high-prestige goods which play an important role in communal ritual systems (e.g., Ford 1972; Micha 1958; Sharp 1952). However, the items just mentioned, together with prestige goods of presumable local manufacture (e.g., gold ornaments, elaborate earthenware pottery), are commonly found associated with each other in graves of the last millennium B.C. and the first millennium A.D. There is good general evidence, although little quantitative information for differential funerary treatment, indicating the existence of social ranking (Brown 1971).

Recent excavations on the island of Negros promise to furnish some more solid evidence in this regard. The site involved is a burial ground excavated in 1973 by two different archaeological teams. Unfortunately, only one of them has so far issued a preliminary report. Tenazas (1974) reports one simple and two complex jar burials at the Magsuhot site, the latter being associated with large and elaborate earthenware coffins and accompanied by extensive grave offerings. The simple burial contained no grave goods, while the complex burials contained 70 and 100 pieces of pottery respectively, some of them figurines and what appear to be other miscellaneous non-utilitarian forms. In addition, the complex burials were associated with iron implements, glass beads, and glass bracelets. No dates for the site or individual graves are yet available, but it should be noted that iron is present while Asiatic trade ceramics are absent. This provides a chronological bracket between ca. 500 B.C. and ca. A.D. 1000.

It is not possible, of course, to draw reliable conclusions from only three graves. It appears, however, that the other archaeological team excavated substantial additional evidence for differential funerary treatment, and further reports are being awaited with great interest. The excavations in Negros constitute the first systematic field investigation of an open site predating porcelain trade. All other sites containing iron but not intrusive glazed ceramics[6] which have been investigated to date are cave sites (Fox 1970; Fox and Evangelista 1957; Hutterer 1974; Kurjack and Sheldon 1970; Maceda 1964b, 1965; Solheim 1964, 1968a; Tuggle and Hutterer 1972). In many cases, site disturbances made it impossible to recover reliable associational patterns while in other cases available site reports are not detailed enough to provide information about the artifactual associations of individual burials. It is quite possible that some or all of the cave sites investigated to date did contain burials of different status. It is also possible, however, that burial in a cave itself may indicate a special status, since cave burial and burial in open site cemetaries seem to have coexisted in space and time. In any case, at this time we simply lack the necessary comparative data.

Assuming that the archaeological evidence from Negros does indicate status differences, the question arises as to whether we are dealing with a segmentary society with a leadership resting purely on achieved status or whether we may actually be observing some kind of ranked society.[7] To demonstrate the existence of a chiefdom organization, we will have to bring in archaeological evidence for such things as settlement hierarchy, reflecting internal economic and political differentiation of the population; consistent differences in mortuary treatment, reflecting the existence of ascribed status and rank; part-time craft specialization and, possibly, some kind of monumental construction, reflecting organization of productive labor beyond the household level (Peebles and Kus n.d.; Renfrew 1973; Sahlins 1972). Little evidence of this sort is available at present although, as usual, some bits and pieces seem to be suggestive.

For instance, looking at the distribution of formal elements of native earthenware pottery, there seem to be indications of internal exchange interactions within the islands in connection with part-time craft specialization and the existence of manufacturing centers. Among the pottery found in sites of the period under discussion are some forms that have exceedingly wide distribution. One such ware is of simple globular form with everted rims, decorated around the neck with parallel incised lines. Solheim (1964) found several specimens of this kind in Masbate and felt that they were so similar to each other that they could well have come from the hand of a single potter. I have found vessels of identical appearance in Samar and have expressed a similar sentiment about them (Hutterer 1969). The same kind of pottery was found in Palawan (Fox 1970), and while there are no detailed descriptions, it seems clear that these finds show much formal consistency and compare closely with those found in Samar and Masbate. There are some other pottery forms which show similar congruence over a comparable area of distribution.

The following considerations are relevant here: considering the wide area of distribution, it is unlikely that these pottery types represent diffuse local manufacture within a contiguous territory occupied by a single ethnic group. In the contemporary ethnographic context, the area includes several ethnic and linguistic subdivisions and it is larger than the area occupied at Spanish contact by the largest ethnic group, the Visayans. Further, if this pottery was exchanged, it would probably not have been an exchange on the subsistence level, since many of the places where the pottery has been found have their own clay sources and, in fact, have produced some utilitarian pottery within historic times. And finally, considering the simplicity of form and decoration of the wares under discussion, it seems unlikely that they would have been a specialized ritual pottery, although they have been found in mortuary contexts. All in all, it is not unlikely that this kind of pottery was made in villages specializing in ceramic production and was traded throughout the Visayan Sea and beyond. The implication is some level of craft specialization and inter-ethnic as well as intra-ethnic trade of non-subsistence goods. Both of these elements are characteristic of societies organized on the level of chiefdoms.

Aware of the danger of presenting a circular argument, this section may be concluded by suggesting that some Philippine groups may have been organized as ranked societies at least by the first millennium A.D. and that this has to be taken into account when assessing the problem of the impetus for foreign trade. It has been pointed out by others (Flannery 1972; Peebles and Kus n.d.; Wilmsen 1972) that chiefdoms not only have the ability but even the need to process a much larger quantity and greater variety of environmental information than societies at simpler levels of organization. Part of this increase in quantity and complexity of information flow is provided by an increase in intergroup exchange.

It would be unrealistic, however, to expect that, one day, we will be able to say with conviction that foreign exchange interactions in the Philippines or elsewhere in Southeast Asia were initiated either by local populations or by foreign traders. The main problem lies not even in the lack of pertinent evidence but the reductionist simplicity of the question. The history of long distance overseas trade in Southeast Asia and the correlated social developments must be seen as the result of complex interactions between several different social and environmental systems over a long period of time. The complexity and systemic nature of these interactions defy any monocausal cause/effect explanation.

C. Philippine Societies of the Sixteenth Century A.D.

Although the reconstruction of past cultural systems is not a primary goal of contemporary archaeology, an assessment of the condition of Philippine societies both at the beginning and end of the period of extensive maritime trade interactions is important for a further understanding of the role long distance exchange may have played in the process of social and cultural change.

In light of the present discussion, it appears that my earlier statements (Hutterer 1973b; 1974) about Philippine lowland societies having been on the verge of urbanism and state formation may have been overly optimistic. Evidence available for three major areas of investigation (settlement patterns, social organization, economic organization) can be accounted for by reconstructing Philippine lowland societies in the sixteenth century along the structural lines of chiefdoms. It is probable, however, that they were different in several respects from chiefdoms found a thousand or so years earlier. Firstly, they seem to have represented new ethnic groupings resulting from the agglomeration of pre-existing ethnic elements. Secondly, they probably had a broader geographical base than the older chiefdoms and, at the time of Spanish conquest, were evidently still expanding. Thirdly, it is likely that the younger lowland societies showed a considerable elaboration of social structure when compared to the earlier chiefdoms. This latter statement is based on, among other things, the apparent change in settlement and community patterns and the expansion of foreign trade relationships. Finally, on the negative side, there is no evidence whatsoever for the formation of bureaucratic structures that would have been interjected between the chief and the daily affairs of politics, commerce and religion, as is usually found in state societies.

In order to be able to carry the discussion further, it will be necessary to collect information in a number of important areas. Archaeologically, as well as ethnohistorically, we know that a wide range of settlement sizes existed, but we know little about settlement location and distribution, the internal structure of settlements, and the relationship between settlement variables and variables of a social and political nature. We know that lowland societies were socially stratified; but, there is insufficient information on the determinants of membership in a social class, how much mobility there was, and what areas of an individual's life were affected by his social status. It is primarily from ethno-historic sources that we know of the existence of political leaders, but descriptions of their roles are ambiguous and so is the information as to what extent both rank and office were hereditary. A particular shortcoming of the ethno-historic sources relates to the fact that the early Spanish observers evidently had some difficulty understanding a cognatic kinship structure and its interaction with a system of social ranking.

Other significant problems revolve around the nature of exchange mechanisms and processes within the islands. There are some suggestions in early historical sources that, at least in some areas and settlements, formal markets may have been present by the sixteenth century. Similarly, there are some intriguing references to gold as an apparent medium of exchange. Historical documents leave no doubt that indenture for nonpayment of debts was common, but the nature of the debts and other circumstances remain largely unclear.

Perhaps one of the most intriguing problems is that of inter-ethnic exchange, since it relates to a larger complex of questions concerning ethnic boundaries, ethnic interaction, and human ecology in tropical environments. I have argued elsewhere (Hutterer 1976) that the scattered distribution of resources in tropical areas tends to favor small populations and high mobility, a situation which expresses itself, in ethnographic terms, in a high degree of social and cultural discontinuity. Because of the scattered nature of resources, the introduction of agriculture and other kinds of exploitative specialization tend to force groups to enter into, or intensify, exchange interactions with other populations. Economic interactions between ethnically distinct groups and groups on different levels of social and economic organization are, therefore, endemic in tropical areas. In any event, it seems to be the case that tropical habitats favor lower limits on the size of homogeneous populations than do other environments. Thus, many societies on the level of stratified chiefdoms and beyond do not have the demographic or economic means to effect a degree of internal economic differentiation necessary on that stage of social development. In the Philippine case, the requisite degree of social differentiation was brought about by restructuring already existing relationships with ethnically different groups, bringing them—at least peripherally—into the realm of the higher economic system.

In view of this argument, it is too narrow a perspective to see (as I have previously done [Hutterer 1973b; 1974]) economic exchanges between lowland and upland societies only as a result of the twin needs of dispersing the imported goods and of collecting forest products for export. The organization of internal exchanges must have been further conditioned by the increasing economic specialization of different ethnic groups, a development which, by itself, is only partially and indirectly tied to the growth of foreign trade. As the social and economic systems of the coastal lowlands expanded, coastal societies probably attempted to bring other ethnic groups as a whole into their social and political ambience and assign them to a (lowly) role within their larger social scheme.

For future archaeological research, the following testable

propositions may be derived from the above considerations:

a) Since economic systems of very different scales and structure articulated in the network of internal exchange, it is likely that the articulation between systems on opposite ends of the scale was very loose and the circumstances of most exchange interactions were arranged on an ad-hoc basis. Systems with similar levels of economic organization, on the other hand, probably articulated quite tightly and transacted exchanges through relatively formalized institutions.

b) It is probable that, as the lowland economies were expanding, they attempted to increase their control of the internal flow of goods. When this could not be done through formalized institutions it was probably attempted through personalized patron-client relationships and probably often entailed some amount of conflict. In fact, ethno-historic sources abound with descriptions of hostility between interior peoples and lowland patrons.

c) There was probably a pronounced cline in the valuation of different goods moving through the exchange networks. In other words, foreign imports were valued most highly and circulated primarily among lowland populations, while goods of lowland manufacture were exchanged with interior cultivators, and only very few goods manufactured in the lowlands and no foreign goods found their way to the hunter/gatherers of the interior forest.

Conclusion

Evolutionary theory postulates that the overall trend of development is in the direction of increasing differentiation between the constituent parts of biological organisms and social groups. Along certain points of this development, when complexity reaches a critical mass, the collapse of the system can only be avoided by the addition of new integrative structural controls. Every new level of structural control is hierarchically superordinate to existing controls and is functionally more generalized. Social scientists have observed such evolutionary changes from several different perspectives: the organization of economic production and consumption, the organization of the social network in the more narrow sense, and the organization of political power. Economic exchange, the topic of special scrutiny for this conference, relates to all three areas of human organization just mentioned. Thus, as the total social fabric increases in complexity and structural sophistication, exchange also undergoes a series of transformations in form, content, and structure. This means that the quality and quantity of exchange interactions constitute a complex measure of the developmental status of a society. Beyond that, the investigation of exchange provides an opportune framework for the observation of social processes crucial for the understanding of basic principles governing the constitution of social entities and their change.

This view of exchange is, of course, not the exclusive intellectual property of neo-Darwinian evolutionism but may be claimed, in some modified form, by virtually any developmental theory of culture. For this reason, and because economic interaction often entails the exchange of material items which survive in archaeological contexts and whose origin and movement through space and time can be studied, archaeologists have long been interested in the problem of exchange. The investigation of prehistoric trade and exchange offers itself as an opportune approach not only for the study of prehistoric economic systems but, far beyond that, as an avenue for the study of cultural and social process.

Notes

1. There has been much discussion and disagreement over the provenance and dating of some of the Chinese ceramics found in insular Southeast Asia. Most Far Eastern ceramicists, being oriented towards the fine imperial and classical wares, have only rather recently become aware of the range and peculiarities of Chinese porcelains excavated in the Philippines, Indonesia and elsewhere outside China. Trade pottery found in the Philippines has been most extensively studied by Aga-Oglu (e.g., 1946; 1949; 1955; 1961; 1972; 1975).

2. This may provide at least a partial explanation for some otherwise puzzling historical events: in 1521, Ferdinand Magellan received a very cordial reception in several places of the Philippines, and his chaplain was able to baptize Rajah Humabon, his wife, and 800 Cebuanos only one week after the arrival of the Spanish ships (Pigafetta 1903-9).

3. This explains why the development of sophisticated metal technologies is found only among highly developed pre-state societies and usually blossoms with the rise of states. Only societies on this level of internal differentiation and structural complexity have the means to maintain this kind of technology, although societies on any level of socio-cultural development may utilize metals acquired from outside sources.

4. Heine-Geldern (1945) is a notable exception. He felt that the introduction of metals to the Southeast Asian islands was chronologically and processually tied to the spread of a 'Dong-son Culture', and that the first metal artifacts came to Indonesia via trade.

5. This is not an unimportant point. Even for the period of porcelain trade for which I postulate the growth of coastal entrepôts, Chao Ju-Kua describes in his Chu Fan Chih how Chinese traders used several different ways of interacting with different groups of Philippine natives. Even such simple expedients are mentioned as throwing porcelain bowls into the jungle which would then be picked up by 'hai-tan' (Aeta, Agta? [Scott 1968]).

6. The cumbersome circumlocution is necessary because, in spite of popular usage, there is no justification for speaking of a Philippine 'Iron Age' (see Hutterer 1976). No generally recognized alternative terminology is presently available.

7. It may be making a mountain out of a molehill, but it is of possible significance that the Negros site is located eight kilometers inland in rugged terrain and is not situated along a navigable river. If this site was indeed part of a central settlement of a chiefdom during the period under discussion, it would contrast with the strong coastal orientation of the lowland settlements of the second millenium A.D.

Markets and Trade in Pre-Majapahit Java

by

Jan Wisseman

Introduction: Early Javanese Trade

The first clear references to Java in Chinese accounts appear in the mid-seventh century. There are a number of earlier references to polities which may have been located on the island, but to date no definite identifications of these early states have been made. The state of Ho-ling, which sent its first mission to China in A.D. 640, has been identified beyond a doubt as the major state then existing on Java. From the time of its first appearance in Chinese histories, Ho-ling was reported to have been a state of considerable commercial importance in the Southern Sea. These reports come not only from the court records (Wang 1958:122-23), but also from Chinese Buddhist sources. Most of the pilgrims who passed through the Southern Sea in the seventh century did so on a series of merchant ships. Of those whose itineraries are known, almost as many sailed with merchants headed for Ho-ling as for Shih-li-fo-shih, or Śrīvijaya (Chavannes 1894),[1] a fact which has been overlooked in the rush of scholarly enthusiasm concerning Śrīvijaya in the last sixty years.

Java's importance in Southeast Asian trade increased steadily in subsequent centuries and after the eleventh century, particularly during the Majapahit period (fourteenth and fifteenth centuries) when it figured as the dominant trading power in the archipelago (Schrieke 1955:19, 29; Wolters 1967:251). External—mainly Chinese—historical sources do not provide any details of the operation of Javanese overseas trade of the late first and early second millennia, nor do they make any mention of economic activity within Java itself. There is, however, a large, as yet untapped, body of indigenous epigraphic material and some spotty archaeological data from which it is possible to elicit a considerable amount of information concerning Java's economy in the period prior to the fourteenth century.

Internal Sources:
Archaeological and Epigraphic Material[2]

The archaeological data from Java are still rather sparse for this period. Although the number of known religious monuments—the bulk of them dating to the late eighth and ninth centuries—well exceeds a hundred, no large population center older than the fourteenth century has yet been found. In fact, in the Jogjakarta-Magelang area of Central Java, where the majority of the temple remains are located, to date no first millennium secular settlement of any size has been found. Problems of chronology, settlement patterns, and economics have been tackled in only two limited areas of Central Java—in the Kebupaten of Rembang on the north coast (Asmar et al. 1975) and in the plains area around Jogjakarata (religious sites only—Asmar and Bronson 1973). Thus, on the basis of archaeological data alone, only tentative conclusions can be drawn about the nature of the political and economic organization of Java before European contact. Even if there were more archaeological data available at present, the information it could provide about the processes involved in economic activity is limited. The mere demonstration of the fact of intra- or inter-regional movement of certain non-perishable goods tells us little about the mechanisms governing the dispersal of these goods or the wider socio-economic setting in which it occurred. No accurate and full reconstruction of any elements of a complex ancient society can be made in the absence of some sort of documentary record.

Luckily, in Java there exists a considerable body of documentary material from the period in question in the form of inscriptions. About two hundred and fifty of these stone and copper-plate inscriptions have been published. Most of this epigraphic material falls into three groups. The earliest group, which dates from the fifth through ninth centuries, is in Sanskrit. All of the twenty or more published Sanskrit inscriptions are metric and either religious or eulogistic in nature. The seven Old Malay documents dating from the seventh through ninth centuries are more varied in character, but also provide little economic information. It is not until the first Javanese language inscriptions appear in the early ninth century that we begin to get any useful economic information. About ninety-five percent of the Javanese language inscriptions written between the ninth and thirteenth centuries are legal documents recording sīma grants—transferals of tax rights by the king or a local petty ruler/district head—the beneficiaries of these grants being in almost every case religious foundations. Of the nearly two hundred and fifty inscriptions reviewed, over sixty, or about twenty-five percent, were found to contain direct references to various forms and levels of economic activity. The format of these documents was, from the earliest examples onward, highly standardized and formalized, giving the impression that this type of transaction had been recorded on more perishable materials for some time before the beginning of the ninth century.

The Socio-Economic Setting:
Central and Early East Javanese Periods

The earliest Javanese language inscriptions, from the beginning of the ninth century, provide us with a picture of a prosperous, densely populated, and politically stable agrarian society. It was characterized by the presence of a true peasantry, well developed social stratification, and a government which, if not completely centralized, was supported by an elaborate bureaucracy and status sytem into which the petty rulers of semi-autonomous districts were already being drawn. This governmental structure was financed by a complex system of direct taxation, corvée labor extractions, and various forms of tax farming ranging from the granting of prebendal domains (involving control of income from the land rather than the land itself) to the creation of a class called the mangilala drwya haji (collectors of the king's due), some at least of whom served in the court in minor capacities, receiving in return the right to collect fees or hospitality in the countryside. [3]

Despite the relatively dense population of the Central and East Javanese plains areas, there seem to have been no large population centers aside from the kraton (palace, capital) until after the beginning of the second millennium. The basic administrative and economic unit appears to have been the wanua (later called thāni, paraduwan, dapur, deśa), [4] or village complex composed of a parent village and several—ideally four or eight—daughter hamlets (Boechari 1973:26, 39; Moertono 1968:27). This pattern is reflected in the present-day mañcapat and mañcalima village administrative groupings (Moertono 1968:27; Koentjaraningrat 1967:270-1). In the early nineteenth century, Crawfurd noted that there were no indigenous Javanese words for town or city and that even the capitals and chief provincial towns were nothing more than assemblages of villages with the palace in the center. He did report, however, that the walled compound of the palace at Jogjakarta contained at that time a population of over 10,000 people (Crawfurd 1856:182-3).

Markets, Trade Networks and Local Commerce

The ninth century Javanese economy was marketized, though probably not fully monetized,[5] with a cyclic five-day market[6] operating within and giving cohesion to the wanua. This market apparently circulated amongst groups of rather tightly packed wanuas. There is no indication of a hierarchy of market centers as described for traditional rural China (Skinner 1964), although the markets at the seat of the king or petty rulers and at some religious centers were undoubtedly larger than the average rural market.

The market (pkĕn/pkan in Old Javanese, though in some later documents the Persian-derived word pasar was used) had a fixed locus. Market places were occasionally cited along with roads and such natural features as rivers and forests in describing the position of a parcel of land, as for example in the Muñcang inscription of A.D. 944:

> (7)...lmah kidul ning pkan ing muñcang...(10)...
> lor ing pkan ing muñcang...—the land to the south
> of the market at Muñcang...north of the market
> at Muñcang...(Brandes and Krom 1913:108).

Occasionally even the names of hamlets within the wanua reflected the position of the market.[7]

The market was in the charge of a local official, the apkĕn or mapkĕn, who controlled access to the market place and collected fees or taxes on goods offered for sale within its precincts.[8] References to these market officials occur in the very earliest Old Javanese inscriptions and continue to appear with relative frequency throughout the period studied, both in lists of wanua officials and of mangilala drwya haji. They appear in at least some cases to have belonged to the class of wanua officials who were paid for their services in usufruct of wanua land,[9] a system which is still used in Java to recompense village officials (Koentjaraningrat 1967:273).

The vendors operating in the rural markets included local farmers, artisans, and several classes of itinerant traders, transporters and professional intermediaries, such as:

adwal: seller, small-scale peddler.

apikul: transporter/vendor who used the pikul or shoulder pole. (Groups of transporters using carts or pack animals appear also to have been present, but the terminology is obscure. There are also occasional mentions of the use of rafts and boats.)

adagang: trader, perhaps relatively small-scale, though a step above the adwal and covering a larger territory. Probably not a foreigner.

abakul or adagang bakulan: a market-based professional intermediary? (see below).

banyaga bantal: (from the Sanskrit vanij, 'merchant', and the Javanese bantal, a smallish unit of measure usually associated with pikul-carried goods) medium-sized trader? The position of the banyaga bantal appears to have been peripheral to the rural market (see note 19). The banyaga, or large-scale merchant, did not operate in the rural market. This class will be discussed in the next section.

The volume and range of goods handled by the individual vendor at this level was evidently small and the number and variety of vendors correspondingly great.[10] The market set-up of this period strongly resembles that described by Raffles in the early nineteenth century (Raffles 1830:193, 220-1), and does not seem greatly different from that found in Java today.

Since none of the inscriptions deal directly with market transactions (they merely list the numbers and classes of artisans and other vendors to be exempted from taxes), we know little about the intra-market economic mechanisms which sustained and regulated the exchange of goods and services. It does, however, appear that the average rural market handled substantially the same types of goods and services as did the nineteenth century market and, to a large extent, the modern rural market, and that the transactions were of much the same scale. The trade goods were usually the easily transportable, relatively non-perishable items such as textiles, hardware, metals, household goods, storable foodstuffs, etc. Most of these items, in the quantity handled by the individual vendor (normally a pikul-worth), probably required no major capital investment, though such prestige goods as gold and jewelry were also traded.

The wanua markets were not isolated or self-sufficient. As noted above, the vendors frequenting them included not only local farmers and artisans, but several classes of itinerant traders and transporters. Sīma grants normally freed traders resident in the wanua of royal taxes not only on commercial transactions within the wanua boundaries, but in all other districts they traveled to as well. Also, many of the products carried by these vendors were clearly of a regional nature: salt and wungkudu dye from the north coast, rice from the plains, tin and possibly other metals from outside Java entirely.

The presence of the abakul in the ninth century market may indicate that the inter-market trading networks of modern Java have their roots in the first millennium. The bakul, an essential part of the modern Javanese market (Dewey 1962:75-81), appears as early as A.D. 880 (Boechari n.d.:23), although, if frequency of mention is any guide, there appear to have been proportionately fewer bakuls among the vendors than there are at present. The modern bakul is a professional middleman vendor, who normally carries on business only within the market precincts, buying in bulk from first-stage carriers (farmers and processors) and selling either retail to individual purchasers or in bulk to second-stage carriers (pikul-carriers, etc.). Since the bakul (abakul) and various groups of transporters appear in the inscriptions, it may indicate that this pattern of economic specialization was present in the ancient markets as well. Then as now the second-stage carriers must have provided essential links tying each market into a regional network. Today, even in the face of competition from other types of transport, the pikul-carriers move massive quantities of goods amongst groups of four or more markets (Dewey 1962:132).

The impression received from the inscriptions of well developed intra- and inter-regional (though not necessarily hierarchical) trade networks is supported by the little archaeological data available at present. A survey of pottery types present at a number of temple sites in the Central Javanese plains (including both excavated and surface-collected material), indicates that by the late eighth or ninth century products of at least three separate pottery making centers circulated throughout the area between Prambanan and Magelang. This same pattern has appeared in the district of Rembang on the north coast: from the tenth century onwards, local wares were distributed throughout the entire surveyed area of roughly 2500 square kilometers (Asmar et al. 1975:98-100).

It has been suggested that the modern Javanese market system is "for the most part not a local growth but was introduced from outside at a point when Java had already achieved very high levels of social, political, and religious development" (Geertz 1963b:42), and that "it was only in the fourteenth century and the centuries immediately following it... (that) the pasar pattern took its characteristic historical form" (p. 43). There is, however, no indication that the Javanese rural market was either imposed or borrowed from outside, nor does it appear to be of such recent origin. Not only was the system closely tied to settlement patterns, but the ancient Javanese market terminology, in contrast to that of some other areas of Southeast Asia, appears to have been almost totally indigenous. It is, in fact, difficult to believe that Java could have achieved its high levels of social and political development without a well developed regional economy.

Merchants, Overseas Trade, and the Growth of Coastal Urban Centers

Although the Javanese rural market system shows little evidence of having been either adopted as a result of overseas contacts or of having been significantly changed in structure by these external influences, other areas of the economy were deeply affected. Changes occurred in economic interactions which lay outside and above the level of the rural market, in the government's attitude towards trade, and in the distribution of population in the Brantas plains area. The impetus for these changes, which began in the ninth century and accelerated in the tenth through twelfth centuries, was provided by the great increase in the volume and economic importance of trade with China during the late T'ang and Sung Dynasties.

During the eighth and ninth centuries the paramount Javanese capital and the bulk of the territory under its control were situated in and around the Kedu Plain of Central Java, to the south of the Perahu-Merapi mountains. That this inland polity had already had longstanding contact with India is known, though the evidence for major commercial activity remains slight. Commercial intercourse with China in the eighth and ninth centuries is evidenced by the moderate quantities of Chinese stoneware present at most if not all of the temple sites in Central Java.

Until the end of the first millennium A.D., sea trade must have dealt largely in relatively small quantities of prestige goods and exotics. There is no sign of the kind of port growth that one would expect if large quantities of goods were being handled. No first millennium port sites have yet been found along the north coast in this region and there is no evidence that the Central Javanese capital exercised direct control over this region before the very end of the ninth century.[11] The capital may even have sought to suppress the rise of any major commerical center on the coast, feeling that the convenience of such a port would be outweighed by the danger of allowing a competing power center to develop so far from the capital. The absence of any direct riverine connection between the interior and the coast directly to the north of it and the relative ease of overland access to the coast meant that no one site on the coast had an overwhelming natural advantage as a trading port. Since there were several overland routes to choose from,[12] it would not have been difficult for the inland government to shift its custom and protection of access roads from one landing place to another.

Alternatively, it is possible that trade with the interior of Central Java was, even at this period, funneled through

East Java. Although no first millennium port sites have yet been found in East Java, there is documentary evidence of commercial activity in the Brantas Delta area by the mid ninth century.[13] It is uncertain, however, whether this area was under the direct control of the Central Javanese capital before the very end of that century.[14] The overseas trade activity in East Java at the time seems to have been centered around the lower Brantas region. The Solo River, which in later centuries provided access to the Central Javanese plains (Schrieke 1957: 296; Crawfurd 1856:170), was apparently not heavily used before the beginning of the tenth century,[15] and there is no record of a port at the mouth of the Solo before the founding of Gresik in the late fourteenth century.

Despite this seeming absence of major ports serving the Central Java plains area, both merchants and merchant communities are mentioned in inscriptions of the region. The large-scale merchant connected with overseas trade (Sanskrit vanij/vanik, Old Javanese banyaga) appears in the inscriptions as early as the late eighth century (Boechari, personal communication). There are several other mentions of the banyaga in Central Javanese inscriptions, although in most cases the word appears to have been used as a personal name. The one mention of interest comes in a metric inscription of A.D. 856, where the merchant is compared with herons, geese, and other migratory birds (Casparis 1956:280).

Mentions of the kabanyagan (merchant community/ settlement/quarter?) appear as early as A.D. 850. The ka--an construction is used in other contexts to denote both groups or classes of people and the land or place associated with them. The Tulang Air inscription of A.D. 850 refers to a priest of the temple of the kabanyagan (Casparis 1956:236). Another inscription, dated A.D. 919 speaks of an official resident in the kabanyagan in the wanua of Galuh (Damais 1970:579). None of the inscriptions of this period mention the nationality of these merchants, but the fact that they formed groups or settlements/ quarters may indicate that at least some of them were foreigners as in other areas of Southeast Asia at the time. Foreigners are mentioned in Central Javanese inscriptions, but only in religious contexts. There is no indication that any merchants or foreigners during this period had any official connection with the Javanese government.

After the removal of the paramount capital to the lower Brantas area of East Java in the early tenth century, the Javanese rulers took a more active and direct interest in overseas trade. Between the tenth and twelfth centuries a large percentage of the sīma documents issued concerned coastal settlements in the Brantas Delta region. Some of these grants were undoubtedly made in order to reduce the power of the local petty rulers who controlled the port areas by depriving them of revenue. Other grants were made with the stated purpose of encouraging settlement in the port areas and thus lessening the danger to merchants and coastal people (hiliran) from banditry.[16] There is also mention in the mid eleventh century of a major royal project involving the damming and diverting into three channels of the Porong branch of the Brantas River. This was done in order to reduce the danger of floods and thus to benefit not only the local farmers, but also the "ship-handlers, pilots and gatherers of goods at Hujung Galuh, including ship captains and merchants (banyaga) originating from the other islands/countries."[17] Perhaps the most important document involving a port area is that of Manañjung (Rempah) dating to the tenth or eleventh century. In it the king outlines rules for quality control, standardization of weights and measures, and apparently sets prices for the produce gathered and stored at the port (Stutterheim 1928:105-8). This apparent attempt to control prices of goods at the ports is interesting, but there is no evidence that such attempts to administer trade directly were anything but sporadic.

In total, the impression one gets from the inscriptions is that there was considerable governmental interest in the Brantas Delta ports, even to the point of encouraging population buildups in the port areas for reasons of security. This trend towards large concentrations of people in coastal areas apparently continued to receive governmental sanction during the Majapahit period. These coastal centers gained in strength as Majapahit disintergrated, and they finally broke away, forming a series of small trade-centered harbor states along much of the north coast.

No direct references to Java's overseas trading partners are found in indigenous sources before the fourteenth century, but lists of trade goods and resident foreigners can be used to supplement references in foreign histories and lists of excavated remains of imported goods to produce a reasonably complete picture of pre-Majapahit trade activities. This picture does not differ greatly from that of trade during the Majapahit and European contact periods. The Manañjung inscription of the late tenth or eleventh century lists trade goods used for external trade, though the list is incomplete as it includes only local produce sold in standard weights or volumes. Of these, rice is stated to be the most important, followed by pepper, salt, beans, dyes and medicines. The majority of these goods clearly were not used in direct trade with China (for Javanese exports to China in the eleventh and twelfth centuries, see Wheatley 1959). If, however, we compare this list with early Dutch and Portuguese records of Javanese exports to other areas in the archipelago, we find clear parallels. In the fifteenth century Javanese rice was sent west to Sumatra and Malacca and east to the Moluccas. So were salt, beans and other foodstuffs. Pepper and dyes were shipped not only to China, but also to Bali where they were exchanged for Balinese ikat cloth which was in great demand in the Moluccas (Schrieke 1955:19-22). The hostilities between Java and Śrīvijaya in the late tenth century must have been tied to this archipelago trade. These hostilities probably arose more through competition for the position as the chief emporium for goods from the other islands than from competition as primary producers of certain products. The trade goods stated by Sung Chinese sources to have originated in Java were largely agricultural produce and manufactured goods, while those originating in Śrīvijaya were forest products (Wheatley 1959). Only in re-exported goods was there any overlap and thus potential for conflict.

Foreigners appear in East Javanese inscriptions in several contexts. Juru cina, juru barata, and juru kling (heads of communities of Chinese, Westerners? and Indians) appear in lists of mangilala drwya haji. Various groups of foreigners appear in contexts implying that they may have functioned as interpreters and intermediaries in negotiations between the court and foreign merchants; similar officials are mentioned in early Portuguese and Dutch accounts (Schrieke 1955:28). There is also mention in six East Javanese inscriptions of the ninth through eleventh centuries of a group of foreigners called the wargga kilalan (group of collectors). This group, which included Khmers, Chams, Ramanyadeśis, Singhalese, Pandikiras, Karnatikas, Dravidians, Aryyas, and Kalingas—some of whom are identified as merchants (Barrett 1968:129)—appears to have had some kind of tax collecting right in the lower Brantas region.[18]

The banigrama (Sanskrit vaniggrāma) or merchant community/guild, which appears in coastal inscriptions of the same period, seems also to have functioned as a tax collecting body. These banigrama groups, which are mentioned only in port areas, were almost certainly foreign trading associations. They appear to have acted in much the same way that the Chinese merchants and merchant groups acted in the Later Mataram period (Moertono 1968:137; Raffles 1830:198-9, 221).

The connection of foreign merchants with tax collecting is not without parallel in Javanese history, but this is the earliest evidence for the presence in the archipelago of classic Southeast Asian tax farming involving foreigners. The Central Javanese inscriptions of the eighth and ninth centuries give no indication that this practice had ever caught on in the interior. This tax farming system may have sprung up not only in response to the king's increasing need for cash and foreign prestige goods but also because it served to reduce the administrative burden of moving trade goods from the wanua to the port in an orderly manner. Since there is no evidence for the existence at that time of a network of intermediate level marketing and collecting centers, the problem of moving predictable amounts of certain goods from large numbers of small rural settlements to the collection centers on the coast must have been acute. Small scale traders undoubtedly participated in this movement of goods, but coordination of supply with demand to produce a guarenteed quantity of goods at the ports at the proper time of year would have been beyond their organizational abilities. The simplest solution for the Javanese government would have been to grant the large scale merchants or merchant groups the right to collect specified amounts of produce from a set number of settlements or districts in return for a periodic payment to the king.[19] This was the manner in which the Javanese kings solved the problem of providing for their various officials: for each new department or expense the king created a new tax and empowered the officials involved to collect it themselves (Moertono 1968:134).

This system of collection of trade goods through taxation may explain why foreign trade goods are not mentioned in rural market trade-good lists but are mentioned in lists of gifts distributed at sīma grant ceremonies. Overseas trade may have bypassed the rural market for the most part, with taxation and gift-giving playing a major role in the movement of the goods involved. This explanation is only a tentative one and is probably only an adequate one for the movement of the more prestigeous trade goods. Non-prestige goods, notably metals and dyes, appear in the market lists and were undoubtedly distributed through the medium of small scale traders.

Notes

1. According to I Ch'ing's biographies of monks, eleven pilgrims broke their journeys at Ho-ling and thirteen at Shih-li-fo-shih.

2. Besides the sources cited in the text and elsewhere in the notes, the following literature on Javanese inscriptions has been consulted: Bhandarkar (1887-9); Bosch (1917; 1925a; 1941); Stein Callenfels (1934); Casparis (1950; 1958; 1961); Damais (1952), Goris (1928; 1930); Kern (1913); Krom (1911; 1913); Naerssen (1937a; 1937b); Poerbatjaraka (1922; 1936), Sarkar (1938); Stuart and Limburg Brouwer (1872); Stutterheim (1925a; 1925b; 1927; 1940); Wibowo (n.d.).

3. For parallel institutions in the Later Mataram period, see Moertono (1968:90-1, 135).

4. Both paraduwan and dapur mean 'group, cluster'.

5. Although a number of silver pieces stamped 'mā' have been recovered in Central Java (Casparis: personal communication), the Javanese economy does not appear to have been generally monetized until after the twelfth century. A large number of Majapahit period coins have been recovered in East Java, and there are mentions in fourteenth and fifteenth century Javanese inscriptions of tax payments made in coins called 'pisis' (Pigeaud 1960-63: 111, 166 and 173; Brandes and Krom 1913: 218-26). These coins were probably either Chinese copper cash or locally minted coins of similarly small denominations, both of which were reported by Chau Ju-kua in the early thirteenth century to have been in use in Java (Hirth and Rockhill 1966: 78).

6. Days of the five-day market week appear in the dates on all Javanese inscriptions. The Waharu inscription of A.D. 931 mentions a 'pkĕn kaliwwan' or Kliwon market (Stuart 1875:16). Kliwon is one of the days of the five-day market week.

7. See the Panumbangan inscription of A.D. 1140 in which there appears a hamlet named 'kidul ing pasar' or South of the Market (Brandes and Krom 1913: 159-63).

8. The market officials are mentioned in lists of mangilala drwya haji (collectors of the king's due). Balinese inscriptions of the same period mention market officials (ser pasar) with similar functions. The fee-collecting market official is still found in Javanese markets (Dewey 1962: 61-2).

9. There are references to 'lmah kapkanan' or land attached to the office of the market official, as well as land attached to other wanua offices.

10. Artisans and processors present in the market included several kinds of smiths, weavers, dye makers, spindle makers, wax processors?, carpenters, potters, basketry and wickerwork makers, net makers, kris sheath makers, etc. Trade goods peddled at the wanua level included clothing, ikat cloth, cadar cloth, thread, cotton, safflower, wungkudu, brazilwood and various other dyes, wax?, spindles, pottery, salt, rice, sesame cake, sugar, onions, lime, ginger, sirih, charcoal, umbrellas, basketry, medicines, sirih boxes, fishing nets, etc.

11. The north coast of Central Java is archaeologically rather puzzling. It has produced a few sixth and seventh century Sanskrit and Old Malay inscriptions and a scattering of apparently early temple remains of a different style from either the Dieng Plateau or Kedu Plains temples, but since most of the epigraphic material is unreadable and no excavation (and little survey) has been done at any of these sites, there is little that can be said about this area at present.

12. There are several mentions of major roads in the late ninth and early tenth century inscriptions. See also Schrieke (1957: 105-11).

13. Kuti, A.D. 840 (Sarkar 1971: I, 76-99)—a late rather defective copy; Waharu, A.D. 873 (Stuart 1875: 7-10); Kañcana, A.D. 860 (Sarkar 1971:I 133-62).

14. Rakryan Kanuruhan, who seems to have controlled the area around Pasuruhan in East Java, appears as one of the donors of minor temples at Prambanan, near Jogjakarta in Central Java, in the early or mid ninth century (Casparis 1956:

310, n. 112). By A.D. 860, the titles of the top administrative officials—<u>Rakryan i Hino</u>, <u>Rakryan i Halu</u>, <u>Rakryan i Sirikan</u>—appear in both Central and East Java. However, it is not until the advent of Balitung in A.D. 899 that the same king's name appears in both regions. It is also significant that the sīma grant documents of Central and East Java, though serving the same purpose, differ considerably in format during the ninth century.

15. First mention comes in a Wanagiri inscription of A.D. 903 (Stutterheim 1934).

16. Kaladi inscription of A.D. 909 (Barrett 1968:107).

17. Kamalagyan inscription of A.D. 1037 (Brandes and Krom 1913:134-6).

18. For lists of foreigners see Kuti, A.D. 840 (Sarkar 1971: I 76-99); Kaladi, A.D. 909 (Barrett 1968:129); Palebuhan, A.D. 927 (Stutterheim 1932:420-37); Turun Hyang, eleventh century (Brandes and Krom 1913:143-6); Cane, A.D. 1021 (ibid.:120-5); and Patakan, eleventh century (ibid.:125-8). All but one of these, an easily portable copper plate inscription, were found in the Brantas Delta region. Inland inscriptions do not mention this group of foreigners.

19. The <u>banyaga bantal</u>, a medium scale merchant, may have acted as agent for the larger scale port-bound merchant. His position in the rural market appears to have been rather peripheral; he is listed more often among the tax collectors than among the traders. There are, in the Later Mataram period, mentions of the subletting of tax farming privileges by Chinese merchant tax farmers (Raffles 1830:198-200). Something of the same sort may have taken place in the eleventh and twelfth centuries.

The Coming of Islam to the Archipelago:

a Re-Assessment

by

Kenneth R. Hall

In the early centuries A.D. Indonesia's archipelago was strategically situated on the great international maritime trade route connecting China and the West, a position which allowed the area numerous contacts with the community of maritime traders. Southeast Asia's role in that route was predominantly one of providing a key link, furnishing the passing traders with supplies, local products, Chinese and Western goods, storage facilities, and hostelries for waiting out the monsoon season. The Chinese viewed the waters stretching from the coast of China and the South China Sea to the Indian Ocean and the coast of Africa as in essence one ocean, the Nan-yang or Southern Seas (Wolters 1963). Laying astride this single ocean and its communications, the Malay Peninsula and the islands adjacent to it possessed a double potential. They could on the one hand disrupt the flow of trade through various forms of piracy; on the other hand, by maintaining political stability and establishing coastal entrepôts they might take advantage of the commercial possibilities offered by the trade route.

The international maritime network has been regarded as a stimulus to the development of Southeast Asia's culture. From earliest times, the maritime network provided a communications channel along which ideologies of Indic and Sinic origin entered Southeast Asia. As reflected in the remaining records of this age, these became important ingredients in the developing systems of Southeast Asian statecraft. In a recently published analysis of earliest Southeast Asian polity, I have argued that the initial forms of statecraft as developed in Burma, Cambodia, Java, Sumatra, and Vietnam were similar in structure and style until the end of the twelfth century when a series of internal changes resulted in a transition to new forms of organization (Hall 1976a). I have proposed that developing indigenous states utilized foreign patterns for their own advantage, and that, despite the outward appearance of Indic or Sinic cultural adaptation, at the heart of the 'classical' Southeast Asian system of state organization lay indigenous ideals of chieftainship, its sacred nature, and its duties, concepts which had previously served as the basis of earlier forms of political organization.[1] During the twelfth through the fourteenth centuries internal changes of a qualitative nature made the old state structures impractical or impossible to maintain. Thus Southeast Asia entered a period of transition from the earlier classical forms of statecraft to those of a 'post-classical' age. Internal developments within the Southeast Asian states provided openings for such formerly peripheral forms of belief as Theravāda Buddhism, Neo-Confucianism, and Sufi Islam, and the adoption of these new ideologies became part of the transition from the 'classical' form of Southeast Asian polity to that of the 'traditional' age.

Little has intrigued scholars more over the past century than the attempt to define the interaction between the international maritime trade routes and the conversion of the Southeast Asian archipelago to Islam. Recently G. W. J. Drewes (1968), in an article entitled "New Light on the Coming of Islam to Indonesia?", surveyed the historiography on this problem, dealing comprehensively with the various interpretations of scholars from as early as the 1850's until the mid 1960's. Reading Drewes' article, one forms the impression that there is little agreement on the ingredients of the archipelago's conversion, nor does Drewes' himself suggest a solution. This paper is intended to extend Drewes' historiographical survey into the 1970's, while at the same time pointing to new research possibilities which I feel are critical to the understanding of the archipelago's history prior to the incursion of the Europeans as well as of the role of the Islamic conversion within this period.

The principal sources for the study of the archipelago's conversion, as described by Drewes, have consisted of Muslim gravestones, the earliest of which may date to the eleventh century (Drewes 1968:454), local histories such as the <u>Hikayat Raja-Raja Pasai</u> (Hill 1960) and the <u>Sejarah Melayu</u> (Brown 1952) which provide us with legends about the conversion, and various external references, notably those of the Chinese and the West. Among the latter, Marco Polo's travel account reported that Samara and Basma(n), local entrepôts on the Sumatra coast, were not Muslim in 1292. Samara and Basma(n) have been identified as Samudra-Pasai, and Polo's report has been related to a Muslim gravestone from Samudra-Pasai, dated 1297, which is purported to have marked the grave of the locality's first Muslim ruler. Polo's record has been held as critical in dating the conversion of Samudra-Pasai to Islam—i.e., to the period between 1292 and 1297 A.D.[2] Drewes, however, argues convincingly that Basma(n) is not Pasai and that Samara is not Samudra, and suggests that Polo's account of Southeast Asia is largely useless except for his note that Perlak was Muslim in 1292 (Drewes 1968:448-9). Further, after evaluating all the various possibilities for Sumatra's conversion, Drewes concludes that people from southern India seem to have played an important role in the spread of Islam in the archipelago—and, more particularly, that the Coromandel Coast of South India seems to have been a likely source for Indonesia's Islam (p. 459). Having eliminated one important literary reference for the study of the conversion and set aside several potential sources for the spread of Islam, Drewes proposed that further analysis must await more research in two areas: new archeological data from northern Sumatra and a definitive study of Islam in southern India.

Almost ten years after Drewes' comments, there has been little attempt to fill the two voids he deemed critical. Only in the 1970's has scholarly archeological research been conducted in Sumatra. In the early 1970's, E. Edwards McKinnon and an Indonesian archeological team excavated what appears to have been a tenth through fourteenth century site at Kota China near Medan.[3] During 1973, Bennet Bronson of the Univeristy of Pennsylvania Museum and Field Museum, in association with the Lembaga Purbakala dan Peninggalan Nasional (The National Archeological Institute of Indonesia), conducted a site survey (Bronson, et al. 1973), and in 1974 undertook excavations at Palembang. It is unfortunate for this paper that the 1974 excavations produced little information for the study of the spread of Islam. The 1973 survey, however, holds considerable promise of things to come. Of particular interest is that Bronson has identified several northern Sumatra sites, on both the east and the west coasts, which are strewn with large quantities of Sung porcelain—the type of evidence we seek to define the centers of international commerce during the period 1000-1400 A.D. Hopefully, excavation of several of these sites will take place during the next decade, and these excavations will allow us to understand better the literary sources we currently possess—the gravestones, local histories, foreign notices, etc.

The second void recognized by Drewes, scholarship on the South Indian Muslim community, has seen no activity. Part of the problem, as with the study of Sumatra's history, seems to be a lack of historical sources. My initial survey of the potential sources for the study of early Muslim contacts with the Coromandel Coast, although this period is in general extremely rich in indigenous documentation, most notably temple inscriptions, does not allow me to predict great things for the future. I will, however, continue to search. While I am not able at present to present a definitive statement on the conversion of the archipelago to Islam, my research on indigenous commercial organization and the ports of trade in early medieval South India (the tenth through the thirteenth centuries) allows me to share with you my impressions of the available data and the directions in which my research on international maritime trade is heading.

South India and the Coming of Islam to Southeast Asia

At the end of the last century, Snouck Hurgronje, the well known Dutch scholar of Islamic civilization in Indonesia, refuted earlier notions that Islam had come directly to Indonesia from the Middle East, holding instead that it was India where scholars should seek the source of Southeast Asia's Islam (Hurgronje 1906). He held that numerous literary traditions of Malay Muslims, including a good many Persian loan words to the Malay language, were borrowed from India. Hurgronje proposed 1200 A.D. as the date of the earliest serious adoption of Islam in the archipelago, and suggested that the participants in the international maritime trade connecting East and West were the source of this Islam.

During the next sixty years scholars attempted to attribute the source of the archipelago's Islam to various areas of the South Asian coast. Suggesting that several of the earliest Muslim gravestones had originated in Gujarat, Dutch scholars (e.g., Kern 1947) first held that Islam came from India's upper west coast, one of India's major centers of commerce over the centuries. But evidence that the 1297 stone of the first Muslim ruler of Pasai (Malik al-Salih) was of a different style than other gravestones of known Gujarat origin—all of which were of a later date—in addition to the fact that Gujarat was not controlled by a Muslim dynasty until 1297, reinforced Hurgronje's conclusion that it was southern India from which Southeast Asia's Islam had come.

In the early 1960s, S.Q. Fatimi (1963) proposed a Bengali origin for the Pasai dynasty. From ancient times, Fatimi noted, the Bengal coast had maintained maritime contact with the archipelago. This communication was highlighted in the ninth century when the Śailendra king Bālaputra Deva founded a Buddhist vihāra (monastery) for Indonesian pilgrims at Nālandā, the Bengal Buddhist center (Bosch 1925b). When Bengal fell to a Muslim conqueror in 1200 A.D., argued Fatimi, it is reasonable to expect that repercussions were felt in Sumatra, i.e., that northern Sumatra, located at the southern end of the Bay of Bengal, converted to Islam to maintain its friendly communications with Bengal. Reinforcing Fatimi's position is Tomé Pires' belief, as expressed in his sixteenth century account of Malacca and the trade of Asia, that Bengal was the source of Southeast Asian Islam. [4]

Malay literature as well as other external evidence does not support Fatimi's Bengali thesis. Most notably the Hikayat Raja-Raja Pasai, the chronicle of the Samudra-Pasai dynasty, is believed to be strongly colored by South Indian tradition. Tamil merchants, jugglers, and wrestlers are repeatedly mentioned in the text, and the chronicle specifically attributes the source of Pasai's Islam to southern India.

To summarize the Hikayat Raja-Raja Pasai conversion legend: Merah Silu, chief of Pasai, had a dream in which the Prophet spit into his mouth and thereby converted him to Islam, and then assigned to him the Muslim name Malik al-Salih. The Prophet announced that in forty days a ship from Mecca would arrive bearing a Muslim holy man who would bestow the Pasai ruler with the vestiges of his office. The Pasai king awoke, finding that he had been circumcised and could recite the entire

Koran and the Islamic confession of faith. Forty days later, the
Pasai ruler received the prophesied ship which bore Shaikh
Ismail, a Muslim holy man, and Sultan Muhammad of Ma'bar who
who had joined the voyage when the ship had stopped at his port
on the South Indian coast (Hill 1960).

The core fact of this tale is that Islam came from Ma'bar,
the term used by western sailors to designate the Coromandel or
eastern coast of southern India.[5] Ma'bar should not be confused
with the modern Malabar or western coast of southern India,
which was identified by early Western sailors as 'Mulaybâr'.
Though a good deal of this conversion story is no doubt symbolic
myth, the stress on a Ma'bar origin for Pasai's Islam must be
considered significant. As emphasized in the Hikayat, it was
from the Coromandel coast that the regalia—portrayed by the
chronicle as the essence of the investiture ceremony and
representing, according to the text, the bestowal of legitimacy
upon the converted monarch—for the coronation of the Pasai
king originated. The royal regalia's most identifiable component
was the nobat, an ankle bracelet, which has had a long
significance in South Indian Tamil tradition.[6] Why, we must ask,
did the Hikayat consider this association with southern India
sufficient to legitimize the new sultan's investiture?

To understand this attitude toward southern India one must
examine the patterns of international trade during this age. The
first critical fact which must be supported is that ports on the
Coromandel coast were populated by Middle Eastern merchants—
mostly Muslims—and that, secondly, these Middle Eastern
merchants normally set out from these Coromandel ports to
Southeast Asia.

In response to our first concern, whether Muslim traders
were resident in Coromandel Coast ports, we may answer with
a qualified 'yes'. My research has yet to discover a specific
reference to a Muslim in the epigraphy of that age. During this
time of Cōḷa hegemony over most of the southeast coast (850-
1265 A.D.), such a void is not unexpected. Temple inscriptions,
the primary source of our knowledge for this period of South
Indian history, make little distinction among the names of
individuals; on the other hand, they do designate the place of
origin of the donor as we will note below. We have argued
elsewhere that foreign merchants and the members of the

indigenous society in southern India were confined to segregated communities; foreign merchants were permitted to interact with the local population only in designated market centers (Hall, in press). This is well shown in several inscriptions of the eleventh century, when Srivijaya's rulers made gifts to temples in Nāgapaṭṭinam, the Cōḷa's favored port, as each gift was arranged not by a foreign merchant, but by a South Indian intermediary who was designated as the 'agent of the Srivijaya king'. There was apparently little opportunity for direct contact betwenn Cōḷa temples and foreign merchants, especially Muslims. There is evidence, however, that there were Muslims resident in the Cōḷa domain. [7] To understand the presence of Muslim merchants in southern India, given the lack of indigenous evidence, it is necessary for us to redirect our focus, for the present, to the definition of the patterns of maritime trade as depicted in external evidence.

Arab sources note that South Indian ports, particularly those on the west coast, were important participants in the commercial patterns of the Indian Ocean (Nilakanta Sastri 1939 and Husayn Nainar 1942). Sources available for the study of pre-eleventh century trading relationships between the Middle East and India consist primarily of collections of the stories of voyages and the merchants who frequented the various ports of the area. These were incorporated by a group of Arab geographers into descriptions and sequences of villages and natural features to be encountered in commercial travel. Until the mid-tenth century, the Persian Gulf port of Sīraf, the official port of Persia's 'Abbāsid dynasty, was the destination for most of these voyages. The last geographer listing Sīraf as his destination has been dated to the mid-tenth century, corresponding to the decline of the 'Abbāsids (Aubin 1959). The 'Abbāsid decline coincides with the rise of the Fatimid dynasty in Egypt (969), whose positive stance toward commerce resulted in a new burst of commercial activity. International trade in the West became focused in the ports of the Arabian Peninsula. Aden became the new center of East-West trade, connecting the Fatimid domain with the ports of southern India. [8] It is from the merchants who traveled between Aden and India that we receive insight into the complexities of the East-West trade.

Of particular value for our analysis are the letters and documents of the Cairo Geniza which have to date been utilized only by Middle East specialists. The Geniza documents are scraps of paper, letters of correspondence, and accounts of business transactions, far more specific and trustworthy than the earlier Arab geographies, which were composed during the tenth through the thirteenth centuries by a group of Jewish merchants, some of whom were active in Indian Ocean commerce. Apparently for religious reasons, these papers were deposited in an enclosed room within a synogogue complex at old Cairo (Fūsṭat). The commercial connections between this community and southern India are of significance for South Indian historiography, as Fūsṭat merchant families established branches of operation in the ports of the Malabar and Coromandel coasts (Hall in press). The remaining Geniza papers document a regular correspondence between the two continents (Goitein 1963).

Of importance for this study are the very clear statements in the Geniza letters that western merchants sailing onward from India to Southeast Asia embarked from al-Ma'bar, i.e., Coromandel coast ports (Goitein 1973:223-9). Letters make specific reference to the travels of Middle Eastern merchants between ports on the Coromandel Coast and Malaya and Indonesia.[9]

The Geniza documents note that the regular maritime route from Egypt terminated on India's Malabar coast. Quilon, in particular, was a major Malabar entrepôt during these times.[10] From Quilon and other southwest coast ports shipping progressed to Ceylon or to ports on the east coast.[11] As depicted in the Geniza letters, regular contact between India and the archipelago was not made from the Ceylon ports but from those of the Coromandel (Ma'bar) coast.

This western evidence of maritime intercourse between the Coromandel Coast and Sumatra is supported by Chinese sources which speak of maritime contact between China and India. Most notably the <u>Yuan-shih</u> reports a Chinese embassy which journeyed to southern India in 1282 A.D. This mission was seemingly undertaken in response to an earlier embassy which the Chinese had attributed to the Pāṇḍyan king of Ma'bar, who by that time had replaced the Cōḷa as the most important among Coromandel Coast rulers. This embassy to China had been led by a Muslim envoy (Nilakanta Sastri 1939:155). After visiting the Pāṇḍya king, the Chinese ambassadors journeyed on to Quilon on the Malabar coast, where they met an official from the Sumatra port of Su-mu-ta (Samudra).[12] The Chinese mission's return voyage set out from Ma'bar and made a visit to Su-mu-ta, where the Chinese ambassadors were warmly welcomed by Su-mu-ta's ruler, who then sent two Muslims[13] as his envoys to the Chinese court.

Of further importance in assigning a South Indian origin to the archipelago's Islam, detailed analysis of the maritime patterns of interaction in the Bay of Bengal during the eleventh through the thirteenth centuries shows conclusively that there was contact between the Coromandel Coast and the archipelago. A joint study conducted by John Whitmore and myself (Hall and Whitmore 1976) concluded the following: during the late eleventh and twelfth centuries, the upper Malay Peninsula and the South Southeast Asian mainland receded from the patterns of power and trade in the island world, including the international maritime trade, and became part of a more regionalized system of communication across the Bay of Bengal connecting Ceylon to Burma and Cambodia. Ports of Java and Sumatra drew the major international trade south and west, while the rise to prominence of the Pagan dynasty in Burma drew the regional trade of the Bay of Bengal north. Bengal, the source of Pasai's Islam in Fatimi's thesis, was a participant in this more regionalized trade and probably did not have a strong maritime relationship with the ports of northern Sumatra. All indications point to such a weak relationship, and the assumption that there was continuous maritime interaction among all those areas sharing the Bay of Bengal would seem to be erroneous.[14]

We may conclude our argument that the archipelago's Islam came from southern India by returning to Malay literary sources. I would argue, firstly, that the important tale of the Ma'bar monarch who left his kingdom to bestow legitimacy upon the Pasai ruler is an adaptation of a South India tradition. An early Kerala legend immortalizes a 'sea king' (As-Samuri) known as Perumal[15] who was convinced by Muslim pilgrims to abdicate his throne and journey to Arabia to study Islam. The legend prophesied that one day As-Samuri, the 'sea king', would return to lead his people to a new era of prosperity. Secondly, one may note the usage of the word lebai in Malay literature to designate the important expert on Muslim religious affairs.

Lebai is derived from a Tamil Source,[16] bearing "testimony to the important role played by people from south India in the spread of Islam in the Archipelago" (Drewes 1968:459).

Thus, the existing evidence supports the Coromandel Coast as the source of the archipelago's Islam, evidence which will hopefully find support from new archeological discoveries. Current archeological evidence is encouraging. In 1088, for instance, Tamil merchants were active at Lobo Tua near Barus.[17] Such evidence may well indicate that the search for data on the coming of Islam to the archipelago should not confine itself to the eastern coast, the focus of this and earlier studies. Three tenth century inscriptions from western Lampung Province, for instance, probably reflect the entry of the western coast as a participant in the patterns of Asian trade.[18] One of these is composed in Old Javanese; one is in Old Malay, but seems to have a Javanese style; the third is in Sanskrit, but is written in Javanese script. All may reflect a Javanese orientation to this early trade. Such west coast evidence is further supported by literary references. Groeneveldt (1960), in Notes on the Malay Archipelago and Malacca Compiled from Chinese Sources, states that it was a five day sail from Java to the port of Ta-tsi, which was inhabited by Arabs.[19] Groeneveldt firmly believed that Ta-tsi was located on Sumatra's west coast. Further, Dutch scholars at one time attempted to locate Basma(n) in Marco Polo's list of Sumatra ports on the west coast (Pelliot 1959:88; Schrieke 1957:255, n. 195). Drewes' 'Reappraisal' dismissed the Polo evidence stating that it was "strange to come across a place located on the west coast of Sumatra in an enumeration of harbour towns on the north coast" (Drewes 1968:448). But Drewes did not know how to handle Groeneveldt's reference to Ta-tsi and its Arab population, suggesting only that the Muslim traders might have occasionally strayed from the normal route (p. 454).

I am suggesting that by the eleventh century the Straits of Malacca were no longer the focal point of the island trade as alternative routes were available and were being used by the various groups of maritime traders. In support of my thesis speak the above mentioned Tamil inscription from the west coast and also Bronson's 1973 survey which found a considerable amount of surface material in the Barus area, particularly pot sherds and Chinese ceramics dating from the Sung period.

Why, we must ask, is there such a concentration? One clue to the answer is a Sung Hui Yao reference (987) to Chinese efforts to acquire Barus camphor (Ma 1971:33).

The Coming of Islam to Pasai

Shifting our focus from external to internal considerations, it is my belief that despite the lack of adequate data to understand the conversion process in detail, the available information affords us more opportunity than has previously been utilized. The Hikayat Raja-Raja Pasai, our major indigenous source for early Sumatra history, may in particular hold the key to future research.

In the Hikayat's story of the conversion to Islam, we are first told about the founding of the Pasai dynasty. Here the chronicle notes that there was a falling out among a number of rulers in Semerlanga in northern Sumatra. This resulted in two brothers, Merah Silu and Merah Hasun, leaving their old 'state', wandering until they settled at the mouth of the Pasangan River. However, a quarrel broke out between the brothers, and Merah Silu left, traveling to the headwaters of the Pasangan River upon the invitation of Megat Iskandar, a local chief. There Merah Silu became very wealthy, collecting worms which miraculously turned to gold when he boiled them. Merah Silu also became very popular among the local population. Megat Iskandar, in consultation with his subordinate chiefs, decided that Merah Silu would be a worthy head chief, a rāja. This action allowed the local population to break their relationship with their former rāja, Sultan Maliku'l-Nasar, who promptly attacked Merah Silu's confederation, only to lose. Merah Silu followed this victory with others and became rāja over all the former territories of Sultan Maliku'l-Nasar.

We may see here the story of a politically 'out' group, as represented by Merah Silu, which was able to gain power by forging new political alliances. One of the most significant aspects of this tale is the theme of upland vs. the coast: Merah Silu went upriver from the coast where he was bestowed with legitimacy by the existing powers of the interior. Once acquiring power, he led the forces of the interior to victory over the coastal sultan, and assumed legitimate control, in the eyes of the Sumatra tribesmen of the interior, over Pasai. The Pasai ruler, thus, owed his initial legitimacy not to Islam, but to Sumatra tradition—legitimacy bestowed by group acclamation—and conquest.

In a similar manner, Diane Lewis' study of the Menangkabau tribes of Negri Sembilan (Lewis 1960), who, I would argue, are of the same general heritage, indicates that the leader of the jungle peoples of the interior was regarded as the original source of political legitimacy, holding hereditary right over all the land. Groups of the tribe desiring to leave the jungle to settle coastal areas came to the 'head chief' (batin) asking his consent. As holder of hereditary titles the batin assigned the title penghulu (territorial chief) to one among the group, and gave him the duty of protecting the people of the tribe who chose to live 'outside' the jungle. Lewis notes that well into the twentieth century the Negri Semilan batin was still performing rituals of sacred installation, burning incense and ritually bathing penghulu, and was still regarded among coastal chiefs as the mythical source of their title.

The tale of Merah Silu follows this same pattern; it establishes legitimacy via the proper channels of Sumatra culture. The Hikayat Raja-Raja Pasai's description of the tribal council states:

> What shall we do about our friend Merah Silu?
> In my opinion it would be a good thing if we made
> him rāja. For in fact he is a rāja, and he is
> wealthy. Then we can all have confidence in
> him (Hill 1960:54, 115).

Merah Silu's wealth was due to his magical power[20] which allowed him to turn worms into gold. Being both royal—the text notes that Merah Silu, who was of the royal lineage of Semerlanga, was indeed rightfully a rāja—and rich was seemingly proof of Merah Silu's ability to promote the general well-being of the tribe. In a sense we are dealing with the anthropologists' concept of gift giving (Sahlins 1963), as Merah Silu was expected to lead his followers to prosperity. This he did by leading his tribal confederacy to victory over surrounding tribes, ultimately establishing control over the coast, and then reaching new levels of prosperity through trading with the international commercial community.

Interestingly, the Hikayat Raja-Raja Pasai informs us that some tribes in Merah Silu's confederacy did not like the new coastal habitat, because of an unwillingness to convert to Islam, and desired instead to return to the jungle.[21] Lewis' study of the Negri Sembilan tribes suggests similarly that the coming of Islam to the Malay Peninsula caused a permanent split of the inhabitants of the region, some choosing to become Muslims and to live in clearings near the banks of rivers, while the remainder retained their traditional jungle life style. The Hikayat notes that contact with the jungle groups continued and mentions royal journeys far up the Pasangan River to the populated interior. It was this interior to which the Pasai ruler looked not only as the source of his legitimacy, but also as the source of trade commodities.[22]

Merah Silu was able to make the Sumatra system work for him. He had been recognized as a rāja via the proper channels, and then had proven himself to be more than a normal chief. He next sought a new legitimacy to signify his very special stature, a search which ultimately lead him to his conversion, by divine intervention, to Islam.

Although international considerations undoubtedly prompted his conversion, Merah Silu's decision to convert may be seen as equally motivated by indigneous considerations. We may regard Islam as representing a new source of prestige for Pasai's rulers. Interestingly, a previous ruler—Sultan Maliku'l-Nasar—had seemingly converted, but was unable to make his power last. Merah Silu, who owed his initial legitimacy to his interior connections, succeeded.

In a sense, the conversion to Islam represented a significant break with the past heritage of Sumatra civilization. The memory of Srivijaya, as O.W. Wolters (1970) has shown, was still a real memory during this age, a tradition to which the Malacca sultans ultimately connected their genealogies. One may argue that the old prestige of Srivijaya was somewhat tarnished by the thirteenth century, and with it the Hindu-Buddhist tradition which was a significant part of Srivijaya's statecraft.[23] Islam could well have been regarded as a powerful new source of prestige, a faith which also benefited the ruler in allowing him to participate in intellectual exchanges with the West.[24] We may note that the world traveler Ibn Battuta, who stopped in Pasai in 1345/6, noticed little difference between his reception at Pasai and that he received at various South Asian courts. A number of the court aristocracy even held Indian titles (Hill 1960:75, 78).

Yet these elite with Indian titles rested on the real power of the Pasai domain, the chiefs (hulubalang and penghulu), and leaders of fighting forces (pendikar, pangilima, phalawan, and penggawa) who are conspicuous in the Hikayat Raja-Raja Pasai chronicle. These were the source of the new Pasai sultan's power, not only in a military sense, but also in the economic sense of enabling the effective flow of commercial commodities into and out of the Pasai port.

I am arguing that the Pasai ruler, despite his conversion to Islam, was still very much a Sumatra chief whose power depended equally upon maintaining his internal and external connections. Islam was the faith of the age, allowing the Pasai ruler a more positive stance in his relationship with the international maritime community which seems to have been dominated by Muslims during these times.[25] I feel, unlike Drewes, that A.H. Johns' argument is correct in stating that the introduction of the less legally oriented Sufi Islam along the trade channels during the late thirteenth century was critical in promoting Pasai's conversion (Johns 1961). In support of this argument one can cite Ibn Battuta's 1345 account that the Pasai ruler took a lively interest in the religious discussion of Sufi theologians resident at his court. The Sufi sect, as noted by Johns, was better able to utilize the existing elements of the pre-Islamic culture which seem so important to the Pasai ruler's political legitimacy. As described by most scholars of Sumatra culture, the conversion process made little real impact upon local social structure or belief (Hurgronje 1906; Winstedt 1925).

O.W. Wolters has explained that we need to view Malay society in terms of the international commercial environment, as "responding to various ever changing influences exerted by external circumstances of Asian trade" (Wolters 1970:3). Modifying Wolters' view, I am placing emphasis not so much on this external environment, but on the internal dynamic of

Sumatra statecraft which promoted the use of these external influences.[26]

Notes

1. This approach disagrees with that of Paul Wheatley in a recent essay (Wheatley 1975) which stresses the role of these external forms in the evolution of Southeast Asian statecraft. My position, as will be argued in the second part of this paper, is that the internal dynamic of existing forms of political organization structured the adoption of Indic and Sinic forms.

2. See for example the use of Polo's account in Schrieke (1957: 230-67).

3. McKinnon's excavations at his east coast site have produced 16 T'ang, 203 Sung, and 11 South Sung coins as well as two Buddha statues of apparent South Indian origin (McKinnon and Tengku Luckman Sinar 1974:73-4, 86).

4. See Pires (1944:142). Drewes suggests that Pires' informant was probably a Bengali and questions Pires' reliability (Drewes 1968:458). Supporting Fatimi's analysis is the fact that the great western traveler of the fourteenth century, Ibn Battuta, visited Samudra-Pasai in 1345, while following a maritime route from Bengal to China (Gibb 1957:273-6).

5. Ma'bar may be translated 'the place of crossing', recognizing the fact that from these ports of India's southeastern coast sailors 'crossed over' to China. See The Encyclopaedia of Islam (1960-) on Ma'bar. 'The place of crossing' may also refer to sailors 'crossing over' to Ceylon.

6. See the Shilappadikaram (Danielou 1965) as an example of South Indian evidence. O.W. Wolters (1970) has focused attention on the use of ankle bracelets as a standard part of the royal regalia of Malay chiefs. On the reliability of the Hikayat tradition see Wolter's presentation in support of the Srivijaya tradition as used in the Sejarah Melayu in the same book. As argued by A.H. Hill (1960), the earliest part of the Hikayat Raja-Raja Pasai—the sections used in this essay—had been composed by the early fourteenth century, suggesting suggesting some authenticity to early sections of the text. As opposed to Hill's dating, A. Teeuw (1964) and R. Roolvink

(1967) have argued that the Hikayat Raja-Raja Pasai and its origin myth were composed later than the earliest sections of the Sejarah Melayu. A more recent article by A. H. Johns (1975) discusses evidence for sixteenth century Islamic intellectual activity in Acheh on the northern Sumatra coast and suggests that Sumatra, and not Malacca, was the earliest center of Muslim culture in Southeast Asia.

7. Sayid Nathar Shah (969-1039), a famous maritime missionary, was said to have settled in the Cōḷa domain. Madurai, the center of Pāṇḍya polity, was said to have had its first Muslim settlers in 1050 (Marrison 1951).

8. In 977, an earthquake was said to have leveled the port of Sīraf. But its ruin was imminent due to the political turmoil associated with the 'Abbāsid dynasty's demise, which had shattered the internal commercial networks in the Persian Gulf area. As a result, Sohar in Oman became the chief port for Persian Gulf trade, and the trade of this area became secondary to that of the Red Sea region (Aubin 1959).

9. Unfortunately, as Goitein explains, medieval seafarers would send messages from Southeast Asia to the southeastern coast of India, but no further. This information was then forwarded in letters written in South India ports to Fūsṭat, leaving no direct communication of the merchants' experiences in Southeast Asia.

10. Supporting the Geniza records are several indigenous sources, most spectacularly a major eleventh century grant made to a Jewish merchant by a Kerala monarch (Kunjan Pillai 1970: 377-88).

11. See 'Letter no. 9' in Gottheil and Worrell (1927). Indigenous sources also note commercial contact between Malabar and Coromandel ports. Most notably, inscriptions in the major ports of the Cōḷa age record visits of merchants from Quilon and other Malabar ports (see Annual Report on Indian Epighraphy 1956-57:152, 157, and South Indian Inscriptions 10:651 as discussed in Hall, in press). Transpeninsular commercial routes also connected the two coasts.

12. The Chinese urged the Su-mu-ta official to have his port send

an envoy to China.

13. Husain and Sulaiman (Parker 1900).

14. Whitmore's study of the commodities of trade, based on Paul Wheatley's research (Wheatley 1959, 1961) supports this thesis. Whitmore notes that the Chinese had little knowledge of the products coming from the upper Malay west coast or the mainland areas of Bengal and Pagan, suggesting little direct commercial interaction between the main commercial route and this northern area of the Bay of Bengal.

15. This is the same name the Hikayat Raja-Raja Pasai assigned to an early Pasai king.

16. The Tamil Lexicon (1936:3441) lists levai as a priest in a mosque.

17. Nilakanta Sastri (1932). Other Tamil inscriptions, all dating to the thirteenth century, have been discovered at Batu Bapahat (Bandar Bapahat) near Suruaso, Padang Highlands (Krom 1931:410) and Porlak Dolok in the Padang Lawas area (Krom 1931:301).

18. L. Damais (1952:98-103): no. 275 (Bawang), no. 283 (Batu Bedil), and no. 289 (Ulu Belu).

19. This reference is from Sung sources (Groeneveldt 1960:15, n. 2). Scholars are not in agreement on the location of Ta-tsi.

20. Magical powers were emphasized as being held by all Sumatra chiefs. See Hall (1976b) for a discussion of early Sumatra chieftainship.

21. The Hikayat Raja-Raja Pasai notes that these people were called Gayau (Gayos) and they still inhabit the interior. Hurgronje (1906) also noted a tradition that the Gayos had once lived on the coast.

22. It may be assumed that the flow of goods to the Pasai port was organized as either a tribute system in which subordinate chiefs were required to supply the port with marketable commodities, or that the Pasai sultans came to control an

indigenous trade cycle in which people of the interior exchanged forest products they had collected for the imported goods which were available in the coastal port. See Bronson (this volume).

23 The success of Pasai seemingly caused the Sejarah Melayu to degrade Pasai because it was a rival to Malacca's claim to be the successor of Srivijaya.

24. This was of no small concern in earlier commercial dealings as may be noted in the gifts from Srivijaya's rulers to South Indian and Bengali Buddhist vihāras (Hall in press).

25. We may note that the South Indian Pāṇḍya king was also using Muslim trade envoys during this time of conversion, though the Pāṇḍya kings themselves were not Muslims. The Pāṇḍya king's personal servant was even said to have been a Muslim (Nilakanta Sastri 1939:155).

26. This essay needs support from archeological data—most notably data showing interrelationships between the coast and the interior. Secondly, further analysis of Sufi Islam and its relationship to the trade routes during the thirteenth century is demanded. On this second point, my own research on southern India will hopefully uncover evidence of Muslim commercial relationships with the South Indian coast, the area from which I have argued Islam spread to the archipelago.

A Chinese Silk Depicted at Caṇḍi Sèwu[1]

by

Hiram W. Woodward, Jr.

On the walls of Caṇḍi Sèwu in central Java there appear depictions of a fabric that can be identified as a Chinese silk (Plates 9-11). The Buddhist temple of Candi Sèwu is now associated with an inscription of 792 A.D. (Soekmono 1965:42; van Lohuizen-de Leeuw 1974). This was a time during which Chinese ceramics were reaching Java in some quantity (Wisseman, this volume), and from literary evidence it is known that Chinese silks had been passing through Southeast Asia for centuries (Wolters 1967:33, 41, 78); it is unlikely, however, that archaeological excavation will even uncover more than the barest traces of an imported fabric. A fabric recreated in stone, however, may tell us more than would actual textile fragments or impressions, for it documents the local response to the imported object.

The Depiction

Framed in a plain molding and carved in low relief is a 110-centimeter-wide section[2] (Plates 10, 11) encompassing three roundels horizontally and eight vertically. A pattern repeats itself four times, after every two of the horizontal rows. Half the roundels are filled by rosettes, and half by animals identifiable as lions and deer; between the roundels are foliate Greek crosses—cusped lozenges surrounded by four floriated balls and, extending from the four corners, foliate arms. The seeming universality of the overall design is due to the long-established interchange between Chinese and Middle Eastern pattern (Meister 1970) and to the fact that during the period in question a network of trade in fabrics covered all of Eurasia. Indeed, the silk whose overall dimensions and structure best match the Caṇḍi Sèwu fabric is not Chinese at all, but Sogdian (though belonging to a group which shows these Central Asian traders succumbing to Chinese influences) and preserved in the Collegiate Church of Notre Dame, Huy, France (Shepherd and

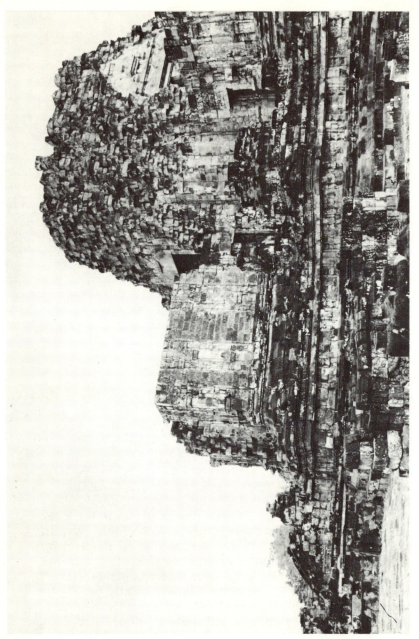

Plate 9. Temple at Chaṇḍi Sèwu.

Plate 10. Portion of temple's exterior wall.

Plate 11. Rosette and Animal Roundels.

Henning 1959:17, Fig. 1). This "ram silk" has three roundels across its weft, and its width is 122 centimeters. The Chinese, however, were weaving silks with a width closer to that of the Sèwu panels; 115 centimeters is attested by a Shosoin fragment which has five medallions across its weft (Shosoin Office 1963-64 (1):vii, 5, Plate 6).

It is these Shosoin fragments, preserved since 756 A.D. in Nara, Japan, that provide the most evidence about eighth-century Chinese silks. Features of the Caṇḍi Sèwu fabric which, on the basis of the Shosoin textiles, can be isolated as Chinese are the wide foliate borders of the roundels and the presence inside roundels of rosettes (Shosoin Office 1964-64 (1):Plates 1, 3, 4, 6, etc.). The rosette also appears as a primary motif on a silk datable to 778 A.D. found by the People's Republic of China near Turfan in Sinkiang, along the silk road in Central Asia (Watson 1974:no. 253). In addition, Sèwu's encirclement of the rosette by secondary flowers is paralleled in this piece. The same kind of encirclement, which seems to be peculiarly Chinese, can be found on late T'ang silver bowls (Singer 1971: Fig. 87). As for the animals, they cannot be matched in any surviving Chinese fabric. Evidence from metalwork, however— in an example from the Ho-chia-ts'un hoard, probably dating from before 756 A.D. (Wen-hua 1972:46; cf. Fontein and Wu 1973:176)—suggests that such a lion, with its elongated tail, might well have appeared in a roundel on a silk. (Another long-tailed lion—a stone lion apparently associated with a Tibetan king who died in 842 [Richardson 1963:Fig. 7] provides tantalizing evidence of the spread of such motifs.) The other animal at Sèwu was perhaps seen by the Javanese as a deer, for the temple, after all, is Buddhist, and a ninth-century Javanese inscription may even refer to a deer-patterned cloth (Śivakidang; Sarkar 1971-72 (1):105, 110). The Chinese model could have depicted a deer (Shosoin Office 1963-64 (1):no. 67; (2):no. 8) or, conceivably, a gazelle, an animal common in Sinkiang (see also Gyllensvärd 1957:Figs. 9 o, 71 b and c); it is easier, however, to find similarly seated animals complete with roundel among Middle Eastern prototypes, in metalwork, for instance (Jettmar 1967:Fig. 131, now in the Hermitage), or wool tapestry (Grabar 1967:Fig. 66). Both examples depict ibexes.

Continued Middle Eastern influence on China is understandable when it is remembered that during the late eighth

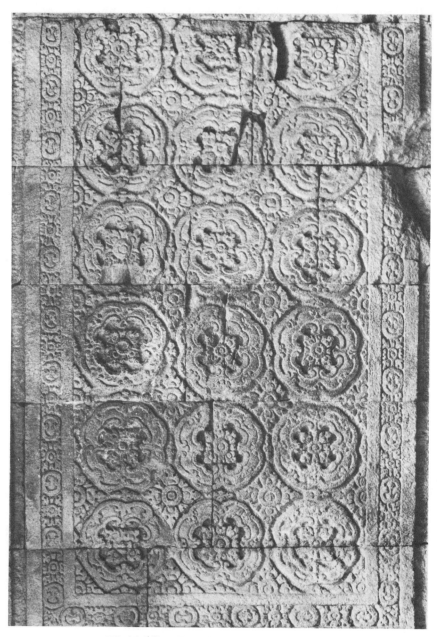

Plate 12. Rosettes at Prambanan.

Plate 13. Circles and Medallions at Prambanan

century huge quantities of Chinese silks were being traded to the then powerful Uighurs of Central Asia for horses (Mackerras 1969). Such trade would have stimulated stylistic developments in directions attractive to the Chinese themselves (cf. Schafer 1963:196-97). The silk depicted at Sèwu might be viewed as one that could equally well have been traded to the Uighurs. It is a document, too, that enriches our knowledge of Chinese textile design, quite independently of what it can tell us about ancient Java.

Associations

The panel at Caṇḍi Sèwu has the proportions and dimensions of a real piece of cloth; an analysis of motifs shows the depicted cloth, in the present state of our knowledge, to have been Chinese (and if not, at least to have been based on a Chinese textile). But other relationships must be explored as well.

On either side of the central panel in Plate 10 are narrower panels, similarly framed, of lacework. What could be represented is, firstly, another textile pattern; secondly, cut-out (e.g., Shosoin Office 1963-64 (2):nos. 9, 10) and stitched-together pieces of cloth that might hang on or above an altar (see Pal 1969:Fig. 39 for a nineteenth-century Tibetan descendant); or, finally, the possible inspiration for the latter, namely elaborate hangings or screens comprised of strung-together garlands of flowers. Similar lacework appears inside a false window on the exterior walls of the ninth-century temple of Plaosan (author's photograph), suggesting that the roundels and the lacework at Sèwu can be supposed to cover apertures in the temple walls.

Both lacework and roundel patterns appear again inside the principal sanctuary of the still later ninth-century Siva Temple at Prambanan (Bernet Kempers 1959:Pl. 157). Roundel patterns appear in two forms. In one (Pl. 12) are rosettes, simpler than Sèwu's, inside broad frames comprised of lobed C-scrolls. In the other (Pl. 13) are circles and eight-pointed medallions that look as if they could have been stamped.

Although similar forms are not unknown in T'ang Chinese

metalwork decor (Gyllensvärd 1957:Fig. 80), we are probably dealing here with a representation of a textile of local manufacture. A figure in the Śiva temple Rāmāyaṇa reliefs wears a sarong with a similar design (Stutterheim 1925b (2): Fig. 37; cf. Solyom n.d.:16).

Modern ethnographic evidence suggests at least one possible answer to the question of why actual cloths should be depicted in such spots. In Bali a corpse is carried to the cremation ground in a tower that is both the formal and connotative descendant of the ancient Hindu-Javanese caṇḍi. Part way up these towers, where a caṇḍi's sanctuary would lie, is the pavilion where the corpse is placed, and valuable pieces of cloth are hung there (Wirz 1928:40 and plates; Covarrubias 1937: 359 and illustration opposite 375; Hooykaas 1973: ill. v. 4). If these Balinese towers had counterparts in ancient Java, then the depiction of fabrics on the stone caṇḍi, which are thought to have had funerary associations (Stutterheim 1931), may have been the result of imitating aspects of towers made of perishable materials, adorned with fabrics, and used in funerals. The apertures or windows covered by the patterns at Sèwu would be like the openings in a Balinese tower's pavilion; inside the Śiva Temple sanctuary we would have the corpse's view of the inside of the same pavilion. If these connections are legitimate, it might even be asked whether the ancient perishable towers had ancestors predating the construction of stone sanctuaries in Java (cf. Stutterheim 1956). As for the lacework pattern, found at both Sèwu and the Śiva temple, if it is to be traced back to a real floral screen, there may exist a tenuous descendant in Malaya. "In each case the bier is covered with a pall...of as good colored cloth...as may be obtainable. There are generally two or three of these coverings, and floral decorations are sometimes thrown across them, the blossoms of the areca-palm and the scented pandanus being woven into exquisite floral strips...about three feet long by two fingers in breadth, and laid at short intervals across the pall" (Skeat 1900:403).

Culture Change

What kind of theory best helps us to understand the adoptions, representations, and shifts that have so far been described? One simple model would have an entrepreneur, in a situation of actual or potential conflict, attaching a foreign object to a known category and thereby redefining his relationship to others; the category becomes expanded and perhaps transformed (cf. Geertz 1963b:147-50). The entrepreneur here would be the builder or builders of the temple; it is their imported silk which expands the category of funerary textiles, and by representing this silk on a temple the builder makes a statement about control of the world of merchants and luxury goods.

Thinking of this entrepreneur as the king himself, rather than as a merchant guild under the protection of the king, brings to mind some Thai material. "Porcelain, carved woodwork and other such items," wrote a seventeenth-century Persian observer, "are brought to Siam from Japan and China but this kind of merchandise is all bought up by the lofty king's administration. The administration buys it in one big purchase and eventually sells it somewhere else at a great profit" (O'Kane 1972:154). But a mythic statement about this kind of reality has more relevance: a nineteenth-century account of royal festivals says that the victory of the king's boat, the Viṣṇu boat, in ceremonial boat races will bring a plenitude of imported goods; the victory of the Lakṣmī boat, the queen's boat, a surfeit of local produce (Nopphamāt 1964:351). These masculine/feminine polarities call to mind others, polarities that can provide a conceptual context for the Caṇḍi Sèwu and Śiva Temple fabrics. The temple visitor, first, is masculine; the temple itself is maternal, is specifically the womb of origin. In a Javanese bilingual inscription of 824 A.D., secondly, the side in Old Javanese (functioning here as a "father tongue") is concerned with the donation of fields to a temple and the presentation of objects—including pieces of cloth—to the witnesses who seal the contract, while matters concerning the royal foundation of the temple itself and of its images are found on the Sanskrit side (Sarkar 1971-72 (1):64-75). The Chinese silk at Sèwu, finally, is recognizably foreign and hangs in an opening; some decades later the cloths at the Śiva Temple no longer look foreign and hang in the womb of the sanctuary.

Notes

1. I wish to thank Jan Wisseman and others at the conference for their helpful comments on an earlier version of this paper.

2. The panel was kindly measured for me by Barbara Wagner and Forrest McGill.

nine, while the number nine was written as it is now. Thirty-nine, while much time checking figures to be sure that the sevens and the nines were correctly coded. In the process, I overlooked a calendar error. I did not discover this until January 8, 1978. In 1889 the Customs Service shifted its accounting from the lunar month, lunar year, to the solar month - following the European pattern, while retaining the lunar. April to March, year. Material coded for January, 1889, should have been coded for January, 1890, while material coded for January and February of 1890 should have been coded for January and February of 1891.

In addition to the calendar error, I also uncovered three other minor errors. The set of cards for 1885 and 1887 each contained one card coded as Western which should have been coded as Chinese. Also, a check on Western firms showed that Arracan had shipped rice in 1889. The Thai in 1889 recorded the name 'Arracan' as 'Hereken' while in 1890 they wrote it down as 'Arikaen'.

All cards have been corrected and the data rerun. The total amount of rice exported in 1889 has dropped from 5,119,040 piculs to 4,503,370 piculs while that for 1890 has dropped from 6,421,341 piculs to 6,346,030 piculs. However, the percentage changes, in terms of the amounts of rice shipped by ethnic groups and by individual brokers, has been very small, 2.1% at the greatest.

Percent Rice Shipped by Ethnic Group,
New Figures

	1885	1886	1887	1888	1889	1890
Indian/Malay	-	-	.1	-	.1	-
Thai	4.9	.6	2.5	2.3	2.6	3.2
Chinese	31.9	40.1	36.2	29.7	24.1	34.8
Western	63.2	59.3	61.2	68.0	73.2	62.0

The calendar changes, then, do not involve any change in the analysis presented in my article, "Ethnic Participation in the Export of Thai Rice, 1885-1890."

I am sending the second article, based on the Customs Service records, "The Thai Rice Trade, 1885-1890," to the Journal of the Siam Society. If the editor of the JSS is willing, I will ask him to publish a complete set of corrected tables for "Ethnic Participation..." as an appendix to "The Thai Rice Trade, 1885-1890."

Constance M. Wilson
February 1978

Ethnic Participation in the Export of Thai Rice, 1885-1890

by

Constance M. Wilson

There exists in the National Archives, Bangkok, Thailand, a set of documents which contains more information about the export of Thai rice between 1885 and 1890 than any other known set of records. These materials, located in the files of Krasuang Phra Khlang Mahasombat (Ministry of the Royal Treasury), numbers Kh. 6 and Kh. 17. 2k, consist of monthly accounts of duties charged to rice exports from Bangkok and Chachoengsao. The accounts begin March 16, 1885, and end December 30, 1890. A thorough search of related files failed to yield additional records. The set of documents is not complete. Accounts are missing for the period from June 21 to July 20, 1887, for December, 1889, and for March and October, 1890. Thus, we have a complete set of accounts for 1886 and 1888, with partial records for 1885, 1887, 1889, and 1890.

These accounts could well be the Thai version of the records which were the original data for the well known British Consular Reports on Thai Trade, reports which for several decades have been the basis of economic studies of Thailand. In the single instance where a direct comparison can be made, for the year 1888, the total figure for rice exports in the Thai accounts is in close accord with the total figure given in the British Consular Report for 1890. The total number of piculs (one picul equals 133 and one-third pounds, 15 piculs equal one short ton, 16.8 piculs equal one British long ton) exported in 1888 according to the Thai records was 7,588,315 piculs. The British Consular Report for 1890, which contains a comparative table of totals for 1888, 1889 and 1890, reports total exports of 7,553,095 piculs for that year.

The Thai accounts provide far greater detail than do the British Consular Reports. The Thai accounts are excellent records, the information in them including the date of the shipment; the name of the person or firm paying the export duty; the type of vessel; the name of the vessel; its tonnage and flag; its destination; the amount of rice shipped; and the amount of tax paid. This information can be used in a number of different ways. The main concern of this paper, however, is a single subject, ethnic participation in the export trade in Thai rice between 1885 and 1890. Other studies, based on this data, are being reserved for future articles.

The titles and names of the export brokers and business firms recorded in these accounts idicate the ethnic group to which these people belong: Indian/Malay, Chinese, Thai, or European. Thai titles belong to people who are either Thai or who are assimilated Chinese who have been granted a Thai title. Chinese are identified by the use of the word chin (Chinese), Malays and Indian by the work kaek, Europeans by such terms as Captain or Mr. The name of the rice broker can also serve to identify his ethnic group. It is, then, a relatively simple matter to determine, in terms of the total amount of rice shipped, or in terms of the percentage of rice shipped, the degree to which various ethnic groups participated in the export of rice from Bangkok and Chachoengsao.

This information is presented in Table 1, Ethnic Participation in the Thai Rice Trade, 1885-1890, which is based on total exports for that period. Examination of the figures given clearly illustrates the preeminent position of the large European and Chinese business houses. During this period, European firms accounted for more than half of all exports of rice from Bangkok and Chachoengsao. The European share ranges from a low of 59.3% in 1886 to a high of 71.6% in 1889. The Chinese share is much less; it ranges from a low of 25.5% in 1889 to a high of 40.1% in 1886. The Chinese were in competition with European rice brokers; when the European business firms increased their share of the export trade, the Chinese share declined and vice versa. Throughout this period, the Thai share of the export trade was very small. However, it was not as minimal as that of the Indians and Malays.

Further breakdowns of this information are available. Table 2 examines the export activities of the business houses and the more important individual traders. The names of the firms and individual traders selected for inclusion in Table 2 were determined by a frequency count. If the name of an export firm or trader turned up five or more times it was listed in Table 2. All other traders with the amounts of rice that they shipped have been dropped from the analysis. Although the selection of the number five as a cut-off point was an arbitrary decision, it has some rationality for it is a number that would cover all individual traders and firms who shipped out an average of at least one load of rice per year during the five year ten month period under study. This cut-off point does indicate the range in the degree of activity involved: that of large, well organized firms; middle level brokers; and marginal traders. Total exports for the Thai, Chinese, and European trade have been brought over from Table 1 in order to provide a base for comparisons. The position of the Indians and Malays in the rice trade was so small that they have been dropped from further consideration. The percentages given in Table 2 refer to the percent of total exports per year handled by a firm or individual broker.

Table 3 examines further the export activities of the firms and individuals listed in Table 2. The trade of each firm and each individual is broken down by the area to which rice exports were sent. The percentages in this case refer to the percent of a firm's or individual's trade with a specific region.

Close examination of Tables 2 and 3 reveals that four types of business activity were represented in the export of Thai rice: (1) that of large European business houses, usually incorporated stock companies with home firms in Europe; (2) large Chinese brokerages, some of which may also have been stock companies, often with bases or branches in Hong Kong or Singapore; (3) small marginal Chinese and Thai brokerages; and (4) private individuals.

European Firms

The most important brokerages are clearly the large European firms: Borneo Company, A. Markwald and Company, and Windsor Rose and Company. Four smaller European business firms also took part in the export of Thai rice: Arracan, Buthmann, Windsor Clarke, and Jucker Sigg and Company. Most of the business houses had other interests in addition to the export of rice. Arracan, Borneo, A. Markwald, Windsor Clarke and Windsor Rose were agents for various insurance companies in Bangkok. Arracan, Borneo, Markwald and Windsor Rose had their own rice mills and may well have shipped their own product. Arracan, Borneo, Buthmann, Markwald, Windsor Clarke and Windsor Rose all had merchant houses in Bangkok. The export of rice, therefore, was but one of their many business activities.

The largest exporter of rice was the firm of Windsor Rose and Company. The Directory for Bangkok and Siam for 1892 (1892:315) lists the head of the company, T. Windsor, as residing in London. In Bangkok, Windsor Rose acted as agent for four steamship companies: the Scottish Oriental Steamship Company, Ltd.; the Ocean Steam Ship Company; La Compagnie Nantaise; and Bradley and Company of Swatow, China.

In 1890 the Scottish Oriental Steamship Company, Ltd., had seven steamers running on regular schedules between Bangkok and Hong Kong: the Mongkut, Kong Beng, Taichow, Phra Chom Klao, Phra Chula Chom Klao, Devawongse, and the Chao Fa. Five of these steamers bear the names and titles of Thai royalty. The agent for the Scottish Steamship Company in Hong Kong was Yuen Fat Hong. The Ocean Steam Ship Company, home office in Liverpool, operated four ships on the Bangkok-Singapore run: the Hecate, Hecuba, Hydra, and Medusa. The agent for the Ocean Steam Ship Company in Singapore was W. Mansfield and Company. Both British companies carried passengers as well as cargo.

Little information is known about La Compagnie Nantaise. Only a single vessel is listed for it in The Directory for Bangkok and Siam for 1892, the J. B. Say which ran between Bangkok and Saigon. Bradley and Company of Swatow owned four vessels in 1892, the Nanshan and Pakshan show up regularly in the Thai records on the Bangkok-Singapore route. The Tongshan and Sishan ran between Bangkok and Hong Kong. Guthrie and Company was their agent in Singapore; the Hong Kong agent is not known.

The bulk of the rice exports of Windsor Rose, over 90 percent, went to Hong Kong and Singapore. Windsor Rose sent little rice to Europe, zero to 7 percent of its exports.

Indeed, Windsor Rose had a major role in the trade with Hong Kong and Singapore. In Table 4, figures for total rice exports on the part of all firms and individual traders were obtained for Hong Kong and Singapore by a second breakdown procedure. It appears that Windsor Rose controlled from 46 percent to 58 percent of all rice exported from Thailand to Hong Kong and from 20 percent to 63 percent of all rice exported from Thailand to Singapore.

A. Markwald and Company, established in 1858, also served as Bangkok agent for a number of steamship agencies: Norddeutscher Lloyd of Bremen; Union Line of London; Kingsing Line of Hamburg; Gellatly, Hankey, Swell and Company of Antwerp and Bordeaux; and the Austro-Hungarian Lloyd firm of Trieste. Norddeutscher Lloyd, subsidized by the German government, was responsible for the Imperial German mail steamers which ran from Bremen to Nagasaki. Its ship, the Schwalbe, ran a regular route between Bangkok and Singapore. A. Markwald apparently owned one vessel itself, the Suriyawong or Sury Wongse, which ran between Bangkok and Singapore. In Singapore, Behn, Meyer and Company handled the vessels sent there by A. Markwald. Most of A. Markwald's exports of Thai rice went to Singapore, 63 percent in 1885, 85 percent in 1886. Although the percentage of Markwald rice reaching Singapore declined in 1887, the amount of rice sent was nearly the same as in 1886. A. Markwald also had a large European trade. In addition, it sent rice to Java and to Australia.

Borneo Company, Ltd., founded in 1856, is an old name in Thailand. In 1892 the head office of the Borneo Company was in London with branches in Bangkok, Sarawak, Singapore, Batavia, and Manchester. In addition to managing the vessels of the home office, Borneo Company was also the Bangkok agent for Les Messageries Maritimes and the Meinam Flotilla Company. In spite of its long time position in Bangkok, the Borneo Company controlled only a small part of the rice trade, from 3 percent to 10 percent depending on the year. Although most of its trade in 1885 and 1886 was with Singapore, in 1887 and 1888 the firm did not send any rice at all to Singapore; all of its rice went to Europe.

The smaller Europen firms, Arracan, Jucker Sigg and Company, and Windsor Clarke, as far as information is available, did not act as agents for other large international shipping companies in Bangkok. There is no clear indication that they owned any vessels of their own. Their overall position in the rice trade was a precarious one. Arracan loaded a total of four vessels in 1890 and is included in Table 3 only because the amount of rice it shipped was relatively high. Jucker Sigg and Company collapsed and went out of business in 1890. Only Windsor Clarke, after a slow start, was able to increase its exports.

None of the above firms were involved in any local coastal trade. Their rice went to Singapore, Hong Kong, Vietnam, Java, Bombay, and Europe. The firm of Buthmann was an exception to this common practice. Its business was entirely local. Although its exports in Tables 2 and 3 are small in size, the tables do not give an accurate picture of Buthmann's role in Thai trade. Captain H. Buthmann is listed in The Directory for Bangkok and Siam for 1892 (1892:296) as manager of the Chantaboon Agency, a merchant firm. Business must have developed well. Six years later The Directory for Bankok and Siam for 1898 carried in its back pages a large advertisement announcing:

> The Buthmann Line of River Steam Boats and Tow Boats.... Regularly Plying Between BANGKOK, PAKLAT, PAKNAM... ETC..., ETC. which have been expecially appointed to convey H.S.M.'s Mails and may be confidently relied on for their regularity and despatch.

The advertisement gives the names of twenty-seven river steamers and four tow boats. The firm had found a niche in Thailand where it could do very well for itself.

The existence of such a firm as Buthmann places the European business houses in an unusual position in Thai shipping. Europeans were the only ethnic group in Thailand to play a role in water transport at every level: local, regional, and international. Neither the Thai nor the Chinese held this position.

Chinese Firms

The second group of rice brokers operating in Bangkok and Chachoengsao were the larger Chinese agencies: Nguan Heng Yu, Huang Li, Ma Hua, Ban Hong, and Lao Bang Seng. All of the Chinese business houses were tied into either Hong Kong or Singapore or both. They did not load any vessels bound for Europe, although, on occasion, they did load ships heading for Manila or for the United States. At times, they were also involved in local trade.

Among the Chinese agencies Nguan Heng Yu held a unique position, for it did very little independent business of its own. Nguan Heng Yu was located at Chachoengsao, on the Gulf of Thailand. In the early part of 1885 Windsor Rose had a branch at Chachoengsao, but that branch was closed shortly after October 13, 1885. Nearly two years later, April 22, 1887, Nguan Heng Yu opened a second branch at Chachoengsao, giving it one branch in the tambon of Thungchang and one in the tambon of Saimun. Nguan Heng Yu's main business was the loading of the vessels of other exporters by lighter outside the sandbar across the Chao Phraya River. Most of its rice went into the holds of vessels managed by Windsor Rose. Nguan Heng Yu also supplied rice for the Hong Kong trade of Huang Li and Ma Hua. The bulk of Nguan Heng Yu's rice went to Hong Kong, a much smaller portion to Singapore.

As is shown in Table 4 those firms which worked together in a cooperative relationship, which is defined here as the joint loading of a vessel while it is in port, dominated the rice export trade from Thailand to Hong Kong and Singapore. Windsor Rose and Nguan Heng Yu, who worked very closely together, handled from 65 percent to 86 percent of all Thai rice exports to Hong Kong. These two firms, plus two other firms, Huang Li and Ma Hua, who also cooperated with Nguan Heng Yu, controlled 87 percent of the rice exports to Hong Kong in 1885 and from 94 percent to 99 percent during the next five years. There was little room for an independent entrepreneur on the Hong Kong route.

Trade with Singapore was more open. Windsor Rose controlled most of the rice exports to Singapore. The contribution of Nguan Heng Yu was very small. Together, the two exporters controlled 29 percent of the rice exports to Singapore in 1885 and 62 percent in 1886. During the first three years of the period under study, 1885-1887, Nguan Heng Yu also helped load the Suriyawong, a Markwald vessel on the Singapore route. This cooperative relationship ended in 1887 and Nguan Heng Yu ceased to do business with A. Markwald and Company. During 1888, 1889, and 1890, Nguan Heng Yu also loaded some vessels for Phraya Samutburanurak, but the amount of rice involved was quite small.

As with the European houses, the strength and durability of the Chinese agencies appears to have been related to outside contacts and to business activities other than shipping. The agency of Huang Li (Wang Lee in the Western press) was especially active. Huang Li was agent for the Ontai Insurance Company. The brokerage firm had its own rice mills, one of which employed a European engineer, and it possessed a branch in Hong Kong. Most of Huang Li's rice went to Hong Kong. The agency controlled from 8 percent to 20 percent of all Thai rice exports to Hong Kong. It often worked with Nguan Heng Yu.

Although it appears to have been a fairly large and stable export firm, little information can be located about Ma Hua which was listed as Koh Mah Wah and Company in the Western press. In addition to its Singapore and Hong Kong trade, Ma Hua also loaded ships bound for Manila and for the United States.

Ban Hong was the Bangkok branch of Low Sam and Company of Singapore, serving as agent for the vessel Borneo, a 440 ton steamship under Captain Bullan. Although the agency managed only a very small portion of the total export trade, its share of the Singapore trade was somewhat larger: 9 percent in 1885; 10 percent in 1886; 8 percent in 1887; 6 percent in 1888; 5 percent in 1889; and 2 percent in 1890.

Lao Bang Seng had its own rice mill in Bangkok, and it also employed a European as an engineer. Lao Bang Seng worked with Ban Seng and Company in Singapore. The two agencies managed the S.S. Ban Seng Guan, a vessel of 551 tons under Captain John E. Geary. Lao Bang Seng's share of the Singapore trade was 3 percent in 1885; 1 percent in 1886; 10 percent in 1887; 9 percent in 1888; 9 percent in 1889; and 9 percent in 1890. By 1888 Lao Bang Seng had overtaken Ban Hong in exports to Singapore. The agency illustrates how a small firm, with its own rice mill and careful management, could provide a stable business with return for its operators.

Small Chinese and Thai Firms

The marginal operations include both Chinese and Thai businesses. The Chinese agencies of Heng Li, Hok Po, and Thai Hua Li were not very successful in this period. They do not appear to be integrated into other networks, neither in terms of the Thai rice trade—none appear to have had their own rice mill—nor in terms of external regional contacts.

Thai trade was occasional and irregular. The Thai rice brokerages shared the same pool of vessels, the <u>Diamond City</u>, the <u>Queen of England</u>, the <u>Independence</u>, the <u>Foochow</u>, the <u>Fortune</u>, the <u>Charoen Wattana</u>, and others. The Thai do not appear to have cooperated in the management and loading of these vessels. The vessels moved around a lot, going from one Thai brokerage to another, at times showing up at the larger European or Chinese houses. There does not seem to be any pattern to their movements, with one destination this month, another the next month. Although Thai rice exporters did send rice to Hong Kong and to Singapore, they did not compete successfully with either the Chinese or European companies on these routes. Nor do they appear to have operated on a regular schedule along the Thai coast.

The main Thai rice exporters were Phraya Boribunranakosakon, Luang Charoenratchathan, Phraya Phisanphonphanit, Phraya Samutburanurak (an inspector in the Thai Rice Department of the Customs House Service), Luang Wisetsunglakakon, and Phraya Anukunsiamnukit (who might not have been Thai as the word <u>siam</u> was often included in titles given to non-Thai as mark of royal favor) who was closely linked with the vessel <u>Singapore</u>, a British steamer out of the Singapore house of Kin Ching and Company. (The Thai accounts sometimes use the long form of these titles, sometimes the short forms.)

Private Individuals

The fourth type of trader, the individual ship owners who dealt directly with the tax collector, form a large group although their share of exports was small. Most were masters of Chinese junks from places like Hainan Island and Amoy. There were a few Malays (or Indians) from Kelantan and Trengganu, turned up in Bangkok every year or two.

General Observations

Unless an individual or business firm had large amounts of capital, outside contacts, and its own rice mill, it was difficult to enter the rice export trade and to remain active in it. All of the major export houses, European and Chinese, appear to have met these qualifications. The small businessman, regardless of his ethnic group, had little chance. The risks of engaging in trade were increased by the perversity of the weather; 1884, 1885, and 1888 were poor years for the rice crop. Low production affected the amount of rice which could be exported after the harvest. In the poor years, export houses needed their rice mills and their local contacts in order to obtain enough rice to stay in business. In good years, when large crops were available, vessels came in from China, Singapore, and Europe. The trade of all agencies, even the marginal ones, improved. The large, integrated firms were able to maintain their position year after year; the smaller firms could not, so that there was a continual overturn in this group.

As has been noted above, cooperative arrangements between export companies did exist, the most important arrangement being the one between Windsor Rose and Nguan Heng Yu, particularly in the trade with Hong Kong. Nguan Heng Yu, with its location at Chachoengsao, was the center of all cooperative arrangements. The firm also worked with Huang Li, Ma Hua and, for brief periods, with A. Markwald and Praya Samutburanurak. There is no evidence of cooperation between Windsor Rose and any other firm. There is a possibility, however, that some cooperation took place between Huang Li and Ma Hua. The cooperative arrangements on the Hong Kong trade enabled four Bangkok trading companies virtually to monopolize rice exports to that city and to control a large share of Thai rice exports to Singapore.

The Thai, faced with the integrated nature of the large export houses with their capital resources, their rice mills, and a scattering of Europeans who turned up in Bangkok, purchased a single load of rice, and then moved on. There is some evidence that certain Chinese, mostly from Hainan Island, their external contacts, and their cooperative arrangements, particularly between the Europeans and the Chinese, had little chance to develop a modern export trade of their own. The earlier trading alliances between the Thai and the Chinese in the export of rice no longer existed. British control over Hong Kong and over Singapore made it more profitable for the Chinese to change their allegiances and to develop new trading arrangements, leaving the Thai outside. It is probable that the Thai role in the Thai export trade, in rice and in other goods, declined in the last half of the nineteenth century.

Sources

Thai Materials

"Phasi Khao Krungtheb lae Chachoengsao," in Records of the Krasuang Phra Klang Mahasonbat, R. 5. Kh. (Ko kwai) 6 and Kh. 17. 2k (Bangkok: National Archives).

English Language Materials, Official Sources

Foreign Office, Annual Series, no. 939 (1891).

Diplomatic and Consular Reports on Trade and Finance (Siam).

Report for the Year 1890 on the Trade, etc., of Siam (London: Harrison and Sons), 1891.

Siam, No. 1 (1886).

Commercial Report by Her Majesty's Acting Consul in Siam for the Year 1885 (London: Harrison and Sons), 1886.

English Language Materials, Other Sources

Bangkok Calendar (Bangkok), 1871, 1873.

The Directory for Bangkok and Siam for 1892 (Bangkok Times office), pp. 296-315 and the advertisements on the back pages.

The Directory for Bangkok and Siam for 1898 (Bangkok Times office), advertisements on the back pages.

Siam Weekly Advertiser (February 21, 1885-August 7, 1886), sections on "Foreign Shipping in Port."

The Straits Times (1890), advertisements of steamship companies and reports of shipping arrivals and departures.

Table 8

Ethnic Participation in the Thai Rice Trade, 1885 through 1890

Ethnic Group	1885			1886			1887		
	Piculs	Tons	%	Piculs	Tons	%	Piculs	Tons	%
Indian/Malay	107	7	-	-	-	-	2,427	162	-
Thai	144,895	9,660	4.9	21,161	1,411	.6	156,234	10,416	2.5
Chinese	928,206	61,880	31.5	1,466,565	97,771	40.1	2,249,463	149,964	36.2
Individual Europeans	-	-	-	-	-	-	-	3	-
Western Firms	1,869,497	124,633	63.6	2,167,602	144,506	59.3	3,811,797	254,120	61.3
TOTAL	2,942,705	196,180	100.0	3,655,328	243,688	100.0	6,219,973	414,665	100.0

Ethnic Group	1888			1889			1890		
	Piculs	Tons	%	Piculs	Tons	%	Piculs	Tons	%
Indian/Malay	5,026	335	-	3,889	259	.1	3,314	221	.1
Thai	173,114	11,541	2.3	144,923	9,662	2.8	226,987	15,132	3.5
Chinese	2,251,794	150,120	29.7	1,304,727	86,982	25.5	2,101,235	140,082	32.7
Individual Europeans	-	-	-	-	-	-	-	-	-
Western Firms	5,158,381	343,892	68.0	3,665,501	244,367	71.6	4,089,805	272,654	63.7
TOTAL	7,588,315	505,888	100.0	5,119,040	341,270	100.0	6,421,341	428,089	100.0

Table 9

Ethnic Participation in the Thai Rice Trade by
Individuals and Business Firms, 1885 through 1890

	1885			1886			1887		
	Piculs	Tons	%	Piculs	Tons	%	Piculs	Tons	%
Thai	144,895	9,660	4.9	21,161	1,411	.6	156,234	10,416	2.5
Phraya Anukun	-	-	-	-	-	-	-	-	-
Luang Boribun	70,383	4,692	2.4	9,133	609	.2	143,542	9,569	2.3
Luang Charoen	3,538	236	.1	3,050	203	.1	7,338	489	.1
Phraya Phisan	37,760	2,517	1.3	5,567	371	.2	3,756	250	.1
Phraya Samut	-	-	-	-	-	-	-	-	-
Luang Wiset	-	-	-	-	-	-	-	-	-
Chinese	928,206	61,880	31.5	1,466,565	97,771	40.1	2,249,463	149,964	36.2
Nguan Heng Yu	313,907	20,927	10.7	506,762	33,784	13.9	695,429	46,362	11.2
Ban Hong	104,314	6,954	3.5	105,440	7,029	2.9	100,451	6,697	1.6
Heng Li	9,447	630	.3	30,429	2,029	.8	25,004	1,667	.4
Hok Po	74,723	4,982	2.5	20,664	1,378	.6	37,352	2,490	.6
Huang Li	218,623	14,575	7.4	443,368	29,558	12.1	785,325	52,355	12.6
Lao Bang Seng	39,456	2,630	1.3	14,143	943	.4	126,860	8,457	2.0
Ma Hua	127,369	8,491	4.3	332,256	22,150	9.1	385,072	25,671	6.2
Thai Hua Li	-	-	-	-	-	-	31,176	2,078	.5
Western Firms	1,869,497	124,633	63.6	2,167,602	144,506	59.3	3,811,797	254,120	61.3
A. Markwald and Co.	318,471	21,231	10.8	226,041	15,069	6.2	500,034	33,336	8.0
Arracan	-	-	-	-	-	-	-	-	-
Borneo Co.	289,289	19,286	9.8	123,311	8,221	3.4	234,245	15,616	3.8
Buthmann	-	-	-	-	-	-	-	-	-
Jucker Sigg and Co.	129,185	8,612	4.4	-	-	-	204,047	13,603	3.3
Windsor Clarke	-	-	-	-	-	-	54,256	3,617	.9
Windsor Rose	1,115,557	74,370	37.9	1,818,250	121,217	49.7	2,806,753	187,117	45.1

259

Table 9 (continued)

	1888			1889			1890		
	Piculs	Tons	%	Piculs	Tons	%	Piculs	Tons	%
Thai	173,114	11,541	2.3	144,923	9,662	2.8	226,987	15,132	3.5
Phraya Anukun	7,390	493	.1	131,810	8,787	2.6	180,123	12,008	2.8
Luang Boribun	129,885	8,659	1.6	–	–	–	26,741	1,783	.4
Luang Charoen	5,969	398	.1	–	–	–	23	2	–
Phraya Phisan	126	8	–	558	37	–	11	1	–
Phraya Samut	24,354	1,624	.3	3,821	255	.1	18,448	1,230	.3
Luang Wiset	3,381	225	–	5,752	383	.1	1,608	107	–
Chinese	2,251,794	150,120	29.7	1,304,727	86,982	25.5	2,101,235	140,082	32.7
Nguan Heng Yu	865,514	57,701	11.4	589,208	39,281	11.5	678,751	45,250	10.6
Ban Hong	124,797	8,320	1.6	104,312	6,954	2.0	24,064	1,601	.4
Heng Li	9,317	621	.1	–	–	–	3,635	242	.1
Hok Po	–	–	–	–	–	–	–	–	–
Huang Li	553,961	36,931	7.3	237,487	15,832	4.6	428,544	28,570	6.7
Lao Bang Seng	205,820	13,721	2.7	166,984	11,132	3.3	140,938	9,396	2.2
Ma Hua	284,605	18,974	3.8	192,229	12,815	3.8	774,837	51,656	12.1
Thai Hua Li	158,794	10,586	2.1	–	–	–	–	–	–
Western Firms	5,158,381	343,892	68.0	3,665,501	244,367	71.6	4,089,805	272,654	63.7
A. Markwald and Co.	830,926	55,395	11.0	464,677	30,978	9.1	358,461	23,898	5.6
Arracan	–	–	–	–	–	–	330,443	22,030	5.1
Borneo Co.	435,990	29,066	5.7	361,001	24,067	7.1	243,585	16,238	3.8
Buthmann	2,860	191	–	16,380	1,092	.3	1,579	105	–
Jucker Sigg and Co.	623,926	41,595	8.2	265,208	17,681	5.2	30,118	2,008	.5
Windsor Clarke	187,055	12,470	2.5	106,968	7,131	2.1	284,570	18,971	4.4
Windsor Rose	3,076,921	205,128	40.5	2,403,471	160,231	47.0	2,841,048	189,403	44.2

260

Table 10

Rice Exports of Individuals and Firms, 1885 through 1890

	1885			1886			1887		
	Piculs	Tons	%	Piculs	Tons	%	Piculs	Tons	%
Thai									
Phraya Anukun	[-]	[-]	-	[-]	[-]	-	[-]	[-]	-
Singapore	-	-	-	-	-	-	-	-	-
Hong Kong	-	-	-	-	-	-	-	-	-
Luang Boribun	[70,383]	[4,692]	-	[9,133]	[609]	-	[143,542]	[9,569]	-
Singapore	8,474	565	12	-	-	-	16,851	1,123	12
Hong Kong	61,909	4,127	88	9,133	609	100	126,691	8,446	88
Luang Charoen	[3,538]	[236]	-	[3,050]	[203]	-	[7,338]	[489]	-
Singapore	-	-	-	-	-	-	-	-	-
Hong Kong	3,499	234	99	3,050	203	100	6,461	431	88
Amoy	39	2	1	-	-	-	-	-	-
Shanghai	-	-	-	-	-	-	5	-	-
Songkhla	-	-	-	-	-	-	861	57	12
Bombay	-	-	-	-	-	-	-	-	-
Java	-	-	-	-	-	-	11	1	-
Phraya Phisan	[37,760]	[2,517]	-	[5,567]	[372]	-	[3,756]	[250]	-
Singapore	26,939	1,796	71	-	-	-	-	-	-
Hong Kong	10,821	721	29	5,365	358	96	2,924	195	78
Chanthaburi	-	-	-	-	-	-	-	-	-
N. Sithammarat	-	-	-	177	12	3	-	-	-
Songkhla	-	-	-	25	2	1	832	55	22
Bombay	-	-	-	-	-	-	-	-	-
Phraya Samut	[-]	[-]	-	[-]	[-]	-	[-]	[-]	-
Singapore	-	-	-	-	-	-	-	-	-
Hong Kong	-	-	-	-	-	-	-	-	-
Trat	-	-	-	-	-	-	-	-	-

261

Luang Wiset	[-]		[-]		[-]		[-]		
Chanthaburi	-		-		-		-		-
Songkhla	-		-		-		-		-
Chinese									
Nguan Heng Yu	[313,907]		[20,927]		[506,762]		[33,784]		[695,429]		[46,362]	
Singapore	102,233		6,815	33	68,104		4,540	13	24,341		1,623	4
Hong Kong	211,674		14,112	67	422,813		28,187	84	670,986		44,732	96
Manila	-		-	-	15,845		1,057	3	-		-	-
Ko Sichang	-		-	-	-		-	-	102		7	-
Ban Hong	[104,314]		[6,954]		[105,440]		[7,029]		[100,451]		[6,697]	
Singapore	104,314		6,954	100	105,440		7,029	100	100,451		6,697	100
Heng Li	[9,447]		[630]		[30,429]		[2,029]		[25,004]		[1,667]	
Hong Kong	9,447		630	-	30,429		2,029	-	24,606		1,640	98
N. Sithammarat	-		-	-	-		-	-	398		27	2
Hok Po	[74,723]		[4,982]		[20,664]		[1,378]		[37,352]		[2,490]	
Singapore	38,047		2,537	51	5		-	-	5,680		379	15
Hong Kong	36,676		2,445	49	10,177		679	49	31,672		2,111	85
Manila	-		-	-	10,482		699	51	-		-	-
Huang Li	[218,623]		[14,575]		[443,368]		[29,558]		[785,325]		[52,355]	
Singapore	63,045		4,203	29	15		1	-	8,678		579	1
Hong Kong	155,578		10,372	71	443,353		29,557	100	776,647		51,776	99
Lao Bang Seng	[39,456]		[2,630]		[14,143]		[943]		[126,860]		[8,457]	
Singapore	39,456		2,630	100	14,143		943	100	126,860		8,457	100
Ma Hua	[127,369]		[8,491]		[332,256]		[22,151]		[385,072]		[25,672]	
Singapore	40,859		2,724	32	-		-	-	43,770		2,918	11
Hong Kong	86,510		5,767	68	305,983		20,399	92	337,783		22,519	88
Manila	-		-	-	13,614		908	4	-		-	-
United States	-		-	-	12,659		844	4	-		-	-
Songkhla	-		-	-	-		-	-	3,519		235	1
Thai Hua Li	[-]		[-]		[-]		[-]		[31,176]		[2,078]	
Singapore	-		-	-	-		-	-	31,176		2,078	100

Table 10 (continued)

	1885			1886			1887		
Western Firms	Piculs	Tons	%	Piculs	Tons	%	Piculs	Tons	%
A. Markwald and Co.	[318,471]	[21,231]		[226,041]	[15,070]		[500,034]	[33,336]	
Singapore	199,049	13,270	63	191,635	12,776	85	187,398	12,493	37
Hong Kong	74,736	4,982	23	34,406	2,294	15	-	-	-
Surabaya	-	-	-	-	-	-	-	-	-
Melbourne	7,726	515	2	-	-	-	-	-	-
Great Britain	-	-	-	-	-	-	20,322	1,355	4
Germany	-	-	-	-	-	-	33,070	2,205	7
Europe	36,960	2,464	12	-	-	-	259,244	17,283	52
Arracan	[-]	[-]		[-]	[-]		[-]	[-]	
Borneo Co.	[289,289]	[19,286]		[123,311]	[8,220]		[234,245]	[15,616]	
Singapore	234,624	15,642	81	69,905	4,660	57	-	-	-
Hong Kong	-	-	-	18,947	1,263	15	-	-	-
Vietnam	-	-	-	-	-	-	-	-	-
Surabaya	-	-	-	-	-	-	-	-	-
Bombay	-	-	-	-	-	-	18	1	-
Great Britain	-	-	-	17,622	1,175	14	-	-	-
Europe	54,665	3,644	19	-	-	-	234,227	15,615	100
Canada	-	-	-	16,837	1,122	14	-	-	-
Buthmann	[-]	[-]		[-]	[-]		[-]	[-]	
Chanthaburi	-	-	-	-	-	-	-	-	-
Trat	-	-	-	-	-	-	-	-	-
Ko Kong (?)	-	-	-	-	-	-	-	-	-
Songkhla	-	-	-	-	-	-	-	-	-
Kelantan	-	-	-	-	-	-	-	-	-
Trengganu	-	-	-	-	-	-	-	-	-
Deli (?)	-	-	-	-	-	-	-	-	-

Jucker Sigg and Co.	[129,185]		[8,612]		[-]		[-]		[204,047]		[13,603]	
Hong Kong	-		-		-		-		-		-	
Manila	43,784		2,919	34	-		-		19,500		1,300	10
United States	16,852		1,123	13	-		-		-		-	
Cairo	21,504		1,434	17	-		-		-		-	
Europe	47,045		3,136	36	-		-		184,547		12,303	90
Windsor Clarke	[-]		[-]		[-]		[-]		[54,256]		[3,617]	
Singapore	-		-		-		-		11,567		771	21
Hong Kong	-		-		-		-		-		-	
Japan	-		-		-		-		-		-	
Bombay	-		-		-		-		-		-	
Europe	-		-		-		-		42,689		2,846	79
Windsor Rose	[1,115,557]		[74,370]		[1,818,250]		[121,217]		[2,806,753]		[187,117]	
Singapore	244,461		16,297	22	564,063		37,604	31	746,554		49,770	27
Hong Kong	852,424		56,828	76	1,239,670		82,645	68	1,916,231		127,749	68
Vietnam	-		-		-		-		-		-	
Manila	-		-		14,517		968	1	-		-	
Surabaya	-		-		-		-		-		-	
Japan	-		-		-		-		-		-	
Europe	18,672		1,245	2	-		-		143,968		9,598	5

Table 10 (continued)

	1888			1889			1890		
	Piculs	Tons	%	Piculs	Tons	%	Piculs	Tons	%
Thai									
Phraya Anukun	[7,390]	[493]		[131,810]	[8,787]		[180,123]	[12,008]	
Singapore	-	-	-	131,810	8,787	100	154,766	10,318	86
Hong Kong	7,390	493	100	-	-	-	25,357	1,690	14
Luang Boribun	[129,885]	[8,659]		[-]	[-]		[26,741]	[1,783]	
Singapore	17,217	1,148	14	-	-	-	-	-	-
Hong Kong	112,668	7,511	86	-	-	-	26,741	1,783	100
Luang Charoen	[5,969]	[398]		[-]	[-]		[-]	[-]	
Singapore	5,936	396	99	-	-	-	-	-	-
Hong Kong	-	-	-	-	-	-	23	2	100
Amoy	3	-	-	-	-	-	-	-	-
Shanghai	-	-	-	-	-	-	-	-	-
Songkhla	-	-	-	-	-	-	-	-	-
Bombay	30	2	1	-	-	-	-	-	-
Java	-	-	-	-	-	-	-	-	-
Phraya Phisan	[126]	[8]		[558]	[37]		[11]	[1]	
Singapore	-	-	-	-	-	-	-	-	-
Hong Kong	-	-	-	-	-	-	-	-	-
Chanthaburi	-	-	-	558	37	100	-	-	-
N. Sithammarat	-	-	-	-	-	-	-	-	-
Songkhla	-	-	-	-	-	-	-	-	-
Bombay	126	8	100	-	-	-	11	1	100
Phraya Samut	[24,354]	[1,624]		[3,821]	[255]		[18,448]	[1,230]	
Singapore	13,257	884	54	-	-	-	-	-	-
Hong Kong	11,097	740	46	3,821	255	100	18,345	1,223	99
Trat	-	-	-	-	-	-	103	7	1

265

Luang Wiset	[3,381]		[225]		[5,752]	[383]	[1,608]	[107]
Chanthaburi	451	13	30		5,752	383	1,608	107
Songkhla	2,930	87	195		–	–	–	–
Chinese								
Nguan Heng Yu	[865,514]		[57,701]		[589,208]	[39,281]	[678,751]	[45,250]
Singapore	31,184		2,079		23,466	1,565	5,167	344	1
Hong Kong	834,330		55,622		565,742	37,716	673,584	44,906	99
Manila	–		–		–	–	–	–
Ko Sichang	–		–		–	–	–	–
Ban Hong	[124,797]		[8,320]		[104,312]	[6,954]	[24,065]	[1,604]
Singapore	124,797	100	8,320	100	104,312	6,954	24,065	1,604	100
Heng Li	[9,317]		[621]		[–]	[–]	[3,635]	[242]
Hong Kong	9,317	100	621	100			3,635	242	100
N. Sithammarat	–		–				–	–
Hok Po	[–]		[–]		[–]	[–]	[–]	[–]
Singapore								
Hong Kong								
Manila								
Huang Li	[553,961]		[36,931]		[237,487]	[15,832]	[428,544]	[28,570]
Singapore	78,482	14	5,232	14	63,245	4,216	27	–
Hong Kong	475,479	86	31,699	86	174,242	11,616	73	428,544	28,570	100
Lao Bang Seng	[205,820]		[13,721]		[166,984]	[11,132]	[140,938]	[9,396]
Singapore	205,820	100	13,721	100	166,984	11,132	100	140,938	9,396	100
Ma Hua	[284,605]		[18,974]		[192,229]	[12,816]	[774,837]	[51,656]
Singapore	38,488	14	2,566	14	87,878	5,859	46	103,614	6,908	13
Hong Kong	173,289	60	11,553	60	104,351	6,957	54	671,223	44,748	87
Manila	72,828	26	4,855	26	–	–	–	–
United States	–		–		–	–	–	–
Songkhla	–		–		–	–	–	–
Thai Hua Li	[158,794]		[10,586]		[–]	[–]	[–]	[–]
Singapore	158,794	100	10,586	100				

Table 10 (continued)

	1888			1889			1890		
	Piculs	Tons	%	Piculs	Tons	%	Piculs	Tons	%
Western Firms									
A. Markwald and Co.	[830,926]	[55,395]		[464,677]	[30,978]		[358,461]	[23,898]	
Singapore	429,919	28,661	52	239,401	15,960	52	120,863	8,058	34
Hong Kong	57,174	5,812	7	16,211	1,081	3	18,389	1,226	5
Surabaya	-	-	-	3,605	240	1	-	-	-
Melbourne	-	-	-	-	-	-	-	-	-
Great Britain	-	-	-	-	-	-	-	-	-
Germany	-	-	-	-	-	-	-	-	-
Europe	343,833	22,922	41	205,460	13,697	44	219,209	14,614	61
Arracan	[-]	[-]		[-]	[-]		[330,443]	[23,898]	
Europe	-	-	-	-	-	-	330,443	23,898	-
Borneo Co.	[435,990]	[29,066]		[361,001]	[24,067]		[243,585]	[16,239]	-
Singapore	-	-	-	28,676	1,912	8	-	-	-
Hong Kong	-	-	-	-	-	-	23,628	1,575	10
Vietnam	-	-	-	5,007	334	1	-	-	-
Surabaya	-	-	-	-	-	-	33,534	2,236	14
Bombay	-	-	-	6	-	-	-	-	-
Great Britain	-	-	-	-	-	-	-	-	-
Europe	435,990	29,066	100	327,312	21,821	91	186,423	12,428	76
Canada	-	-	-	-	-	-	-	-	-
Buthmann	[2,860]	[191]		[16,380]	[1,092]		[1,579]	[105]	
Chanthaburi	-	-	-	11,296	753	69	1,535	102	97
Trat	-	-	-	1,663	111	10	-	-	-
Ko Kong (?)	-	-	-	-	-	-	44	3	3
Songkhla	-	-	-	1,447	96	9	-	-	-
Kelantan	-	-	-	1,974	132	12	-	-	-
Trengganu	1,621	108	57	-	-	-	-	-	-
Deli (?)	1,239	83	43	-	-	-	-	-	-

Jucker Sigg and Co.	[623,926]	[41,595]		[265,208]	[17,681]		[30,118]	[2,008]	
Hong Kong	15,347	1,023	3	–	–	–	–	–	–
Manila	–	–	–	–	–	–	–	–	–
United States	–	–	–	–	–	–	–	–	–
Cairo	–	–	–	–	–	–	–	–	–
Europe	608,579	40,572	97	265,208	17,681	100	30,118	2,008	100
Windsor Clarke	[187,055]	[12,470]		[106,968]	[7,131]		[284,570]	[18,971]	
Singapore	8,355	557	4	–	–	–	–	–	–
Hong Kong	–	–	–	–	–	–	31,336	2,089	11
Japan	–	–	–	–	–	–	54,756	3,650	19
Bombay	65	4	1	59	4	–	–	–	–
Europe	178,635	11,909	95	106,909	7,127	100	198,478	13,232	70
Windsor Rose	[3,076,921]	[205,128]		[2,403,471]	[160,232]		[2,841,048]	[189,402]	
Singapore	1,079,381	71,959	35	1,073,455	71,564	45	941,798	62,787	33
Hong Kong	1,777,378	118,492	58	1,188,885	79,259	49	1,654,070	110,271	58
Vietnam	–	–	–	–	–	–	1,329	87	–
Manila	–	–	–	–	–	–	–	–	–
Surabaya	–	–	–	–	–	–	22,742	1,516	1
Japan	–	–	–	–	–	–	46,931	3,129	2
Europe	220,162	14,677	7	141,131	9,409	6	174,178	11,612	6

Table 11

Cooperative Relationships: Thai Rice Trade, 1885 through 1890

Hong Kong Trade	1885			1886			1887		
	Piculs	Tons	%	Piculs	Tons	%	Piculs	Tons	%
Cooperative Arrangements									
Windsor Rose	852,424	56,828	57	1,239,670	82,645	49	1,916,231	127,749	49
Nguan Heng Yu	211,674	14,112	14	422,813	28,187	17	670,986	44,732	17
SUBTOTAL	[1,064,098]	[70,940]	[71]	[1,662,483]	[110,832]	[66]	[2,587,217]	[172,481]	[66]
Huang Li	155,578	10,372	10	443,353	29,557	17	776,647	51,776	20
Ma Hua	86,510	5,767	6	305,983	20,399	12	337,783	22,519	9
Phraya Samut	-	-	-	-	-	-	-	-	-
TOTAL	[1,306,186]	[87,079]	[87]	[2,411,819]	[160,788]	[95]	[3,701,547]	[246,776]	[95]
Independents									
Phraya Anukun	-	-	-	-	-	-	-	-	-
Luang Boribun	61,909	4,127	4	9,133	609	-	126,691	8,446	3
Luang Charoen	3,499	234	-	3,050	203	-	6,461	431	-
Phraya Phisan	10,821	721	1	5,365	358	-	2,924	195	-
Heng Li	9,447	630	1	30,429	2,029	1	24,606	1,640	1
Hok Po	36,676	2,445	2	10,177	679	-	31,672	2,111	1
A. Markwald and Co.	74,736	4,982	5	34,406	2,294	1	-	-	-
Borneo Co.	-	-	-	18,947	1,263	1	-	-	-
Jucker Sigg and Co.	-	-	-	-	-	-	-	-	-
Windsor Clarke	-	-	-	-	-	-	-	-	-
Total Exports to Hong Kong	1,506,916	100,461	100	2,526,402	168,427	100	3,902,703	260,180	100

Table 11 (continued)

Hong Kong Trade	1888			1889			1890		
	Piculs	Tons	%	Piculs	Tons	%	Piculs	Tons	%
Cooperative Arrangements									
Windsor Rose	1,777,378	118,492	51	1,188,885	79,259	58	1,675,070	110,271	46
Nguan Heng Yu	834,330	55,622	24	565,742	37,716	28	673,584	44,906	19
SUBTOTAL	[2,611,708]	[174,114]	[75]	[1,754,627]	[116,975]	[86]	[2,327,654]	[155,176]	[65]
Huang Li	475,479	31,699	14	174,242	11,616	8	428,544	28,570	12
Ma Hua	173,289	11,553	5	104,251	6,957	5	671,223	44,748	19
Phraya Samut	11,097	740	-	3,821	255	-	18,345	1,223	-
TOTAL	[3,271,573]	[218,105]	[94]	[2,037,041]	[135,803]	[99]	[3,445,766]	[229,718]	[96]
Independents									
Phraya Anukun	7,390	493	-	-	-	-	25,357	1,690	1
Luang Boribun	112,668	7,511	3	-	-	-	26,741	1,783	1
Luang Charoen	-	-	-	-	-	-	23	2	-
Phraya Phisan	-	-	-	-	-	-	-	-	-
Heng Li	9,317	621	-	-	-	-	3,635	242	-
Hok Po	-	-	-	-	-	-	-	-	-
A. Markwald and Co.	57,174	3,812	2	16,211	1,081	1	18,389	1,226	-
Borneo Co.	-	-	-	-	-	-	23,628	1,575	1
Jucker Sigg and Co.	15,347	1,023	-	-	-	-	-	-	-
Windsor Clarke	-	-	-	-	-	-	31,336	2,089	1
Total Exports to Hong Kong	3,473,660	231,577	100	2,053,252	136,883	100	3,604,624	240,308	100

269

Table 11 (continued)

Singapore Trade	1885			1886			1887		
	Piculs	Tons	%	Piculs	Tons	%	Piculs	Tons	%
Cooperative Arrangements									
Windsor Rose	244,461	16,297	20	564,063	37,604	55	746,554	49,770	56
Nguan Heng Yu	102,233	6,815	9	68,104	4,540	7	24,341	1,623	2
SUBTOTAL	[346,694]	[23,113]	[29]	[632,167]	[42,144]	[62]	[770,895]	[51,393]	[58]
A. Markwald and Co.	199,049	13,270	17	191,635	12,776	19	187,398	12,493	14
Phraya Samut	–	–	–	–	–	–	–	–	–
TOTAL	[545,743]	[36,383]	[46]	[823,802]	[54,920]	[81]	[958,239]	[63,886]	[72]
Independents									
Phraya Anukun	–	–	–	–	–	–	–	–	–
Luang Boribun	8,474	565	1	–	–	–	16,851	1,123	1
Luang Charoen	–	–	–	–	–	–	–	–	–
Phraya Phisan	26,939	1,796	2	–	–	–	–	–	–
Ban Hong	104,314	6,954	9	105,440	7,029	10	100,451	6,697	8
Hok Po	38,047	2,537	3	5	–	–	5,680	379	–
Huang Li	63,045	4,203	5	15	1	–	8,678	579	1
Lao Bang Seng	39,456	2,630	3	14,143	943	1	126,860	8,457	10
Ma Hua	–	–	–	–	–	–	–	–	–
Thai Hua Li	–	–	–	–	–	–	31,176	2,078	2
A. Markwald and Co.	–	–	–	–	–	–	–	–	–
Borneo Co.	234,624	15,642	20	69,905	4,660	7	–	–	–
Windsor Clarke	–	–	–	–	–	–	11,567	771	1
Total Exports to Singapore	1,182,233	78,816	100	1,022,763	68,184	100	1,330,247	88,683	100

Table 11 (continued)

Singapore Trade	1888			1889			1890		
	Piculs	Tons	%	Piculs	Tons	%	Piculs	Tons	%
Cooperative Arrangements									
Windsor Rose	1,079,381	71,959	49	1,073,455	71,564	56	941,798	62,787	63
Nguan Heng Yu	31,184	2,079	1	23,466	1,565	1	5,167	344	-
SUBTOTAL	[1,110,565]	[74,038]	[50]	[1,096,921]	[73,128]	[57]	[946,965]	[63,131]	[63]
A. Markwald and Co.	-	-	-	-	-	-	-	-	-
Phraya Samut	13,257	844	1	-	-	-	-	-	-
TOTAL	[1,123,822]	[74,921]	[51]	[1,096,921]	[73,128]	[57]	[946,965]	[63,131]	[63]
Independents									
Phraya Anukun	-	-	-	131,810	8,787	7	154,766	10,318	10
Luang Boribun	17,217	1,148	1	-	-	-	-	-	-
Luang Charoen	5,936	396	-	-	-	-	-	-	-
Phraya Phisan	-	-	-	-	-	-	-	-	-
Ban Hong	124,796	8,320	6	104,312	6,954	5	24,064	1,601	2
Hok Po	-	-	-	-	-	-	-	-	-
Huang Li	78,482	5,232	4	63,245	4,216	3	-	-	-
Lao Bang Seng	205,820	13,721	9	166,984	11,132	9	140,938	9,396	9
Ma Hua	38,488	2,566	2	87,878	5,859	5	103,614	6,908	7
Thai Hua Li	158,794	10,586	7	-	-	-	-	-	-
A. Markwald and Co.	429,919	28,661	20	239,401	15,960	12	120,863	8,058	8
Borneo Co.	-	-	-	28,676	1,912	1	-	-	-
Windsor Clarke	8,355	557	-	-	-	-	-	-	-
Total Exports to Singapore	2,193,954	146,263	100	1,919,227	127,948	100	1,508,274	100,551	100

BIBLIOGRAPHY

Symbols Used in the Bibliography

AP	Asian Perspectives. Honolulu
BEFEO	Bulletin de l'École Française d'Extrême-Orient. Hanoi/Paris.
BKI	Bijdragen, Koniklijk Instituut voor Taal-, Land-, en Volkenkunde. The Hague.
BKS	Berita Kajian Sumatera [Sumatra Research Bulletin].
JMBRAS	Journal of the Malayan Branch, Royal Asiatic Society. Kuala Lumpur.
OV	Oudheidkundige Verslagen van de Comissie in Nederlandsch-Indië voor Oudheidkundig Onderzoek op Java en Madoera en van den Oudheikundigen Dienst in Nederlandsch-Indië. Batavia.
TBG	Tijdschrift voor Indische Taal-, Land-, en Volkenkunde. Koninklijk Bataviaasch Genootschap van Kunsten en Wetenschappen. The Hague.
VBG	Verhandelingen van het Baraviaasch Genootschap van Kunsten en Wetenschappen. Bandung.

Adams, R. Mc.
- 1965 Land Behind Bagdad. Chicago: University of Chicago Press.

Adams, R. Mc., and H. J. Nissen
- 1972 The Uruk Countryside. Chicago: University of Chicago Press.

Aga-Oglu, K.
- 1946 "Ying Ch'ing Porcelain Found in the Philippines." Art Quarterly 9:314-27.
- 1949 "The Relationships Between the Ying Ch'ing and Early Blue and White." Far Eastern Ceramic Bulletin 8:27-33.
- 1955 "The So-Called 'Swatow' Wares: Types and Problems of Provenance." Far Eastern Ceramic Bulletin 30:1-34.
- 1961 "Ming Porcelain From Sites in the Philippines." AP 5:243-52.
- 1972 The Williams Collection of Far Eastern Ceramics. Ann Arbor: University of Michigan Museum of Anthropology.
- 1975 The Williams Collection of Far Eastern Ceramics: Tonnancour Section. Ann Arbor: University of Michigan Museum of Anthropology.

Allen, D. L.
- 1954 Our Wildlife Legacy. New York: Funk and Wagnalls Co.

Andaya, L. Y.
- 1971 "The Kingdom of Johore, 1641-1728: A Study of Economic and Political Developments in the Straits of Malacca." Ph.D. dissertation, Cornell University.

Anderson, J.
1971 Mission to the East Coast of Sumatra in 1823. Kuala Lumpur: Oxford University Press.

Anonymous
1972 "The Lampang Field Station in Thailand." Newsletter of the Scandinavian Institute of Asian Studies 5:3-8.

Arensberg, C.
1968 The Irish Countryman. New York: Natural History Press.

Asmar, T., and B. Bronson
1973 Laporan Ekskavasi Ratu Baka. Jakarta: Lembaga Purbakala dan Peninggalan Nasional.

Asmar, T., B. Bronson, Mundarjito, and J. Wisseman
1975 Laporan Penelitian Rembang. Jakarta: Lembaga Purbakala dan Peninggalan Nasional.

Aubin, J.
1959 "Le ruine de Siraf et les routes du Golfe Pérsique aux XIe et XIIe siécles." Cahiers de Civilization Médiévale 2:295-301.

Aung Thwin, M. A.
1976 "Kingship, the Sangha, and Society in Pagan." In Explorations in Early Southeast Asian History, edited by K. R. Hall and J. K. Whitmore, pp. 205-56. Michigan Papers on South and Southeast Asia, no. 11. Ann Arbor: CSSEAS Publications.

Barnett, P. G.
1943 "The Chinese in Southeastern Asia and the Philippines." Annals of the American Academy of Political and Social Science 226:32-49.

Barrett, A. M.
　1968　"Two Old Javanese Copper-plate Inscriptions of Balitung." M.A. thesis, University of Sydney.

Barth, F.
　1959　"The Land Use Pattern of Migratory Tribes of South Persia." Norse Geografisk Tidsskrift 17:1-11.
　1969　Ethnic Groups and Boundaries. Boston: Little, Brown Co.

Bassett, D. K.
　1964　"British Commercial and Strategic Interest in the Malay Peninsula During the Late Eighteenth Century." In Malayan and Indonesian Studies, edited by J. Basin and R. Roolvink, pp. 122-40. Oxford: Clarendon Press.

Bastin, J.
　1961　"The Changing Balance of the Southeast Asian Pepper Trade." In Essays on Indonesian and Malayan History, pp. 19-52. Singapore: Donald Moore Books.

Bayard, D. T.
　1970　"Excavations at Non Nok Tha, Northeastern Thailand, 1968: An Interim Report." AP 13:109-43.
　1971　"Non Nok Tha: The 1968 Excavation." Mimeographed. University of Otago, Studies in Prehistoric Anthropology 4.
　In press　"An Early Indigenous Bronze Technology in Northeast Thailand: Its Implications for the Prehistory of East Asia." Paper read at the 28th International Congress of Orientalists, Canberra, Jan. 1971, to appear in Proceedings.

Bayard, D. T., T. T. Marsh, and D. N. H. L. Bayard
　1974　"Pa Mong Archaeological Survey Programme. Preliminary Report." Mimeographed. University of Otago: Department of Anthropology.

Benda, H. J., and J. A. Larkin

    1967   The World of Southeast Asia. New York: Harper and Row Publishers.

Bernet Kempers, A. J.

    1959   Ancient Indonesian Art. Cambridge: Harvard University Press.

Beyer, H. O.

    1947   "Outline Review of Philippine Archaeology by Islands and Provinces." Philippine Journal of Science 77:205-374.

Beyer, H. O., G. N. Steiger, and C. Benitez

    1926   A History of the Orient. Boston: Ginn and Co.

Bhandarkar, R. G.

    1887-89   "A Sanskrit Inscription from Central Java." JMBRAS 17 (2):1-10.

Blair, E. H., and J. A. Robertson

    1903-09   The Philippines, 1493-1898. 55 vols. Cleveland: Arthur H. Clark Co.

Boechari

    1973   "Some Considerations on the Problem of the Shift of Mataram's Center from Central to East Java in the 10th Century." Paper presented at the London Colloquy on Early Southeast Asia. University of London: School for Oriental and African Studies.

    n.d.   Prasasti-prasasti Jawa Tengah II. Mimeographed. Jakarta.

Bosch, F. D. K.

    1917   "Een Koperen Plaat van 848 Śaka." OV 1917:88-98.

    1925a   "De Oorkonde van Kembang Aroem." OV 1925:41-9.

    1925b   "Een Oorkonde van het Groote Klooster te Nālandā." Tijdschrift van het Kon. Bat. Genootschap 65:509-88.

    1941   "Een Maleische Inscriptie in het Buitensorgsche." BKI 100:49-53.

Boxer, C.

1947 The Topasses of Timor. Amsterdam: Koningklijk Vereenniging Instituut. Mededelingen 73.

1948 Fidalgos in the Far East, 1550-1770. The Hague: Martinus Nijhoff. Reprint. London: Oxford University Press, 1968.

1967 Francisco Vieira de Fiegueiredo: A Portuguese Adventurer in South East Asia, 1624-1667. The Hague: Martinus Nijhoff.

Brandes, J. L. A., and N. J. Krom

1913 "Oud-Javaansche Orkonden nagelaten Transscripties van wijlen Dr. J. L. A. Brandes uitgegeven door Dr. N. J. Krom." VBG 60.

Bronson, B.

1973 "Prehistory and Early History of Central Thailand with Special Reference to Chansen." Manuscript.

1975 "A Lost Kingdom Mislaid: A Short Report on the Search for Srivijaya." Field Museum of Natural History Bulletin 46(4):16-20.

Bronson, B., and G. F. Dale

1972 "Excavation at Chansen, Thailand, 1968 and 1969." AP 15:15-46.

Bronson, B., and J. Wisseman

1974 "An Archaeological Survey in Sumatra, 1973." BKS 4(1):87-94.

In press "Palembang and Srivijaya: The Lateness of Early Cities in Southern Southeast Asia." AP.

Bronson, B., Basoeki, M. Soehadi, and J. Wisseman

1973 Laporan Penelitian Arkeologi de Sumatera. Jakarta: Lembaga Purbakala dan Peninggalan Nasional.

Brookfield, H. C.

1968 "New Directions in the Study of Agricultural Systems

(Brookfield, H. C.)

(1968) "in Tropical Areas." In Evolution and Environment, edited by E. T. Drake, pp. 413-39. New Haven: Yale University Press.

Brookfield, H. C., and D. Hart

1971 Melanesia: A Geographical Interpretation of an Island World. London: Methuen and Co.

Brown, C. C.

1952 "Sejarah Melayu or 'Malay Annals': A Translation of Raffles Ms. 18." JMBRAS 25(2 and 3).

Brown, J. A.

1971 Approaches to the Social Dimensions of Mortuary Practices. Memoirs of the Society for American Archaeology 25.

Bruder, J. S., E. G. Large, and B. L. Stark

1975 "A Test of Aerial Photography in an Estuarine Mangrove Swamp in Veracruz, Mexico." American Antiquity 40:330-7

Byrne, J. V., D. LeRoy, C. M. Riley

1959 "The Chenier Plain and Its Stratigraphy, Southwestern Louisiana." Transactions, Gulf Coast Association of Geological Societies 9:237-59.

Carson, G.

1965 The Old Country Store. New York: E. P. Dutton.

Casparis, J. G. de

1950 Prasasti Indonesia I: Inscripties uit de Çailendra-Tijd. Bandung: A. C. Nix and Co.

1956 Prasasti Indonesia II: Inscripties uit de Çailendra-Tijd. Bandung: Masa Baru.

1958 Short Inscriptions from Tjandi Plaosan Lor. Berita Dinas Purbakala 4. Jakarta: Lembaga Purbakala dan Peninggalan Nasional.

(Casparis, J. G. de)

    1961   "New Evidence on Cultural Relations Between Java and Ceylon in Ancient Times." Artibus Asiae 24: 241-8.

Chambers, M. J. G., and A. Sobur

    1975   "The Rates and Processes of Recent Coastal Accretion in the Province of South Sumatra: A Preliminary Survey." Paper presented at the Regional Conference on the Geolgoy and Mineral Resources of South East Asia, Jakarta.

Chang, K. C.

    1975   "Ancient Trade as Economics or as Ecology." In Ancient Civilization and Trade, edited by J. A. Sabloff and C. C. Lamberg-Karlovsky, pp. 201-24. Albuquerque: University of New Mexico Press.

Chavannes, E.

    1894   Mémoirs Composé à l'Époque de la Grande Dynastie T'ang sur les Religieux Eminents qui Allèrant Chercher la Loi dans les Pays d'Occident (I Ching 634-713). Paris: E. Leroux.

Chen, Ta

    1940   Emigrant Communities in South China. New York: Institute of Pacific Relations.

Ch'en, C. A.

    1974   Historical Notes on Hoi-An (Faifo). Monograph Series IV. Carbondale, Ill.: Center for Vietnamese Studies.

Chorley, R. J., and P. Haggett

    1967   Socio-Economic Models in Geography. London: Methuen and Co.

Chou, T. K.

    1967   Notes on the Customs of Cambodia. Translated by

(Chou, T. K.)
(1967) J. G. d'A. Paul (from P. Pelliot). Bangkok: Social Science Association Press.

Coedès, G.
1918 "Le Royaume de Crivijaya." BEFEO 18(6):1-36.

Cole, F. C.
1945 The Peoples of Malaysia. New York: D. van Nostrand Co.

Collins, R.
1975 Conflict Sociology. New York: Academic Press.

Conklin, H. C.
1957 Hanunóo Agriculture. Rome: UN/FAO.

Coser, L.
1956 The Functions of Social Conflict. New York: The Free Press.

Courtier, D. B.
1962 Notes on Terraces and Other Alluvial Features in Parts of Province Wellesley, South Kedah, and North Perak. Ipoh: Director of the Geological Survey.

Covarrubias, M.
1937 Island of Bali. New York: Knopf.

Crawfurd, J.
1856 A Descriptive Dictionary of the Indian Islands and Adjacent Countries. London: Bradbury and Evans.

Crumley, C. L.
1976 "Toward a Locational Definition of State Systems of Settlement." American Anthropologist 78:59-73.

Cunningham, C. E.
1965 "Order and Change in an Atoni Diarchy."
Southwestern Journal of Anthropology 21:359-82.

Cushman, J. W.
1975 "Fields from the Sea: Chinese Junk Trade with Siam During the Late Eighteenth and Early Nineteenth Centuries." Ph.D. dissertation, Cornell University.

Dahrendorf, R.
1959 Class and Class Conflict in Industrial Society. Stanford: Stanford University Press.

Damais, L. C.
1952 "Études d'Épigraphie Indonésienne III: Liste des Principales Inscriptions Datées de l'Indonésie." BEFEO 46:1-105.
1970 "Répertoire Onomastique de l'Épigraphie Javanaise (Jusqu'a Pu Sindok Śri Iśānawikrama Dharmmotuṅgadewa): Étude d'Épigraphie Indonésienne." BEFEO 66.

Danielou, A. (translator)
1965 Shilappadikaram. New York: New Directions Publishing Corp.

Dasmann, R. F.
1964 Wildlife Biology. New York: Wiley and Sons.

Davis, W. G.
1973 Social Relations in a Philippine Market. Berkeley: University of California Press.

Denton, R. K.
1968 The Semai. New York: Holt, Rinehart and Winston.

de Sá, A. B.
1949 A Planta de Cailaco (1727). Lisboa: Agencia Geral das Colonias.

Dewey, A. G.
1962 *Peasant Marketing in Java*. Glencoe, Ill.: Free Press.

Dinas Purbakala
1955 "Kissah perdjalanan ke Sumatra Selatan dan Djambi." *Amerta Warna Warta Kepurbakalaan* 3.

Dirks, R.
1975 "Ethnicity and Ethnic Group Relations in British Virgin Islands." In *The New Ethnicity: Perspectives from Ethnology*, edited by J. Bennett, pp. 95-109. St. Paul: West Publishing Co.

Doeppers, D.
1971 "Ethnicity and Class in the Structure of Philippine Cities." Ph.D. dissertation, Syracuse University.
1975 "Chinese Communities and Resdential Patterns in Philippine Cities and Towns During the Late Nineteenth Century." Paper read at the 13th Pacific Science Congress, August 1975, Vancouver.
1976 "Contributions of Geography to the Social History of the Philippines." Paper read at the 28th Annual Meeting of the Association for Asian Studies, March 1976, Toronto.

Drewes, G. W. J.
1968 "New Light on the Coming of Islam to Indonesia?" *Bijdragen tot de Taal-, Land-, en Volkenkunde* 124:433-59.

Dunmore, J.
1973 "French Visitors to Trengganu in the 18th Century." JMBRAS 46:144-59.

Dunn, F. L.
1964 "Excavations at Gua Kechil, Pahang." JMBRAS 37:87-124.

(Dunn F. L.)

   1966   "Radiocarbon Dating of the Malayan Neolithic."
Proceedings of the Prehistoric Society 32:352-3.

   1975   Rain-Forest Collectors and Traders. A Study of
Resource Utilization in Modern and Ancient Malaya.
Malaysian Branch of the Royal Asiatic Society,
Monograph No. 5. Kuala Lumpur.

Durkheim, E.

   1964   The Division of Labor in Society. New York: The
Free Press.

Ellen, R. F., and I. C. Glover

   1974   "Pottery Manufacture and Trade in the Central
Moluccas, Indonesia: The Modern Situation and the
Historical Implications." Man, n.s., 9:353-79.

Encyclopedia of Islam

   1960f   Leiden: E. J. Brill.

Evans, I. H. N.

   1928   "On Ancient Remains from Kuala Selinsing, Perak."
Journal of the Federated Malay States Museums
12(5):121-32.

   1932   "Excavations at Tanjong Rawa, Kuala Selinsing,
Perak." Journal of the Federated Malay States
Museums 15(3):79-134.

Fatimi, S. Q.

   1963   Islam Comes to Indonesia, edited by Shirle Gordon.
Singapore: Malaysian Sociological Research Institute,
Ltd.

Flannery, K. V.

   1972   "Summary Comments: Evolutionary Trends in Social
Exchange and Interaction." In Social Exchange and
Interaction, edited by E. N. Wilmsen, pp. 129-35.
Ann Arbor: University of Michigan Museum of
Anthropology.

Flemming, N. C.

   1969   Archaeological Evidence for Eustatic Change of Sea Level and Earth Movements in the Western Mediterranean During the Last Two Thousand Years. Geological Society of America, Special Paper 109.

Fontain, J., and Tung Wu

   1973   Unearthing China's Past. Boston: Museum of Fine Arts.

Ford, R. I.

   1972   "Barter, Gift, or Violence: An Analysis of Tewa Intertribal Exchange." In Social Exchange and Interaction, edited by E. N. Wilmsen, pp. 21-45. Ann Arbor: University of Michigan Museum of Anthropology.

Forman, S., and Nanai'e Nau Naha

   In press   "Descent, Alliance, and Exchange Ideology Among the Makassae of Portuguese Timor: A Preliminary Statement." In The Flow of Life (Essays in Honor of Van Wouden), edited by J. Fox

Foster, B.

   1974   "Ethnicity and Commerce." American Ethnologist 1:437-48.

   1975   "Mon Commerce and the Dynamics of Ethnic Relations." Paper read at the 28th Annual Meeting of the Association for Asian Studies, March 1976, Toronto.

Fox E. (translator)

   1954   Bisayan Accounts of Early Bornean Settlements in the Philippines Recorded by Fr. Santarén. Chicago: University of Chicago Press.

Fox, R. B.

   1953   "The Pinatubo Negritos." The Philippine Journal of Science 81(3-4).

   1967   "The Archaeological Record of Chinese Influences in the Philippines. Philippine Studies 15:41-62.

(Fox, R. B.)

   1970   The Tabon Caves: Archaeological Explorations and Excavations on Palawan Island, Philippines. Manila: National Museum.

Fox, R. B., and A. E. Evangelista

   1957   "The Cave Archaeology of Cagrayray Island, Albay Province." Journal of East Asiatic Studies 6(1): 57-68.

Francillon, G.

   1967   "Some Matriarchic Aspects of the Social Structure of the Southern Tetum." Ph.D. dissertation, Australian National University.

Freedman, J. D.

   1961   "The Concept of Kindred." Journal of the Royal Anthropological Institute 91:192-220.

Gardner, P. M.

   1972   "The Paliyans." In Hunters and Gatherers Today, edited by M. G. Bicchieri, pp. 404-47. New York: Holt, Rinehart and Winston.

Garvan, J. M.

   1963   The Negritos of the Philippines, edited by H. Hockegger. Horn-Wien: Verlag F. Berger.

Geertz, C.

   1963a   "Indonesian Cultures and Communities." In Indonesia, edited by R. T. McVey, pp. 24-96. New Haven: Human Relations Area Files Press.

   1963b   Peddlars and Princes. Chicago: University of Chicago Press.

Gibb, H. A. R. (translator)

   1957   Ibn Battuta, Travels in Asia and Africa, 1325-1354. London: Routledge and Kegan Paul Ltd.

Gibson-Hill, C. A.

1949 "Cargo Boats of the East Coast of Malaya." JMBRAS 22:106-25.

1953 "The Origin of the Trengganu Perahu Pinas." JMBRAS 26:206-210.

Glover, I. C.

1972 "Excavations in Timor. A Study of Economic Change and Cultural Continuity in Prehistory." Ph.D. dissertation, Australian National University.

Gluckman, M.

1956 Customs and Conflict in Africa. Oxford: Basil Blackwell.

Goitein, S. D.

1963 "Letters and Documents on the India Trade in Medieval Times." Islamic Culture 37:188-205.

1973 Letters of Medieval Jewish Traders. Princeton: Princeton University Press.

Goris, R.

1928 "De Oudjavaanische Inscripties uit het Śrī-Wedari te Soerakarta." OV 1928:63-70.

1930 "De Inscriptie van Koeberan Tjandi." TBG 70: 157-70.

Gorman, C. F.

1970 "Excavations at Spirit Cave, North Thailand: Some Interim Interpretations." AP 13:79-107.

1971 "The Hoabinhian and After: Subsistence Patterns in Southeast Asia During the Late Pleistocene and Early Recent Periods." World Archaeology 2:300-20.

n.d. "A Priori Models and Thai Prehistory: A Reconsideration of the Beginnings of Agriculture in Southeast Asia." Manuscript.

Gottheil, R., and W. H. Worrell
   1927   Fragments from the Cairo Genizah in the Freer Collection. New York: The Macmillan Company.

Gould, W. G., and E. McFarlane, Jr.
   1959   "Geological History of the Chenier Plain, Southwestern Louisiana." Transactions, Gulf Coast Association of Geological Societies 9:261-70.

Grabar, O.
   1967   Sasanian Silver. Ann Arbor: University of Michigan Museum of Art.

Groeneveldt, W. P.
   1960   Notes on the Malay Archipelago and Malacca, Compiled from Chinese Sources. Jakarta: C. V. Bhratara.

Groube, L. M.
   1965   "The Dynamics of Culture Change in Prehistoric New Zealand." Paper read at Congress, Australia and New Zealand Association for the Advancement of Science, Hobart, August 1965.
   1967   "Models in Prehistory: A Consideration of the New Zealand Evidence." Archaeology and Physical Anthropology in Oceania 2:1-27.

Gyllensvärd, B.
   1957   T'ang Gold and Silver. Bulletin of the Museum of Far Eastern Antiquities 29.

Haggett, P.
   1965   Locational Analysis in Human Geography. New York: St. Martin's Press.

Haile, N. S.
   1969   "Quaternary Deposits and Geomorphology of the Sunda Shelf of Malaysian Shores." In Proceedings of the International Quaternary Association Congress. Paris.

(Haile, N. S.)

1971   "Quaternary Shorelines in West Malaysia and Adjacent Parts of the Sunda Shelf." Quaternaria 15: 333-43.

Hall, K. R.

1975   "Khmer Commercial Development and Foreign Contacts under Suryavarman I." Journal of the Economic and Social History of the Orient 18:318-36.

1976a   "An Introductory Essay on Southeast Asian Statecraft in the Classical Period." In Explorations in Early Southeast Asian History, edited by K. R. Hall and J. K. Whitmore, pp. 1-24. Michigan Papers on South and Southeast Asia No. 11. Ann Arbor: CSSEAS Publications.

1976b   "State and Statecraft in Early Srivijaya." In Explorations in Early Southeast Asian History, edited by K. R. Hall and J. K. Whitmore, pp. 61-105. Michigan Papers on South and Southeast Asia No. 11. Ann Arbor: CSSEAS Publications.

In press "International Trade and Foreign Diplomacy in Early Medieval South India." Journal of the Economic and Social History of the Orient.

Hall, K. R., and J. K. Whitmore

1976   "Southeast Asian Trade and the Isthmian Struggle, 1000-1200 A.D." In Explorations in Early Southeast Asian History, edited by K. R. Hall and J. K. Whitmore, pp. 303-40. Michigan Papers on South and Southeast Asia No. 11. Ann Arbor: CSSEAS Publications.

Harding, T. G.

1967   Voyagers of the Vitiaz Strait: A Study of a New Guinea Trade System. Seattle: University of Washington Press.

Harrison, T., and S. J. O'Connor

1969   Excavations of the Prehistoric Iron Industry in

(Harrisson, T., and S. J. O'Connor)

(1969) West Borneo. Cornell Southeast Asia Program Data Paper 72. Ithaca: Cornell University.

Hedland, T. N., and E. P. Wolfenden

1967 "The Vowels of Casiguran Dumagat." In Studies in Philippine Anthropology, edited by M. Zamora, pp. 592-6. Manila: Alemar-Phoenix Publishing House.

Heekeren, H. R. van

1958 The Bronze-Iron Age of Indonesia. The Hague: Marinus Nijhoff.

Heine-Geldern, R. von

1932 "Urheimat und frueheste Wanderungen der Austronesier." Anthropos 27:543-619.

1945 "Prehistoric Research in the Netherlands Indies." In Science and Scientists in the Netherlands Indies, pp. 129-67. New York: Board for the Netherlands Indies, Surinam, and Curacao.

Higgs, E. S.

1972 Papers in Economic Prehistory. Cambridge: Cambridge University Press.

Higham, C. F. W.

1972 "Initial Model Formation in Terra Incognita." In Models in Archaeology, edited by D. L. Clarke, pp. 453-76. London: Methuen and Co.

1975 "Non Nok Tha: The Faunal Remains." Mimeographed. University of Otago: Studies in Prehistoric Anthropology Anthropology 7.

In press a The Prehistory of the Southern Khorat Plateau, with Particular Reference to Roi Et Province.

In press b "Economic Change in Prehistoric Thailand." To appear in World Anthropology. The Hague: Mouton.

Higham, C. F. W., and R. H. Parker
1970   "Prehistoric Research in Northeastern Thailand, 1969-1970: A Preliminary Report." Mimeographed. University of Otago: Department of Anthropology.

Hill, A. H. (translator)
1960   "Hikayat Raja-Raja Pasai." JMBRAS 33(2).

Hirth, F., and W. W. Rockhill
1966   Chau Ju-kua: His Work on the Chinese and Arab Trade in the Twelfth and Thirteenth Centuries, Entitled 'Chu-fan-chi'. New York: Paragon.

Hollwoger, F.
1966   "Progress of River Deltas in Java." In Scientific Problems of the Humid Tropical Zone Deltas and Their Implications, pp. 347-55. Paris: UNESCO.

Holmes, N. H., Jr., and E. B. Trickey
1974   "Late Holocene Sea Level Oscillations in Mobile Bay." American Antiquity 39:122-4.

Holt, C.
1967   Art in Indonesia, Continuities and Change. Ithaca: Cornell University Press.

Hoop, A. N. J. Th. àTh. van der
1938   "De praehistorie." In Geschiedenis van Nederlandsch-Indië, edited by F. W. Stapel, vol. 1: 7-111. Amsterdam: N. v. uitgeversmaatschappij "Joost van den Vondel."

Hooykaas, C.
1973   Religion in Bali. Iconography of Religion 13, no. 10. Leiden: E. J. Brill.

Hurgronje, C. S.
1906   The Achehnese, translated by A. W. S. O'Sullivan. Leiden: E. J. Brill.

Hurt, W. R.

1974 The Interrelationships Between the Natural Environment and Four Sambaquis, Coast of Santa Catarina, Brazil. Indiana University Museum, Occasional Papers and Monographs 1. Bloomington.

Husayn Nainar, S. M.

1942 Arab Geographers' Knowledge of South India. Madras: University of Madras.

Hutterer, K. L.

1969 "Preliminary Report on Archaeological Fieldwork in Southwestern Samar." Leyte-Samar Studies 3:37-56.

1973a An Archaeological Picture of a Pre-Spanish Cebuano Community. Cebu City: University of San Carlos.

1973b "Basey Archaeology: Prehistoric Trade and Social Evolution in the Philippines." Ph.D. dissertation, University of Hawaii.

1974 "The Evolution of Philippine Lowland Societies." Mankind 9:287-99.

1976 "An Evolutionary Approach to the Southeast Asian Cultural Sequence." Current Anthropology 17:221-41.

Ileto, R. C.

1971 Magindanao, 1860-1888: The Career of Dato Uto of Buayan. Cornell Southeast Asia Program Data Paper 82. Ithaca: Cornell University.

Indrapala

1971 "South Indian Mercantile Communities in Ceylon, circa 950-1250." Ceylon Journal of Historical and Social Studies, n.s. 1(2):101-13.

Jaspan, M. A.

1975 "A Note on Palembang in 1832: A Note on Urban Manufacturing and the Work Force." BKS 4(2):5-8.

Jettmar, K.

1967   Art of the Steppes. New York: Crown.

Johns, A. H.

1961   "Sufism as a Category in Indonesian Literature and History." Journal of Southeast Asian History 2(2).

1975   "Islam in Southeast Asia: Reflections and New Directions." Indonesia 19:33-55.

Jones, S.

1972   "Finance in Ningpo: The 'Ch'ien Chuang', 1750-1880." In Economic Organization in Chinese Society, edited by W. Willmott, pp. 47-77. Stanford: Stanford University Press.

Kasetsiri, Charnuit

1973   "The Rise of Ayudhya. A History of Siam in the Fourteenth and Fifteenth Centuries." Ph.D. dissertation, Cornell University.

Keesing, F. M.

1962   The Ethnohistory of Northern Luzon. Stanford: Stanford University Press.

Keller, G. K., and A. F. Richards

1967   "Sediments of the Malacca Strait, Southeast Asia." Journal of Sedimentary Petrology 37:102-27.

Kern, H.

1913   "Sanskrit-Inscriptie ter Eere den Javaanschen Vorst Erlanga." BKI 67:610-22.

Kern, R. A.

1947   De Islam in Indonesie. The Hague.

Koentjaraningrat

1967   "Tjelapar: A Village in South Central Java." In Villages in Indonesia, edited by Koentjaraningrat, pp. 244-80. Ithaca: Cornell University Press.

Kraft, J. C.
1972 A Reconnaissance of the Geology of the Sandy Coastal Areas of Eastern Greece and the Peloponnese. College of Marine Studies Technical Report 9. Newark, Delaware.

Kraft, J. C., G. Rapp, Jr., and S. E. Aschbrenner
1975 "Late Holocene Paleogeography of the Coastal Plain of the Gulf of Messina, Greece, and Its Relationships to Archaeological Settings and Coastal Change." Geological Society of America Bulletin 86:1191-1208.

Kroeber, A. L.
1919 Peoples of the Philippines. New York: American Museum of Natural History.

Krom, N. J.
1911 "Over Inscriptie's van Middenen Oost Java w. o. die van 829 Ś. op den Ganeśa van Blitar." Rapporten van den Oudheidkundigen Dienste in Nederlandsch-Indië 1911:138.

1913 "Epigraphische Aanteekeningen I: Erlangga's Oorkonde van 963." TBG 60:585-91.

1931 Hindoe-Javaansche Geschiedenis. The Hague.

Kung, H. W.
1962 Chinese in American Life. Seattle: University of Washington Press.

Kunjan Pillai, P. N. E.
1970 Studies in Kerala History. Trivandrum: (distributors) National Book Stall, Kottayam.

Kurjack, E. B., and C. T. Sheldon
1970 "The Archaeology of Seminoho Cave in Lebak, Cotabato." Silliman Journal 17(1):5-18.

La Capra, D.
1972 Emile Durkheim: Sociologist and Philosopher. Ithaca: Cornell University Press.

Lach, D. F.
1965 Asia in the Making of Europe. Vol. 1. Chicago: University of Chicago Press.

Lamb, A.
1959 "Recent Archaeological Work: Kedah." JMBRAS 32: 214-32.
1960 Chandi Bukit Batu Pahat. Monographs on Southeast Asian Subjects 1. Singapore: Eastern Universities Press.
1970 The Mandarin Road to Old Hue. London: Chatto and Windus.

Lane, F. C.
1966 Venice and History. Baltimore: Johns Hopkins Press.

Leach, E. R.
1954 Political Systems of Highland Burma. Cambridge: Harvard University Press.
1964 "Anthropological Aspects of Language: Animal Categories and Verbal Abuse." In New Directions in the Study of Language, edited by E. Lenneberg, pp. 23-63. Cambridge: MIT Press.

Lee, R.
1972a "The !Kung Bushmen of Botswana." In Hunters and Gatherers Today, edited by M. G. Bicchieri, pp. 327-68. New York: Holt, Rinehart and Winston.
1972b "!Kung Spatial Organization: An Ecological and Historical Perspective." Human Ecology 1:125-47.
1972c "Social Life Among the !Kung Bushmen." In Population Growth: Anthropological Implications, edited by B. Spooner, pp. 329-50. Cambridge: MIT Press.

Leopoldo, A.
 1933 Game Management. New York: Charles Scribner's Sons.

Leur, J. C. van
 1955 Indonesian Trade and Society. The Hague: W. van Hoeve.

Lewis, D.
 1960 "Inas: A Study of Local History." JMBRAS 33:65-94.

Lohuizen-de Leeuw, J. E. van
 1974 "Van Erp's Suggestion for the Date of Barabudur." Paper read at the International Conference on Barabudur, Ann Arbor. To appear in Essays on Barabudur, edited by L. Gomez and H. W. Woodward, Jr.

Lombardi, J. R.
 1975 "Reciprocity and Survival." Anthropological Quarterly 48:245-54.

Lombard-Salmon, C.
 1972 "Un Chinois a Java (1729-1736)." BEFEO 59:281-318.

Loy, W. G., and H. E. Wright
 1972 "The Physical Setting." In The Minnesota Messenia Expedition, edited by W. A. McDonald and G. Rapp, pp. 36-46. Minneapolis: University of Minnesota Press.

Lugo, A. E., and S. C. Snedaker
 1974 "The Ecology of Mangroves." Annual Review of Ecology and Systematics 5:39-64.

Ma, L. J. C.
 1971 Commercial Development and Urban Change in Sung China (960-1279). Michigan Geographical Publications No. 6. Ann Arbor: University of Michigan.

Maceda, M. N.

1964a　The Culture of the Mamanua. Manila: Catholic Trade School.

1964b　"Preliminary Report on Ethnographic and Archaeological Fieldwork in the Kulaman Plateau, Island of Mindanao, Philippines." Anthropos 59: 75-82.

1965　"Second Preliminary Report on the Archaeological Excavation in the Kulaman Plateau (Cotabato), Island of Mindanao, Philippines." Anthropos 60:237-40.

Mackerras, C.

1969　"Sino-Uighur Diplomatic and Trade Contacts (744 to 840)." Central Asiatic Journal 13:215-40.

Macknight, C. C.

1973　"The Nature of Early Maritime Trade: Some Points of Analogy from the Eastern Part of the Indonesian Archipelago." World Archaeology 5:198-208.

Malinowski, B.

1961　Argonauts of the Western Pacific. New York: E. P. Dutton.

Malleret, L.

1959-63　L'Archéologie du Delta du Mékong. 4 vols. Paris: Publications de l'École Française d'Extrême Orient.

Marrison, J. E.

1951　"The Coming of Islam to the East Indies." JMBRAS 24:28-37.

Marschall, W.

1968　"Metallurgie und fruehe Besiedlungsgeschichte Indonesiens." Ethnologica 4:29-263.

Mauss, M.

1967　The Gift. Translated by I. Cunnison. New York: Norton.

McDonald, W. A.

1972 "The Problems and the Program." In The Minnesota Messenia Expedition, edited by W. A. McDonald and G. R. Rapp, pp. 3-17. Minneapolis: University of Minnesota Press.

McDonald, W. A., and G. R. Rapp, Jr.

1972a "Perspectives." In The Minnesota Messenia Expedition, edited by W. A. McDonald and G. R. Rapp, Jr., pp. 240-63. Minneapolis: University of Minnesota Press.

1972b The Minnesota Messenia Expedition. Minneapolis: University of Minnesota Press.

McIntire, W. G.

1958 Prehistoric Settlements of the Changing Mississippi River Delta. Coastal Studies Series 1. Baton Rouge: Louisiana State University.

1959 "Methods of Correlating Cultural Remains with Stages of Coastal Development." In Second Coastal Geomorphology Conference, edited by R. J. Russell, pp. 347-59. Washington, D.C.: Office of Naval Research.

McKinnon, E. E.

1973 "Kota Tjina: A Site with T'ang and Sung Period Associations." BKS 3(1):46-52.

McKinnon, E. E., and Tengku Luckman Sinar

1974 "Notes on Further Developments at Kota China." BKS 4(1):63-86.

Meilink-Roelofsz, M. A. P.

1962 Asian Trade and European Influence, 1500-1620. The Hague: Martinus Nijhoff.

Meister, M. W.

1970 "The Pearl Roundel in Chinese Textile Design." Ars Orientalis 8:255-67.

Micha, F. J.

1958 "Der Handel der zentralaustralischen Eingeborenen."
Annali Lateranensi 22:41-228.

Moertono, S.

1968 State and Statecraft in Old Java: A Study of the Later
Mataram Period, 16th to 19th Century. Cronell
Modern Indonesia Project Monograph Series 43.
Ithaca: Cornell University.

Mohr, E. C.

1944 The Soils of Equatorial Regions. Ann Arbor: J. W.
Edwards.

Moormann, F. R., and S. Rajanasoonthon

1972 The Soils of the Kingdom of Thailand. Bangkok:
Ministry of Agriculture, Soil Survey Division.

Morison, S. E.

1961 The Maritime History of Massachusetts, 1783-1860.
Boston: Houghton Mifflin Co.

Morse, H.

1932 The Gilds of China with an Account of the Gild
Merchant of Canton. 2nd ed. London: Longmans,
Green, and Co.

Muller, J.

1975 "Pollen Analytical Studies of Peat and Coal from
Northwest Borneo." In Quaternary Research in
Southeast Asia, edited by G. J. Bartstra and W. A.
Casparis, pp. 83-6. Rotterdam: A. A. Balkema.

Naerssen, F. H. van

1937a "Een Hindoe-Balineesche Oorkonde Gevonden in Oost
Java." TBG 77:602-10.

1937b "Twee Koperen Oorkonden van Balitung in het
Koloniaal Instituut te Amsterdam." BKI 95:441-61.

Nguyen Thanh Nha

1970 Tableau économique de Viet-Nam aux 17e et 18e siècles. Paris: Editions Cujas.

Nilakanta Sastri, K. A.

1932 "A Tamil Merchant Guild in Sumatra." TBG 72: 314-27.

1939 Foreign Notices of South India. Madras: University of Madras.

Norduyn, J., and H. Th. Verstappen

1972 "Purnavarman's River-works near Tugu." BKI 128: 298-306.

Nopphamât, Nâng

1964 Phra râtchakaranyânusôn phra râtchaniphon nai phra bât somdet phra Chunla Chôm Klao čhao yû hua lae rüang Nâng Nopphamât. Bangkok: Khlang Witthayâ.

Obdeyn, V.

1941-43 "Zuid-Sumatra Volgens de Oudste Berichten I-III." Tijdschrift Konink. Ned. Aardr. Gen. 58:190-217, 322-43, 476-503; 59:46-76, 742-71; 60:102-11.

Odum, E. P.

1959 Fundamentals of Ecology. Philadelphia: W. B. Saunders Co.

O'Kane, J. (translator)

1972 The Ship of Sulaimān. New York: Columbia University Press.

Omohundro, J. T.

1974 "The Chinese Merchant Community of Iloilo City, Philippines." Ph.D. dissertation, University of Michigan.

1976 "Merchant Culture and Chinese Ethnicity in the Philippines." Paper read at the 28th Annual Meeting

(Omohundro, J. T.)

(1976)   of the Association for Asian Studies, March 1976, Toronto.

Ormerling, F. J.

1957   The Timor Problem: A Geographical Interpretation of an Underdeveloped Island. The Hague: Martinus Nijhoff.

Owen, N. G.

1971   "The Rice Industry of Mainland Southeast Asia, 1850-1914." Journal of the Siam Society 59(2): 75-143.

1976   "Kabikolan in the Nineteenth Century: Socio-Economic Change in the Provincial Philippines." Ph.D. dissertation, University of Michigan.

Pal, Pratapaditya

1969   The Art of Tibet. New York: The Asia Society.

Paris, P.

1931   "Anciens canaux reconnus sur photographies aériennes dans les provinces de Ta-keo et du Chaudoc." BEFEO 31:221-4.

1941   "Notes et mélanges: anciens canaux reconnus sur photographies aériennes dans les provinces de Ta-keo, Chau-doc, Long-xuyen et Rach-gia." BEFEO 41:375-80.

Parker, E. H.

1900   "The Island of Sumatra." The Imperial and Asiatic Quarterly Review, 3rd series, IX.

Parker, R. H.

1971   "Continuity and Change in Two Areas of Northeastern Thailand." Paper read at the 28th International Congress of Orientalists, January 1971, Canberra.

Peacock, B. A. V.
- 1964 "A Preliminary Note on the Dong-so'n Bronze Drums from Kampong Sungai Lang." Federation Museums Journal 9:1-3.
- 1965 "Recent Archaeological Discoveries in Malaya 1964." JMBRAS 38:248-55.

Pearson, R. J.
- 1962 "Dong-so'n and Its Origin." Bulletin of the Institute of Ethnology, Academia Sinica 13:27-50.

Peebles, C. S., and S. M. Kus
- n.d. "Some Archaeological Correlates of Ranked Societies." Manuscript.

Pelliot, P.
- 1959 Notes on Marco Polo. Paris: Adrien-Maisonneuve.

Pendleton, R.
- 1949 Soils and Land Use in Peninsular Thailand. Bangkok: Department of Agriculture.

Peterson, J. T.
- 1975 "Hunter-Gatherer/Farmer Food Exchange." Paper read at the 13th Pacific Science Congress, August 1975, Vancouver.
- 1976 "Folk Traditions and Interethnic Relations in Northeastern Luzon, Philippines." In Directions in Pacific Traditional Literature, edited by A. L. Kaeppler and A. H. Nimmo. Honolulu: Bishop Museum Press.
- In press a The Ecology of Social Boundaries. Monograph Series in Anthropology. Urbana, Ill.: University of Illinois Press.
- In press b Merits of Margins. University of Ohio series on Southeast Asia.
- In press c "Hunter-Gatherer/Farmer Exchange." American Anthropologist.

Peterson, J. T. , and W. E. Peterson

In press "Implications of Contemporary and Prehistoric Exchange Systems." In Sunda and Sahul, edited by J. Golson, R. Jones, and J. Allen. London: Academic Press.

Peterson, W. E.

1973 "A New Perspective on the Relationship Between Migration, Diffusion and Cultural Evolution." Paper read at the 25th Annual Meeting of the Association for Asian Studies, March 1973, Chicago.

1974 "Summary Report of Two Archaeological Sites from Northeastern Luzon." Archaeology and Physical Anthropology in Oceania 9:26-35.

In press Anomalous Archaeological Sites of Northeastern Luzon and Models of Southeast Asian Prehistory. Manila: National Museum.

Pigafetta, A.

1903-09 "Primo Viaggio Intorno al Mondo." In The Philippine Islands, 1493-1898, edited by E. H. Blair and J. A. Robertson, vol. 33:25-366; 34:38-180. Cleveland: Clark.

Pigeaud, Th. G. Th.

1960-63 Java in the 14th Century: A Study in Cultural History. The Nāgera-Kĕrtāgama by Rakawi Prapañca of Majapahit, 1365 A.D. 3rd ed. The Hague: Martinus Nijhoff.

Pires, T.

1944 The Suma Oriental of Tomè Pires. Edited and translated by A. Cortesao. London: The Hakluyt Society.

Plog, R. , and J. N. Hill

1971 "Explaining Variability in the Distribution of Sites." In The Distribution of Prehistoric Population Aggregates, edited by G. J. Gumermann, pp. 7-36. Prescott College: Anthropological Reports, 1.

Poerbatjaraka, R. Ng.
1922 "Transcriptie van een Koperen Plaat in het Museum te Solo." OV 1922:29.
1936 "Vier Oorkonden in Koper." TBG 76:373-90.

Polanyi, K.
1957 "The Economy as Instituted Process." In Trade and Markets in the Early Empires, edited by K. Polanyi, C. M Arensberg, and H. W. Pearson, pp. 243-69. Glencoe, Ill.: Free Press.

Radcliff-Brown, A. R.
1964 The Andaman Islanders. New York: Free Press.

Raffles, Sir T. S.
1830 The History of Java. 2nd ed. London: J. Murray.

Rahmann, R., and M. N. Maceda
1962 "Notes on the Negritos of Antique, Island of Panay, Philippines." Anthropos 57:626-43.

Rappaport, R. A.
1971 "Ritual, Sanctity, and Cybernetics." American Anthropologist 73:59-76.

Ras, J. J.
1968 Hikajat Bandjar, a Study in Malay Historiography. The Hague: Martinus Nijhoff.

Reber, A. L.
1966 "The Sulu World in the Eighteenth and Early Nineteenth Centuries." M.A. thesis, Cornell University.

Reed, W. A.
1904 Negritos of Zambales. Department of the Interior, Ethnological Survey Publications 2(1). Manila: Bureau of Printing.

Renfrew, C.

1969a "Trade and Culture Process in European Prehistory." Current Anthropology 10:151-74.

1969b Review of "Locational Analysis in Human Geography," by P. Haggett. Antiquity 43(169):75-6.

1972 The Emergence of Civilization; the Cyclades and the Aegean in the Third Millenium B.C. London: Methuen and Co.

1973 "Monuments, Mobilization and Social Organization in Neolithic Wessex." In The Explanation of Culture Change: Models in Prehistory, edited by C. Renfrew, pp. 539-58. Pittsburgh: University of Pittsburgh Press.

Renfrew, C., J. E. Dixon and J. R. Cann

1968 "Further Analysis of Near Eastern Obsidians." Proceedings of the Prehistoric Society 34:319-31.

Richardson, H.

1963 "Early Burial Grounds in Tibet and Tibetan Decorative Art of the 8th and 9th Centuries." Central Asiatic Journal 7:73-92.

Ricklefs, M. C.

1973 "Jogjakarta under Sultan Mangkabumi, 1749-1792. A History of the Division of Java." Ph.D. dissertation, Cornell University.

Roolvink, R.

1967 "The Variant Versions in the Malay Annals." BKI 73(3):311.

Rubin, J., and B. Brown

1975 The Social Psychology of Bargaining and Negotiation. New York: Academic Press.

Sahlins, M. D.

1963 "Poor Man, Rich Man, Big Man, Chief: Political

(Sahlins, M. D.)

(1963) "Types in Melanesia and Polynesia." Comparative Studies in Society and History 5: 285-303.

1965 "On the Sociology of Primitive Exchange." In The Relevance of Models for Social Anthropology, edited by M. Banton, pp. 139-236. London: Tavistock.

1968 Tribesmen. Englewood Cliffs, N. J.: Prentice-Hall.

1972 Stone Age Economics. Chicago: Aldine, Atherton.

Sakamaki, S.

1964 "Ryu-kyu and Southeast Asia." The Journal of Asian Studies 23:383-389.

Sarkar, H. B.

1938 "Copper-plates of Kembang Arum 824 Saka." Journal of the Greater India Society 5:31-50.

1971-2 Corpus of the Inscriptions of Java (up to 928 A.D.). 2 vols. Calcutta: Firma K. L. Mukhopadhyay.

Schafer, E. H.

1963 The Golden Peaches of Samarkand. Berkeley: University of California Press.

Schebesta, P.

1952-7 Die Negrito Asiens. 2 vols. Wien-Moedling: St. Gabriel Verlag.

Schnitger, F. M.

1936 Outheidkundige Vondsten in Palembang. Leiden: E. J. Brill.

1937 The Archaeology of Hindoo Sumatra. Internationales Archiv fuer Ethnographie 35.

Schrieke, J. J. O.

1955 Indonesian Sociological Studies: Selected Writings of B. Schrieke, Part 1. The Hague: W. van Hoeve.

1957 Indonesian Sociological Studies, Part 2: Ruler and

(Schrieke, J. J. O.)

(1957) Realm in Early Java. The Hague: W. van Hoeve.

Schulte Nordholt, H. G.

1971 The Political System of the Atoni of Timor. The Hague: Martinus Nijhoff.

Schurz, Wm. L.

1939 The Manilla Galleon. New York: Dutton.

Scott, W. H.

1968 A Critical Study of the Prehispanic Source Materials for the Study of Philippine History. Manila: University of Santo Tomas.

Service, E. R.

1962 Primitive Social Organization: An Evolutionary Perspective. New York: Random House.

Sharp, L.

1952 "Steel Axes for Stone-Age Australians." Human Organization 11:17-22.

Shepard, F. P., et al.

1967 "Holocene Changes in Sea Level: Evidence in Micronesia." Science 157:542-4.

Shepherd, D. G., and W. B. Henning

1959 "Zandaniji Identified?" In Aus der Welt der islamischen Kunst, edited by R. Ettinghausen, pp. 15-40. Berlin: Verlag Gebr. Mann.

Shiba, Y.

1970 Commerce and Society in Sung China. Translated by Mark Elvin. Ann Arbor: Center for Chinese Studies.

Shosoin Office

1963-4 Shōsōin hōmotsu kaisetsu: senshoku [Textiles in the Shosoin]. Tokyo: Asahi Shimbun Publishing Co.

Sieveking, G. de G.
- 1954-5 "Ancient Shorelines." Federation Museums Journal, n.s. 1-2:140.

Simmons, H. B., and F. A. Herrmann
- 1972 "Effects of Man-made Works on the Hydraulic Salinity, and Shoaling Regimen of Estuaries." Geological Society of America Memoir 133:555-70.

Singer, P.
- 1971 Early Chinese Gold and Silver. New York: China House Gallery.

Sinha, D. P.
- 1972 "The Birhors." In Hunters and Gatherers Today, edited by M. G. Bicchieri, pp. 371-403. New York: Holt, Rinehart and Winston.

Skeat, W. W.
- 1900 Malay Magic. Repr. London: Frank Cass and Co., 1965.

Skeat, W. W., and O. Blagden
- 1906 Pagan Races of the Malay Peninsula. 2 vols. London: Macmillan.

Skinner, C.
- 1963 Sja'ir pareng Mengkasor (The Rhymed Chronicle of the Macassar War) by Enti Amin. The Hague: Martinus Nijhoff.

Skinner, G. W.
- 1957 Chinese Society in Thailand. Ithaca: Cornell University Press.
- 1964 "Marketing and Social Structure in Rural China." Journal of Asian Studies 24:3-43.

Snow, D. R.
1972 "Rising Sea-level and Prehistoric Cultural Ecology in Northern Maine." American Antiquity 37:211-21.

Sobur, A. S., et al.
1975 "Remote Sensing Applications for Environmental and Resource Management Studies in the Musi-Banyuasin Coastal Zone, South Sumatra." Paper presented at the UN/FAO Regional Seminar on Remote Sensing Applications, Jakarta.

Soekmono, R.
1963 "Geomorphology and the Location of Criwijaya." Madjallah Ilmu-Ilmu Sastra Indonesia 1(1):79-90.

1965 "Archaeology and Indonesian History." In An Introduction to Indonesian Historiography, edited by Soedjatmoko, pp. 36-46. Ithaca: Cornell University Press.

1967 "A Geographical Reconstruction of Northeastern Central Java and the Location of Medang." Indonesia 4:2-7.

Solheim, W. G. II
1964 The Archaeology of Central Philippines, a Study Chiefly of the Iron Age and Its Relationships. Manila: Bureau of Printing.

1968a "The Batungan Cave Sites, Masbate, Philippines." In Anthropology at the Eighth Pacific Science Congress, edited by W. G. Solheim II, pp. 21-62. Asian and Pacific Archaeology Series No. 2. Honolulu: University of Hawaii, Social Science Research Institute.

1968b "Thailand." AP 9:36-44.

1969 "Reworking Southeast Asian Prehistory." Paideuma 15:125-39.

1970 "Northern Thailand, Southeast Asia and World Prehistory." AP 13:145-58.

Solheim, W. G. II, R. H. Parker, and D. T. Bayard

    1966   "Preliminary Reports on Excavations at Ban Nadi, Ban Sao Lao, Pimai No. 1." Mimeographed. University of Hawaii, Social Science Research Institute.

Solyom, G., and B. Solyom

    n.d.   Textiles of the Indonesian Archipelago. Asian Studies at Hawaii, No. 10. Honolulu: The University Press of Hawaii.

Sopher, D.

    1965   The Sea Nomads. Singapore: Singapore National Museum.

Spencer, J. E.

    1954   Asia, East by South: A Cultural Geography. New York York: John Wiley and Sons.

Spencer, J. E., and F. L. Wernstedt

    1967   The Philippine Island World. Berkeley: University of of California Press.

Stargardt, J.

    1973a   "Southern Thai Waterways: Archaeological Evidence on Agriculture, Shipping and Trade in the Srivijayan Period." Man 8:5-29.

    1973b   "The Srivijayan Civilization in Southern Thailand." Antiquity 47(187):225-33.

Stauffer, P. H.

    1973   "Cenozoic." In Geology of the Malay Peninsula, edited by D. J. Gobbet and C. S. Hutchinson, pp. 143-76. New York: Wiley-Interscience.

Steensgaard, N.

    1974   The Asian Trade Revolution of the 17th Century. Chicago: University of Chicago Press.

Stein Callenfels, P. V.

1934 "De Inscriptie van Soekaboemi." Mededeelingen der Koninklijk Akademie van Wetenschappen, Afdeeling Letterkunde 1934:115-30.

Steinberg, D. J.

1971 In Search of Southeast Asia. New York: Praeger Publishers.

Stuart, A. B. C.

1875 Kawi Oorkonden in Facsimilie met Inleiding en Transscriptie. Leiden: E. J. Brill.

Stuart, A. B. C., and J. J. Limburg Brouwer

1872 "Beschreven Steenen op Java." TBG 18:91-117.

Stutterheim, W. F.

1925a "Een Oorkonde op Koper uit het Singosarische." TBG 65:208-81.

1925b Rama-Legenden und Rama-Reliefs in Indonesien. 2 vols. Munich: Georg Muller Verlag.

1925c "Transscriptie van Twee Jayapattras." OV 1925: 57-60.

1927 "Een Belangrijke Ookonde uit Kedoe." TBG 67: 172-215.

1928 "Transscriptie van een Defecte Oorkonde op Bronzen Platen uit het Malangsche." OV 1928:105-8.

1931 "The Meaning of the Hindu-Javanese candi." Journal of the American Oriental Society 51:1-15.

1932 "Een Oorkonde van Koning Pu Wagiswara uit 927 A.D." TBG 72:420-37.

1934 "Een Vrij Overzetveer to Wanagiri (M. N.) in 903 A.D." TBG 74:269-95.

1940 "Oorkonde van Balitung uit 905 A.D. (Randoesari I)." Inscripties van Nederlandsch-Indie, uitgegeven door het Koninklijk Bataviaasch Genootschap van Kunsten en Wetenschappen 1:3-28.

(Stutterheim, W. F.)

1956 "Some Remarks on Pre-Hinduistic Burial Customs on Java." In Studies in Indonesian Archaeology, edited by W. F. Stutterheim, pp. 65-90. The Hague: Martinus Nijhoff.

Swift, M. G.

1965 Malay Peasant Society in Jelebu. London: Athlone Press.

Tamil Lexicon

1928-36 Mylapore: University of Madras.

Tarling, N.

1963 Piracy and Politics in the Malay World. Melbourne: Cheshire.

Taylor, K. W.

1976 "Madagascar in the Ancient Malayo-Polynesian Myths." In Explorations in Early Southeast Asian History, edited by K. R. Hall and J. K. Whitmore, pp. 25-60. Michigan Papers on South and Southeast Asia No. 11. Ann Arbor: CSSEAS Publications.

Teeuw, A.

1964 "Hikayat Raja-Raja Pasai and Sejarah Melayu." In Malayan and Indonesian Studies, edited by J. Bastin and R. Roolvink, pp. 222-34. Oxford: Clarendon Press.

Tenazas, R. C. P.

1974 "A Progress Report on the Magsuhot Excavations in Bacong, Negros Oriental, Summer 1974." Philippine Quarterly of Culture and Society 2:133-55.

Tjia, H. D.

1973 "Geomorphology." In Geology of the Malay Peninsula, edited by D. J. Gobbett and C. S. Hutchinson, pp. 13-24. New York: Wiley-Interscience.

Tjia, H. D., S. Asikin, and R. S. Atmadja
1968   "Coastal Accretion in Western Indonesia." Bulletin, National Institute of Geology and Mining 1(1):15-45.

Tuggle, H. D., and K. L. Hutterer
1972   "Archaeology of the Sohoton Area, Southwestern Samar, Philippines." Leyte-Samar Studies 6(2).

Turnbull, C.
1965   Wayward Servants: The Two Worlds of the African Pygmies. Garden City, N.Y.: Natural History Press.

UN/ECAFE
1973   Archaeology and the Mekong Project. Bangkok: ECAFE.

Vanoverbergh, M.
1925   "Negritos of Northern Luzon." Anthropos 20:148-99; 399-442.

Verstappen, H. Th.
1953   Jakarta Bay. The Hague: Drukkerij Trio.
1966   "The Use of Aerial Photographs in Delta Studies." In Scientific Problems of the Humid Tropical Zone Deltas and Their Implications, UNESCO, pp. 29-33. Paris: UNESCO.
1973   A Geomorphological Reconnaissance of Sumatra and Adjacent Islands (Indonesia). Groningen: Wolters and Noordhoff.

Vita-Finzi, L.
1969   The Mediterranean Valleys. Cambridge: Cambridge University Press.

Volker, T.
1954   Porcelain and the Dutch East India Company. Leiden: E. J. Brill.

(Volker, T.)
1959 The Japanese Porcelain Trade of the Dutch East India Company after 1683. Leiden: E. J. Brill.

Wake, C. H.
1964 "Malacca's Early Kings and the Reception of Islam." Journal of Southeast Asian History 5:104-28.

Wales, H. G. Q.
1940 "Archaeological Researches on Ancient Indian Colonization in Malaya." JMBRAS 18:1-85.
1974 "Langkasuka and Tambralinga: Some Archaeological Notes." JMBRAS 47:15-40.

Wallace, B. J.
1970 Hill and Valley Farmers. Cambridge, Mass.: Schenkman.

Wang, Gungwu
1958 "The Nanhai Trade: A Study of the Early History of Chinese Trade in the South China Sea." JMBRAS 31(2).
1959 A Short History of the Nanyang Chinese. Singapore: Eastern Universities Press.

Warren, C. P.
1964 The Batak of Palawan: A Culture in Transition. Research Series, No. 3. University of Chicago: Philippine Studies Program, Department of Anthropology.

Watson, W.
1968 "The Thai-British Archaeological Expedition." Antiquity 42:302-6.
1974 The Chinese Exhibition. Toronto: Royal Ontario Museum.

Weide, D. L., and M. L. Weide
1973 "Application of Geomorphic Data to Archaeology: A Comment." American Antiquity 38:428-31.

Wen-hua....
1972 Wen-hua Ta-ko-ming ch'i-chien ch'u-t'u wen-wu (Cultural Relics Discovered During the Period of the Great Cultural Revolution). Peking: Wen Wu Press.

Wheatley, P.
1959 "Geographical Notes on Some Commodities Involved in Sung Maritime Trade." JMBRAS 32(2).
1961 The Golden Kersonese. Kual Lumpur: University of Malaya Press.
1964 Impressions of the Malay Peninsula in Ancient Times. Singapore: Eastern Universities Press.
1971 The Pivot of the Four Quarters. Chicago: Aldine.
1975 "Satyānṛta in Suvarnadvīpa: From Reciprocity to Redistribution in Ancient Southeast Asia." In Ancient Civilization and Trade, Edited by J. A. Sabloff and C. C. Lamberg-Karlovsky, pp. 227-38. Albuquerque: University of New Mexico Press.

Wibowo
n.d. "Prasasti Alasantan." Typescript. Modjokerto.

Wickberg, E.
1965 The Chinese in Philippine Life, 1850-1898. New Haven: Yale University Press.

Williams, B. J.
1968 "The Birhor of India and Some Comments on Band Organization." In Man the Hunter, edited by R. B. Lee and I. DeVore, pp. 126-31.

Williams-Hunt, P. D. R.
1949 "An Introduction to the Study of Archaeology from the Air." Journal of the Siam Society 37:85-100.

Wilmsen, E. N.

1972 "Introduction: The Study of Exchange as Social Interaction." In Social Exchange and Interaction, edited by E. N. Wilmsen, pp. 1-4. Ann Arbor: University of Michigan Museum of Anthropology.

Winstedt, R. O.

1925 Shaman, Saiva, and Sufi, a Study of the Evolution of Malay Magic. London: Constable and Co., Ltd.

Wirz, P.

1928 Der Totenkult auf Bali. Stuttgart: Strecker und Schroeder.

Wolters, O. W.

1963 "China Irredenta: The South." The World Today 19 (12):540-52.

1967 Early Indonesian Commerce: A Study of the Origins of Śrivijaya. Ithaca: Cornell University Press.

1970 The Fall of Śrivijaya in Malay History. Ithaca: Cornell University Press.

1975 "Landfall on the Palembang Coast in Medieval Times." Indonesia 20:1-57.

Woodburn, J.

1968 "An Introduction to Hadza Ecology." In Man the Hunter, edited by R. B. Lee and I. DeVore, pp. 49-55. Chicago: Aldine.

Wu, D. Ye-ho

1974 "To Kill Three Birds with One Stone: Revolving Credit Associations Among Papuan Chinese." American Ethnologist 1:565-84.

Wyatt, D. K.

1968 "Family Politics in Nineteenth Century Thailand." Journal of Southeast Asian History 9:208-28.

Yü, Ying-shih

1967 *Trade and Expansion in Han China*. Berkeley: University of California Press.

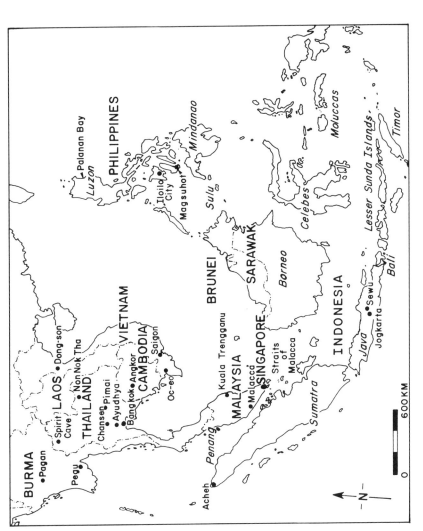

Map 4. Southeast Asia.